Gulf Coast Fish

A Cookbook

Gulf Coast Fish
A Cookbook

ROY F. GUSTE, JR.

illustrations by Mark Green

W. W. Norton & Company • New York • London

Dedication:

To Tabitha, my editor, who made it right,
and to my sweet Cybil.

～～～～～～～～
～～～～～～～～

The text of this book is composed in Devinne
with display set in Duchamp
Composition by Bytheway Typesetting Services
Manufacturing by Tien Wah Press
Book design by Antonina Krass
Cover Illustration: Credit Melanie Marder Parks

Library of Congress Cataloging-in-Publication Data
Guste, Roy F.
Gulf coast fish : a cookbook / Roy F. Guste, Jr. ; with illustrations by Mark Green.
p.   cm.
Includes index.
1. Cookery (Fish)   2. Fishes – Mexico, Gulf of.   I. Title.
TX747.G876   1997
641.6'92 – dc20   95-319

ISBN 0-393-03425-9

W. W. Norton & Company, Inc., 500 Fifth Avenue, New York, N.Y. 10110
W. W. Norton & Company Ltd., 10 Coptic Street, London WC1A 1PU
1 2 3 4 5 6 7 8 9 0

CONTENTS

Drum

Jack

Mackerel

Marlin

Mullet

Porgy

Ray

Sawfish

Shark

Spadefish

Squirrelfish

Swordfish

Tarpon

Threadfin

Tilefish

Triggerfish

Tripletail

Wrasse

PREFACE

～～～～～～～～～

The Gulf Coast: A Heritage of Many Cultures and Cuisines

The American coast of the Gulf of Mexico is an unusually bountiful area of the world that has had the culinary good fortune of having been influenced by several important cultures and cuisines. It was the American Indian who first developed a seafood cuisine and culture utilizing the many species of fish swimming in the plentiful waters, rich in abundant varieties of fish and seafood.

Along our American Gulf Coast, beginning where Mexico meets Texas, we find the marvelous Mexican cuisine including dishes made from Mexico's famous peppers and the slow simmering sauces of the *caldero*, the traditional clay pot of the Mexicans. Dishes borrowed from the Yucatan are found both in Texas and in Florida, the two ends of our Gulf Coast, both having easy access to the Yucatan Peninsula. The pungent cilantro, brought by the earliest Spanish explorers, found a welcoming home in Mexico, so welcome that it now seems there would be no Mexican cuisine without it, or hard to imagine one without.

From there we cross into Texas and the coast of Tex/Mex cuisine. This is the true Southwestern cuisine so well known and loved by all Americans. Then we move on to Louisiana, with its vast legacy of Creole cuisine, influenced by French, Spanish, and Caribbean cooking, and Cajun cuisine, developed from French Canadian and Louisiana Indian influences. Finally we move to Mississippi and Alabama, where Southern cuisine meets the Gulf, and on to Florida, where the cuisines of Puerto Rico, Cuba, and all the Caribbean islands have taken hold and become American.

The recipes delivered here are less likely to be found in the restaurants than in the homes of families who for generations have developed and maintained their own special dishes.

A rich harvest of fish is what this book is about — a rich harvest of fish and a solid grouping of tried and true recipes, compiled to open the secrets of this harvest so it may visit your table in a most delicious way.

A Note About the Illustrations

In this book I have introduced over seventy Gulf Coast fish for your enjoyment. The beautiful illustrations of each fish, done by Florida graphic artist Mark Green, show these colorful creatures as they appear underwater. When you see the actual fish in the market, they will appear less colorful even when still whole, much the less when cut into fillets or steaks. Fish lose their color quickly after they leave the water. Some fish that live deep in the Gulf actually lose their normal coloration as they near the surface as a catch. Artist Mark Green is a professional diver. He knows these fish and their brilliant colors at the depths at which they live, and has labored to correctly capture the fish as they appear there.

INTRODUCTION

The Fish of the Gulf Coast, and How to Handle Them

In New Orleans and the Gulf South, we have grown up with an old adage that was a wise one: "Eat fish: live longer."

This adage was intended to encourage us to eat fish by reminding us of its health benefits; however, the reminder was hardly necessary. We who have eaten fish regularly for our entire lives have always recognized its health benefits—and its gastronomic benefits as well.

Fishing on the Gulf Coast is marvelous. The absolute joy of the fishing expedition, however simple it may be, the catching of the fish, the cooking and eating of the catch, and the camaraderie that generally exists through all phases of this exercise is what encourages us to bring the fish to the table. And that is just the beginning.

Eating the fish is the crowning glory. And what an event we have turned it into. Our cooking and enjoyment of fish is as important to us, if not more, than any other food that we eat. We love fish! Forget the health benefits . . . we just love fish.

We love the beauty of the animal, we love the salt-sea-air smell of its fresh flesh, we love its wonderfully variable flavors and the variable colors of the meat, from pearly white to ruddy red. Give us a fillet of pompano over a *filet de boeuf* any day.

But many of the species of fish that are available from the Gulf of Mexico are unfamiliar to many Americans. And now that these fish are being transported across the states, to the delight of fish eaters in every corner of the country, it is time to make a few suggestions as to recipes that might best, yet simply, introduce our bounty to you. Herein lies the *raison d'être*, the purpose, of this book.

Ask your fish merchant if he has something new from the Gulf Coast . . . then grab this book and enjoy!

SELECTING FISH AND PREPARING IT FOR COOKING

Choosing the Fish Market

Finding the best possible available fish is where this gastronomic fishing trip sets sail. Unless you are actually doing the fishing yourself or are close to a fishing area where you might be able to purchase fresh fish directly from the local fishermen, you will probably be making your way to the local fish market or seafood department of a large grocery store. In major cities, fish markets may specialize in different kinds of fish, and that will contribute to your choice of shop. Once you have arrived at the door of the fish market the work begins.

On entering the store, the odor of the shop should be like the odor of the sea— that of fresh salt air and water. The shop should be clean. If there is a fishy smell, as of old fish, this could be the first indicator of some less than acceptable product offerings. This is just a warning. It may not actually indicate to you that the shop does not have the fish you want. These odors can come from areas other than the fresh fish themselves, such as a trash bin or used delivery cartons that are headed for the dumpster.

The way the fish is displayed is the first real indicator. The whole fish should be displayed on crushed ice, mostly covered with the ice, to be slipped out for your view as you make your selections. There should be no standing water in the display bins for the fish to slush around in.

Fillets, steaks, or chunks of fish, where the skinless flesh is exposed, should not be displayed lying directly in the ice. This exposure to the ice will drain away some of the precious fresh fish taste that you are making your best effort to locate. These cuts of fish should be displayed in plastic-wrap-covered trays on the ice or in a display refrigerator with no ice or standing water in the trays. They could also be displayed individually tightly wrapped in plastic wrap on the crushed ice.

The way the merchant handles the fish will also indicate the care the shop takes with the product they sell. All fish—whole, fillets, steaks, large chunks—should be handled with both hands by the seller when he or she shows and packs the fish. Picking up any fish or cut and letting its own weight stretch it out begins a slight tearing of the firm texture you want. Professionals know this. Find a store that employs professionals and you will have found a store that purveys an acceptable, if not exceptional product.

Watch the way the fish is packaged for the trip home. It should be well wrapped in waxed paper, and then perhaps in a plastic bag to prevent leaking. Fillets and whole fish should never be folded or twisted around in the bag. This action will also contribute to the gradual tearing of the firm texture of the fresh fish.

Once you have found a market that is clean, has the selection you want, and displays and handles the fish properly, you can proceed with choosing your purchase.

This is the optimum situation. We all know that much of the seafood and many of the markets available to us are not as perfect as we might want them to be. Do *your* best to find the best and proceed from there.

Determining the Freshness of Fish at the Market

There are varying degrees of "fresh" to be found when shopping for fish. The freshest fish, of course, have been caught that day or the day before; not so fresh are the ones caught several days before. Be aware that some fish are called fresh simply because they have never been frozen, when perhaps they should have been.

When you look for fresh fish, I suggest you search out the fish that are caught that day or the day before. Only the most reputable shops will be completely honest in their information to the buyer, particularly when they are dealing with cuts such as fillets, steaks, or chunks that are missing several of the primary parts from which "fresh" can be determined by the buyer. In a whole fish the job is sometimes easier because there are more ways to determine the freshness visually.

The eyes are a good place to start. The eyes of the fish should be clear, bright, and shiny. Any dullness or cloudiness will indicate a lack of freshness. Sometimes, however, fish eyes have clouded due to the close exposure to the ice, so you should also look to the gills.

To check the gills of the fish, lift up the gill covers behind the cheeks of the fish head and check the color. They should be clearly red as well as moist and shiny. Any graying in coloration or stickiness to the touch will indicate lack of freshness.

The fish itself should have a nice shine from the natural protective slime and the scales should be tight to the skin. Dullness of the fish body, stickiness or cloudiness of the slime, and loosening of scales are all indicators of lack of freshness or improper handling and refrigeration.

Touch the fish. If the fish texture is not firm and springy, if the indentation made from your touch does not spring back, then the fish is not absolutely fresh.

If you are shopping for a fillet, steak, or chunk, the same holds. If the flesh of the fillet or steak is not firm, if it appears to be stretching apart, it is not fresh. If the coloration of the flesh is not the way it should be for that particular fish—pearly translucent, opaque white, orange-pink, or ruddy red—or if there are dark or discolored areas, it is not absolutely fresh.

The final, most absolute and endurable freshness check for all fish is its odor. Smell the fish. Have the merchant hold it up to you for a sniff. Don't be shy. If the fish does not smell of the sea, of salt breezes and waves, if it smells "fishy," it is not suitably fresh. Trust yourself on this, and learn to do it if you don't know how already.

Determining the Quality of Frozen Fish

Some of the fish that you can buy at large grocery store chains that have a fish department, as well as some varieties shipped to your local fish market, have been previously frozen and defrosted for sale. It is an unfortunate state of affairs, but the processing of much of our nation's catch is actually done on shipboard, even before the ship returns to dock. Much of this fish is cut into fillets, quick-frozen, and made ready for packing and shipping as soon as the boat returns to port. In other cases the fish is unloaded from the fishing boats at dockside processing plants where all is processed, frozen, and packaged for facility of shipment and delivery. Be sure that this fish looks fresh. You won't have eyes or gills to check for freshness in these cases. These fish most frequently are in the form of small dressed fish, fillets, or whole dressed larger fish for display from which fillets and steaks can be cut to order.

If these fish have been properly handled from boat to shelf, they can resemble fresh fish to an acceptable degree in both taste and texture. As in fresh fish, the flesh should have a firmness to it and no discernible discoloration. The ultimate test remains the odor of the fish. Do not accept any "fishy" smelling products here. Even a frozen fish, if touched, can impart a fishy smell from the melting surface ice onto your fingertips. If it does, this frozen fish is unacceptable.

Good frozen fish is certainly an acceptable alternative to no fish at all. The greatest benefit of the freezing process is that fish previously unavailable in one area can now be enjoyed by so many more seafood enthusiasts in this country. It is also a general fact that people buying a fish different in taste and texture from their local varieties are happy with the opportunity for a change of pace, and less demanding of the absolute freshness of the cut.

Deciding What Fish to Buy: The Principle of Substitution

There are two approaches to shopping for fish. You can decide on a recipe and then go out and find the fish, or, as I do more often than not, you can determine the recipe by the best fish choice available that day. The latter schedules fewer disappointments at the market, where they may not have exactly what you are looking for, but it can require a lot of last-minute decision making.

Your job will be much easier if you realize that you need not be tied down to the one fish indicated in a particular recipe. Fish with similar meat types can be substituted for one another.

The characteristics to consider in substituting fish are oil content, color, and texture. Oil content affects the flavor and moistness of the fish. The oilier the fish, the stronger and richer the flavor; the lower the oil content, the more delicate the flavor. Oilier fish are also more moist, which in turn affects the cooking method you use. Fish with lower oil content require cooking methods that add moisture so that they do not dry out. (The fish oil, by the way, is very healthful. Although it is fat, it contains Omega-3 fatty acids that actually help in the reduction of cholesterol levels.)

Color indicates the richness of the fish flavor. A fish that is dark red in coloration will have a full-bodied flavor, whereas a fish that is cottony-white will taste far lighter and more delicate, and will need milder, accompanying ingredients so as not to be overwhelmed. (The lighter colored fish are the best choice for any individual just beginning to enjoy the taste and healthful benefits of fish.)

Texture refers to the density of the flesh and the way in which it separates when cut with a fork after cooking. Flaky fish are loosely, coarsely textured and will come apart in well-defined lines, holding together in pieces much like the pieces you might find in lump crabmeat. Fish with a finer, delicate texture have a more closely knit mass that cooks into a more tender, softer product and separates into tiny flakes. Both flaky and delicate fish need careful handling in cooking. Firm, dense fish, on the other hand, have a texture more like a meat, with less breakdown of the fiber in the cooking process; they are the best fish to use for grilling.

To substitute fish successfully, all of these factors must be considered. However, finding fish of similar meat types need not be a difficult process. Each recipe in this book specifies other Gulf Coast fish that can be used instead. In addition, meat characteristics are listed with each fish, and you can find a match by consulting the chart of the meat types of Gulf Coast fish in the appendix.

If you cannot find a compatible Gulf Coast fish in your fish market, you can substitute fish from other regions as long as the meat type is similar. Your fish merchant should be able to advise you on this. For example, if your recipe specifies scamp and you find a beautiful piece of halibut, that will work instead; both fish are white and flaky with a low oil content. Or if your recipe calls for weakfish and your market has brook trout or salmon, go for it—they are compatible.

Deciding How Much Fish to Buy

Of course, if you are shopping for a specific recipe, it will have specified the amount to buy. But if you are using the best-fish-available approach, you may not be sure how much fish you need.

For different cuts, you will use different portion weights. If serving a whole fish per person, use a 1- to 1 1/2-pound fish for each. If serving fillets or chunks, use 6- to 8-ounce portions. For steaks including bone and skin, plan on about 8 ounces a portion. Often you must choose from the pieces available and that is how final weight will be determined.

Larger fish, scaled and drawn (eviscerated) and including the head, yield approximately 1 pound of meat to every 3 pounds of total weight. If you plan to bake a

6

fish for six, you would buy an 8- to 9-pound fish, scaled and drawn, head on, which would yield up to 8 ounces of meat per person. Eight ounces is a fairly healthy portion of fish and can be reduced to as little as half of that, or 4 ounces of fish, if served with enough other accompanying dishes. Thus, a 5-pound dressed fish could actually serve six persons small 4-ounce portions. The portion weight on which you will decide will sometimes be determined by the available fish. An absolutely fresh red snapper that would serve six people 5 ounces each is hard to turn down for being light on meat weight.

Having the Market Prepare the Fish for Cooking

Most fish markets either sell fish already prepared for use or will prepare it for you according to your needs. Take the opportunity of having the fish merchant clean and cut the fish for you. The tasks of scaling, eviscerating, degilling, filleting, skinning, et cetera, may not excite you, and in today's small apartment and home kitchens, it is sometimes difficult to do a proper job, and proper cleanup. If, however, you prefer to prepare the fish yourself, you will find instructions for doing so on pages 10–15.

Market to Home

This leg of the voyage is now highly dependent on you. Handling the fish properly while getting it from the store to your home is an important step.

Be sure that the properly packaged fish is not put in a bag with other groceries where it can get crushed, folded, or stretched. If your purchase was made at a grocery store, hold the fish back until it can be properly placed on the top of other groceries, or preferably in a bag of its own.

Make the grocery or fish market your last stop before you head home and make the fish your last purchase. Treat the time you keep your fish in the car the same way you would treat ice cream—don't let it melt.

If you have some distance to drive to purchase your fish, you might consider taking along a small cooler with several quart plastic bags of ice cubes to keep things at a proper storage temperature for the drive home. Leave the fish wrapped and lay it on top of the ice bags. Get it home as cold or colder than when you bought it.

Once home with your fresh fish, prepare it immediately for refrigerated storage.

If the fish is already in the form in which you will use it, requires no further work, and is to be used that day or night, remove it from the store packaging, wipe it gently with a damp towel, and place it on a clean dish or tray large enough for it to be laid out in a single layer. Cover it with a clean, damp towel or a sheet of plastic wrap and refrigerate in the coldest part of the refrigerator. Use both hands to handle the fish. You want to continue to preserve the firm texture of the flesh as best you can now that things are in your hands.

If the fish is to be used that night but is not in the form you will need, clean and prepare it when you get home from the market, then wrap it in plastic and refrigerate it until you are ready to cook.

If your fresh fish is to be kept for the next day's meal, remove it from the store packaging and wipe it gently with a clean, damp cloth. If you are dealing with a whole fish with skin and perhaps scales, it should be eviscerated before storing (see page 12). Leave the skin and scales on, however, until just before cooking. This may add some inconvenient last-minute work, but it assures the finest flavor from your fish. The skin and scales provide powerful protection for the delicate fresh taste of the fish, and an equally powerful barrier against dehydration and the absorption of odors from other foods. Then lay the whole fish in a tray of crushed ice so that it is completely submerged. Cover the tray with a damp cloth and store in the coldest part of the refrigerator. As the ice melts, the water must be drained from the tray. The fish should never be allowed to lie in standing water.

If the fresh fish cuts to be used the next day are without scales and skin—fillets, steaks, chunks, etc.—they should be wrapped tightly in plastic wrap so that no air is left within the wrap. They can now be stored in crushed ice or simply on a dish in a single layer. Again, it is particularly important with skinless fish that they not be allowed to sit in standing water. Water will pull delicate fresh tastes from the flesh.

When you are ready to use the fish, remove it from the tray and wraps, if any, and gently wipe it dry with a clean, damp cloth.

Fresh fish brought home to be frozen must be carefully handled.

There are several ways to package and freeze fish to best maintain its fresh qualities. A common and suitable method is to freeze the fish completely submerged in water. In this case, the fish cut or cuts are placed in a cleaned milk carton or plastic freezer container and the container is filled with water. The fish must be completely submerged and the water should not reach the top of the container. As the water freezes into ice, it expands. A 1-inch level from the water's surface to the top edge of the container is sufficient to allow for the expansion of volume. When filling the container, cold water with ice is preferable because it will hasten the freezing of the whole contents, lessening the damage to the fish texture by freezing.

Fish can also be placed in plastic freezer bags with a little water. Be sure to squeeze all the air out of the bag as you secure it closed. This can be done with small bags and the fish pieces can be frozen individually for ease later when only a certain amount of fish needs to be defrosted.

Another method is to tightly wrap the fish individually in plastic wrap and eliminate all air from the enclosure.

In all cases, the fish must never be folded or curled or pressed tightly together. Do not stack the fish in the freezer where they will be crushed before freezing. Preserve the texture as well as the taste.

Freezing fish with skin and/or scales on helps protect the taste from dehydration and odor absorption. However, since when defrosted for cooking the texture of the fish will be less firm than before freezing, scaling and skin removal at this juncture must be done very gently, handling the fish as carefully as possible.

LENGTH OF TIME FROZEN FISH CAN BE STORED:

There are differing opinions on the length of time that frozen fish can be properly stored and lose the least of its good qualities. I suggest that some fish can be stored up to one month and other types up to two months.

The oil content in the fish is what determines the length of time it can be frozen successfully. Delicious fish oils will change in flavor while the fish is frozen. In effect, the flavor gradually changes from savory to rancid. It is this distasteful "oily" flavor that most fish eaters reject as unacceptable in a piece of fish served.

Low-oil-content fish can be frozen successfully for two months, and high-oil-content fish can be frozen for one month. If you are freezing fish yourself, you can adhere to this suggestion. Store-bought frozen fish is anybody's guess. All store-bought frozen fish should be thawed and used immediately.

Defrosting Fish

Fish that is frozen needs to be defrosted in the refrigerator. If it is individually wrapped, it should be allowed twenty-four hours to defrost. If it is packed in a carton of ice, it will take two days.

Allow frozen fish the time to defrost slowly. The faster it defrosts, the more the firm texture will deteriorate.

Fish can also be defrosted in the microwave. The key is to turn and rotate it frequently, no matter what size it is, until it is defrosted. Leave the protective plastic wrapping on the fish and place it on a microwave-safe plate. Defrosting one 6- to 8-ounce fillet takes about 4 minutes at 100 percent power, turning and rotating the fish every minute. Handle the fish gently during this process, and check it frequently—if you leave it in too long it will start to cook. Steaks or whole fish will take longer. You can average about 6 minutes per inch of thickness of the steak or whole fish, turning a quarter turn every minute to assure even defrosting before the fish begins to cook.

Cleaning Fish

As was pointed out earlier—but can't be emphasized enough—by all means take advantage of your fishmonger's offer of service in the cleaning of the fish. The market is the best place to have the fish scaled, eviscerated, degilled, pan-dressed, filleted, steaked, chunked, etc.

If some or all of these services have not yet been performed on your fish to accommodate your needs, however, you will have to do it at home. The following instructions will give you an idea of how to perform these processes yourself, in the order that you would need to follow if you had a whole and completely undressed fish before you.

Depending upon how you want to serve your fish, you may not need to perform all these procedures. A fish that is going to be filleted does not have to be eviscerated or dressed in any way. A fillet that is going to be skinned does not have to be scaled. A fish that is going to be pan-dressed does not have to be degilled, unless the head is used for stock. Skip the unnecessary steps.

SCALING:

This may be the first step you need to perform on your whole fish. You will want to perform this first, even before evisceration, because when the fish is still plumped with all its natural contents (the viscera) it is more manageable. Once the fish has surrendered its entrails, there is less form to the body and the scaling is more difficult.

Scaling a fish can be done with a knife or a fish-scaler—a special tool that can be found in sporting good stores and some cooking equipment shops or grocery store utensil sections. The fish should be laid upon a flat surface parallel to your body, perhaps on a damp towel to prevent slipping during the process.

Some people prefer to hold the fish by the tail, others by the head. I find it easier to scale small fish by holding the head and larger fish by holding the tail. In either case, the knife or fish-scaler is scraped across the body of the fish from tail to head, against the lay of the scales, so that the scales are lifted up and pulled away from the skin. Wrap the tail or head, whichever you are holding, with a kitchen towel to give yourself a good grip on what otherwise might be a slippery handful.

If a knife is used, always use a dull one. There is no need for a sharp cutting blade; a blunt blade works better because it can lift and scrape while not penetrating the skin and flesh under the scales. Also, if you hold the fish by the head as opposed to the tail, the dull knife will not cut you in the event it slips to your hand. In all of cooking and chopping, the cardinal rule of knife use is never, never to cut toward yourself. I break this rule here in the case of a knife that is too dull to cut you, yet ideal for the job at hand.

Hold the knife at a forty-five degree angle so it lifts but doesn't dig. When one side of the fish is scaled completely, turn the fish over and do the other side. Run your fingers over the entire fish to be sure that you have done a thorough job. Then rinse the fish free of loose scales and pat it dry.

EVISCERATING:

Evisceration is the removal of the viscera or entrails of the fish from the stomach cavity—though I don't believe in my entire life I have ever heard the process referred to by any fisherman or fish seller other than as "gutting" the fish.

This operation is a most important step, as the viscera of the fish will spoil the flesh if it is not removed in a timely fashion.

When you buy fish, sometimes the viscera have not yet been removed. My feeling about this is that it allows the fish merchant—provided the fish is quite fresh—to attach a price to it that appears to be less expensive than had the fish already been gutted. The lower the weight and higher the percentage of flesh to total weight, the more expensive the price would have to be per pound for the fish. It is a normal practice.

The actual process of evisceration begins with the insertion of a sharp knife blade into the underside of the fish, beginning at the vent—the small opening near the tail of the fish—and moving the blade of the knife toward the head until you have cut an opening that is large enough to remove the entrails themselves; from the body cavity. Do not cut into the entrails themselves; they can leave a bitter flavor on the flesh. Remove all the entrails and, using your fingers or a clean, damp cloth, wipe out any dark blood that may adhere to the interior of the cavity walls. Discard the viscera. Your fish is now eviscerated, or "drawn."

DEGILLING:

Removing the gills of the fish is an important next step if you are cooking the fish with its head on—or if you plan to use the head and bones to make stock.

It is always my preference to cook whole fish with its head on. I truly appreciate the presentation of a single whole fish on a plate for each person or a large fish on a serving platter to be served up to the dining party. Leaving the head on also means the cooked fish will be juicier. The gills, however, can leave a bitter taste in the pan drippings and the flesh of the fish nearby. Remove them.

To remove the gills, lay the fish flat on a surface and, using your thumb, lift up the gill cover on the rear of the head, just behind the fish cheek. With scissors or a small knife, cut the red, semicircular gills from the inside of the fish. Perform the same exercise on the other side of the fish head. Discard the gills.

Dressed and Pan-Dressed Fish

A fish that has been scaled, eviscerated, and degilled is "dressed." It is ready to be cooked whole. Some people prefer to also remove the head, fins, and tail; a fish so treated is "pan-dressed."

Filleting a Fish

Filleting a fish brings it to its cleanest and purest state of flesh. The fillet of the fish—the single whole width and length of meat from one side of a fish—is by far the most popular cut for serving. It is virtually boneless, depending on the fish, and delivers an ease of handling from kitchen to table, in the cooking and particularly in the eating, that is preferred by most fish lovers, both cooks and diners alike.

The fillet can be served with the skin on or off. This is determined by the firmness of the texture of the fish and the preparation in which it is to be used. A fish that might be preferred skinless for poaching may well be preferred skin-on for grilling. The skin helps hold the flesh together in the cooking and the lifting and is a delicious component of many fish fillets.

There are two general shapes of fish: round and flat. Round fish—round in width, not the circumference of the entire fish—include most fish that we eat; it is the standard fish body type. Flat fish are those that are just that—flat—such as flounder and sole. Flounder is the only flat fish in this book; it is a most popular and widely available fish and is preferred by many aficionados.

The tool used for filleting can greatly help the procedure. A filleting knife, a *sharp* filleting knife, is a near necessity. This knife would be one with a long, thin, flexible blade. If you don't have a knife designed for filleting, use your knife with the thinnest blade.

The filleting is slightly different for the two fish body types.

FILLETING ROUND FISH:

Lay the fish flat on a surface before you, holding the head in your left hand, tail toward your right. Make your first cut into the side of the fish behind the gill and pectoral fin—the fin on the side of the fish just behind the head. Cut into the width of the fish to the bone. Turn your knife flat, blade toward the tail, and cut as you

13

slide the blade along the backbone of the fish all the way to the tail. Remove the fillet and trim off any bony areas that may have come off in the fillet. Turn the fish over and repeat the process. You now have the two fillets of the round body-type fish.

The degilled head and bones of the fish that you have remaining should be used for stock.

FILLETING FLAT FISH:

More often than not, the fillets of flat fish are taken off two from the top and two from the bottom, as opposed to a single top fillet and a single bottom fillet.

Lay the fish flat on a surface before you. Make a cut across the width of the fish behind the head and pectoral fin. Make a second cut to the depth of the backbone from behind the head down the backbone the length of the fish to the tail. Insert your knife into the intersection of the cuts behind the head and slide it along the backbone and ribs of the fish, cutting from backbone to outer perimeter as you move across the fish to the tail. Remove this single half top fillet and repeat the process for the other half top fillet. Turn the fish over and repeat the entire process for the two half bottom fillets. The two half top fillets will be thicker than the two half bottom fillets.

The remaining degilled head and bones of the flat fish should be used for stock.

SKINNING FISH FILLETS:

If your recipe calls for a skinned fillet, the fillets you now have are ready for the final procedure of skinning. Use your sharpest filleting knife, or at least your sharpest available knife.

Lay the fillet flat before you, skin side down, with the tail end at your left hand. Grip the small tail end between your left-hand thumb and forefinger. Use a towel to secure that hold if it is easier for you. Make a cut across the width of the fillet about 1/2 to 1 inch from the tail end through the flesh to the skin, but not through the skin. Turn your knife flat, blade toward your right hand and the wide end—previously the head end—of the fillet. Now slide your knife beneath the fillet, between the flesh and the skin, until you have completely separated the two.

Repeat the process for all fillets to be used.

Steaking a Fish

A popular way of cutting larger fish into portions for cooking and serving is to cross-section it into steaks.

Steaks are cut from a large fish that is eviscerated, but need not be scaled or skinned. There are differing preferences on this. Some people prefer the steak skinned. It will depend on the fish and your personal likes.

To cut a fish into steaks, place the fish, belly side down, before you on a cutting board. Using a large, very sharp knife, or a cleaver, begin behind the head (if there is still a head) and cut straight down into the fish across the width. Make the cut clean. Move down the fish toward the tail the distance that you want the steak to be thick. A normal thickness is 1/2 to 1 inch, depending on the size and the circumference of the fish. Make another clean cut to separate the steak from the remaining fish body. Continue the process for the entire fish, or for as many steaks as you want to take from the fish.

As you move from the head to the tail—the large to small end of the fish—you will want to increase the thickness of the steak to accommodate for the diminishing circumference of the fish. In this way each portion will have an equal weight, if not an equal circumference. The thicker pieces will need to be cooked longer than the thinner ones.

Chunking a Fish

Very large fish that are too big even to cut into steaks are often cut into chunks. A chunk of a fish is a piece of the very large and thick fillet that has been cut into manageable lengths.

Such a piece can be left whole for baking or cut into strips width-wise to produce portions that would be a boneless half-steak. The chunk can also be cut into cubes for skewers, kebabs, or brochettes.

COOKING GULF COAST FISH

You are now ready to sample the recipes. I hope that they will inspire you to want to use the Gulf Coast fish introduced in this book in other ways as well. To that end, I have included in the last chapter of the book instructions for basic cooking methods, and suggestions about choosing sauces. Following this general advice, you should be able to create your own delicious recipes.

TO THE PIANO!

Almost twenty-five years ago, I attended my first cooking class at the Cordon Bleu in Paris. I arrived with a solid knowledge of Creole cuisine, having already apprenticed in the kitchen at Antoine's Restaurant in New Orleans.

Our instructor, Chef Narcisse, who was a tyrant of the art, began our session with sketchy instructions for the fish recipe we were going to prepare and the command for us to begin the recipe's execution. That command, which he bellowed to the small group, was "Au piano!" In due course we learned that his expression for "cooking at the stove" was "playing the piano." And so to you, my friends, I cry the same command, *To the piano!*

Great Barracuda

Group: Barracuda

Other common name(s):
Barracuda
Cuda

Latin name:
Sphyraena barracuda
Family Sphyraenidae

Maximum length:
6 1/2 feet

Maximum weight:
106 pounds

Cuts:
whole (small)
steak
fillet

Meat characteristics:
tender, white, flaky
low oil content

Preferred cooking methods:
bake
braise
fry
poach
steam

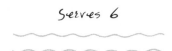
1 3-pound whole great barracuda, scaled
    and drawn (see Note)
1 stick salted butter, melted

Juice of 2 lemons
Salt and freshly ground black pepper
Vegetable oil for grilling

Serves 6

Light the charcoal 1 hour before cooking. "Butterfly" the barracuda to ready it for the grill. To butterfly the fish, the head and tail can be removed, or not, as you desire. Split the full length of the fish from the underside, almost but not completely through. Remove the backbone and any other bones in the flesh. Cut out and discard any dark parts of the meat. Slash the skin side of the fish diagonally four times on each side, about 1/2 inch deep.

In a small bowl, combine the melted butter and lemon juice and paint it on all sides of the fish. Sprinkle the fish lightly with salt and pepper.

When the grill is ready, place the fish on an oiled grill rack or grill screen, or on oiled heavy foil on the grill rack. Baste the fish with the butter and lemon juice. Cover the grill and cook, skin side down, for approximately 15 minutes, or until the flesh is white and flaky all the way through when broken with the tines of a fork. Baste regularly. Do not turn the fish during cooking.

When the fish is opaque and flaky all the way through, remove it to a heated serving platter and cut it all the way across into serving portions. Serve with the remaining butter and lemon juice basting liquid poured over.

Notes: If you prefer, you can have the fish butterflied at the market. The same preparation can be used for a larger barracuda. The fish can be cut into steaks 1 inch or so thick, or a whole fillet, or portioned cuts of fillets, and cooked 8 to 10 minutes per inch of thickness.

Gulf kingfish, Spanish mackerel, spotted sea trout, striped bass, and weakfish are also excellent in this recipe.

1 3-pound whole great barracuda, scaled
    and drawn (see Note)
2 tablespoons chili powder
2 tablespoons Hungarian paprika
2 tablespoons salt
1 teaspoon cayenne pepper
4 cloves garlic, pressed

1/4 cup olive oil
Juice of 1 lime
Vegetable oil for grilling
1/4 cup melted salted butter
Juice of 1 lime
1 tablespoon minced fresh cilantro leaves

Serves 4-6

~~~~~~~~~~~~~

~~~~~~~~~~~~~

Light the grill or charcoal 1 hour before cooking. Butterfly the barracuda (see instructions on page 18).

In a small bowl, combine the chili powder, paprika, salt, cayenne, pressed garlic, olive oil, and lime juice, and work them together into a paste. Rub the fish, flesh side and skin side, with the seasoning paste.

When the grill is ready, oil the rack and grill the barracuda, flesh side down, for about 5 minutes. Carefully turn the fish over and continue cooking another 4 minutes until the fish is opaque and flaky all the way through.

Carefully remove the barracuda from the grill to a heated serving platter. Combine the hot melted butter, lime juice, and minced fresh cilantro leaves, paint it over the fish, and serve.

Notes: If you prefer, you can have the fish butterflied at the market.

Atlantic bonito, creolefish, hard-tail jack, scamp, and Spanish mackerel also work well in this recipe.

Other Delicious Recipes for Great Barracuda include:

Great Barracuda Baked with Onion and Lime (see spotted jewfish, page 42)

Broiled Great Barracuda Fillets with Cilantro Butter (see weakfish, page 123)

Ceviche of Great Barracuda (see creolefish, page 28)

Corn-Flour-Fried Great Barracuda Fillets (see dog snapper, page 300)

Grilled Great Barracuda Steaks with Onions, Green Bell Peppers, and Eggplant (see ling cobia, page 84)

Grilled Great Barracuda with Tomato Sauce (see lookdown, page 179)

Panfried Great Barracuda with Bienville Sauce (see wahoo, page 207)

Tamales with Great Barracuda and Roasted Tomato and Chili Sauce (see common jack, page 156)

Whole Panfried Great Barracuda with Onion, Garlic, and Red Wine Sauce (see pilot fish, page 190)

Wood-Grilled Great Barracuda Steaks with Achiote-Garlic Paste (see black grouper, page 49)

Black Sea Bass

Group: Sea Bass

Other common name(s):
  Black Bass
  Sea Bass
  Bass
Latin name:
  Centropristes striatus
  Family Serranidae
Maximum length:
  2 feet

Maximum weight:
  10 pounds
Cuts:
  whole
  steak
  fillet
Meat characteristics:
  firm, white
  low-to-medium
  oil content

Preferred cooking methods:
  bake
  broil
  fry
  grill
  poach
  sauté

Cold Poached Black Sea Bass Fillets with Green Onion Mayonnaise

Green Onion Mayonnaise (recipe follows)
2 quarts water, or enough to cover fish
    (about 2 inches deep in skillet)
1 lemon, thinly sliced
1 medium onion, thinly sliced
2 sprigs fresh parsley
2 bay leaves
1 clove garlic, mashed

6 whole black peppercorns
2 teaspoons salt
1/4 teaspoon cayenne pepper
6 6-ounce pieces black sea bass fillet,
    skinned
6 large lettuce leaves
3 cups chopped lettuce

Serves 6

Prepare the Green Onion Mayonnaise Sauce, and refrigerate or hold aside at room temperature.

In a wide skillet, bring the water to a boil with the lemon, onion, parsley, bay leaves, garlic, peppercorns, salt, and cayenne. Let boil for 3 minutes to allow the water to draw the flavor from the seasoning ingredients. Lower the heat to a simmer and lay in the black sea bass fillets. Poach for 10 minutes, or until the fish is flaky when broken with a fork. With a long spatula, carefully remove the fillets from the water and drain. Cover and chill.

To serve: Place a lettuce leaf on each of six chilled salad plates, and layer the leaf with chopped lettuce. Lay each cold black sea bass fillet on a bed of chopped lettuce. Nap the fillets with the dressing and serve the remaining dressing on the side.

Green Onion Mayonnaise Sauce

2 egg yolks
3/4 teaspoon salt
1/4 teaspoon freshly ground white pepper
1/4 teaspoon cayenne pepper
1 teaspoon Dijon mustard
1/4 cup freshly squeezed lemon juice

1 1/4 cups light olive oil
1/4 cup cold reduced fish stock (see
    page 372)
1/2 cup chopped green onions
1/4 cup dry white wine

In a bowl, beat the egg yolks together with the salt, white pepper, cayenne, and mustard. Add 1 tablespoon of the lemon juice, and beat in a quarter of the oil 1 tablespoon at a time. Add the remaining lemon juice, and beat in the rest of the oil, a little at a time, until the dressing is completely emulsified and very thick. Beat in the cold fish stock.

In a small saucepan, simmer the green onions in the wine until the wine has almost completely reduced. Stir the onions and wine into the mayonnaise. Adjust seasonings, if necessary. Refrigerate or hold aside at room temperature until ready to use.

Note: Also excellent in this recipe are black drum, jolthead porgy, tripletail, and white grunt.

Criolla Sauce (recipe follows)
Vegetable oil for grilling

6 8-ounce black sea bass steaks
2 tablespoons salted butter

Serves 6

Light the grill or charcoal 1 hour before cooking. Prepare the Criolla Sauce.

When the grill is ready, brush the rack with oil. Brush one side of the black sea bass steaks with oil and place them oil side down on the rack. Grill for 5 minutes, or until they are turning white even on the top side. Brush the top of the steaks with oil and carefully turn them over. Cook for another 4 minutes or so, until the flesh is white all the way through when broken with the tines of a fork.

Remove the steaks to warm plates and top each with 1 teaspoon butter. Serve with the Criolla Sauce on the side.

Criolla Sauce

2 tomatoes, skinned (see Note), seeded, and finely chopped
1/2 cucumber, seeded and finely chopped
1/2 green or red bell pepper, seeded and finely chopped
1/2 yellow onion, finely chopped
2 cloves garlic, minced
1 tablespoon capers, minced
1 1/2 teaspoons minced fresh tarragon, or 1/2 teaspoon dried tarragon

1/4 cup minced fresh parsley
2 tablespoons Creole mustard
2 tablespoons red wine vinegar
4 teaspoons light-flavored olive oil
1 teaspoon Louisiana hot sauce, or to taste
Salt and freshly ground white pepper

In a bowl, combine all the ingredients and season to taste with salt and white pepper. Reserve at room temperature until ready to use.

Notes: To skin the tomatoes, immerse them in boiling water for 1 to 2 minutes, then plunge them into cold water.

Atlantic spadefish, common jack, Florida pompano, king mackerel, largetooth sawfish, ling cobia, lookdown, queen triggerfish, sand perch, and yellowfin tuna can also be used with this recipe. Use 6 8-ounce Florida pompano fillets or 6 6-ounce sand perch fillets; cooking times are approximately the same. For the Atlantic spadefish, lookdown, and queen triggerfish, use 6 1-pound whole fish, scaled and drawn. Grilling times for these fish is slightly longer, about 7 minutes or until the tops start to turn white, then brush the top with oil and turn over to cook through.

Other Delicious Recipes for Black Sea Bass include:

Baked Black Sea Bass with Bacon and Onion (see red grouper, page 52)

Baked Crabmeat-Stuffed Black Sea Bass (see gulf kingfish, page 106)

Black Sea Bass Fillets with Mornay Sauce (see yellowtail snapper, page 314)

Black Sea Bass Fillets Simmered in Leek and Tomato Sauce (see hard-tail jack, page 174)

Black Sea Bass with Pecans (see lookdown, page 181)

Breaded Black Sea Bass with Creole Tomato Sauce (see black grouper, page 47)

Broiled Black Sea Bass (see gulf founder, page 131)

Broiled Black Sea Bass with Poulette Sauce (see red porgy, page 260)

Grilled Black Sea Bass with Tomato Butter (see sand perch, page 32)

Poached Black Sea Bass Fillets with Maltaise Sauce (see common dolphin, page 88)

Poached Black Sea Bass Fillets with Rockefeller Sauce (see tripletail, page 363)

Sautéed Black Sea Bass Steaks Marseilles-Style (see rainbow runner, page 194)

Creolefish

Group: Sea Bass

Other common name(s):
  "Snapper" (sic)

Latin name:
  Paranthias furcifer
  Family Serranidae

Maximum length:
  1 foot 3 inches

Maximum weight:
  10 pounds

Cuts:
  whole
  steak
  fillet

Meat characteristics:
  firm, white, flaky
  low-to-medium oil
  content

Preferred cooking methods:
  bake
  broil
  fry
  grill
  sauté

2 habañero (Scotch bonnet) chilies, stemmed, seeded, and minced (see Note)
1 large onion, chopped
2 large tomatoes, chopped
2 large cloves garlic, minced
1 cup freshly squeezed lime juice

1/4 cup olive oil
1/4 cup minced fresh cilantro
1/2 teaspoon salt
1 1/2 pounds creolefish fillets, skinned
6 large lettuce leaves

Serves 6

In a large bowl, combine the chilies, onion, tomatoes, and garlic. Stir in the lime juice, olive oil, cilantro, and salt.

Cut the creolefish fillets into bite-sized pieces and fold them into the other ingredients in the bowl, being sure that they are completely covered. Cover the bowl with plastic wrap and refrigerate for at least 3 hours, but no more than 5. The lime juice will cause the creolefish to "cook" and become opaque as it marinates. Stir the fish around in the bowl once or twice during the marinating period to be sure all pieces are well exposed to the marinade. The ceviche is done when the fish pieces are opaque all the way through. Adjust salt if desired.

Serve the ceviche in glass dessert dishes or parfait glasses lined with lettuce leaves.

Notes: Jalapeño peppers can be used in place of the habañeros. The amount of peppers used should be adjusted to suit your own tastes.

Black grouper, dog snapper, great barracuda, sheepshead, and shortfin mako shark also go well in this recipe.

Creole Mustard Sauce (recipe follows)
6 1-pound whole creolefish, scaled and
   drawn (see Note)
1 cup corn flour (see Note)
2 teaspoons salt
1/2 teaspoon freshly ground white pepper
1/2 teaspoon cayenne pepper

Peanut oil for frying
6 8-inch-long diagonally cut slices French
   bread
2 tablespoons melted salted butter
6 4-ounce slices cooked ham
Hungarian paprika

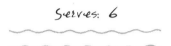

Serves: 6

Prepare the Creole Mustard Sauce, and hold aside warm.

Heat 1/2 inch oil in a heavy, wide skillet to 375°. In a bowl, combine the corn flour with the salt, white pepper, and cayenne. Dredge the creolefish in the corn flour mixture, and fry, without crowding the pan, about 5 minutes on each side, or until golden brown. Drain on absorbent paper and hold aside warm.

Place the French bread slices on a cookie sheet and brush them with the melted butter. Lay a slice of ham on each slice of bread and broil about 3 minutes, or until the ham is thoroughly heated and the bread slices are lightly toasted. Top each serving with a fried fish, nap with the warm Creole Mustard Sauce, sprinkle with paprika, and serve immediately.

Creole Mustard Sauce

6 egg yolks
2 1/2 tablespoons freshly squeezed lemon
   juice
1/4 teaspoon freshly ground white pepper

1/4 teaspoon cayenne pepper
2 sticks salted butter
2 tablespoons Creole mustard

Combine the egg yolks, lemon juice, white pepper, and cayenne in a blender and process for a few seconds. In a saucepan, heat the butter to a bubbling boil, and add it in a thin stream to the blender while processing, until all is incorporated. Add the Creole mustard, and blend the sauce for a few seconds more. Serve warm.

Notes: The heads of the fish may be removed if desired. Fillets of creolefish are equally enjoyable in this recipe, though they lack the adventure of deboning the flesh as you eat; use 6 6-ounce skinned fillets.

Corn flour is often used in the frying of seafood rather than white flour. It can be bought as plain corn flour in specialty stores or as corn masa flour or "masa harina" in stores that sell Mexican or Central and South American food products. It is the flour that corn tortillas are made from. It can also be gotten in the form of "fish-fry," which is corn flour that is already seasoned with salt and pepper.

Pinfish, red porgy, speckled hind, and striped mullet are also excellent fried this way.

Other Delicious Recipes for Creolefish include:

Baked Crabmeat-Stuffed Creolefish (see gulf kingfish, page 106)
Broiled Creolefish with Balsamic Vinegar (see Atlantic moonfish, page 153)
Creolefish Barbacoa (see great barracuda, page 20)
Creolefish Fillets Simmered in Leek and Tomato Sauce (see hard-tail jack, page 174)
Grilled Creolefish Fillets with Tomato Butter (see sand perch, page 32)
Panfried Creolefish with Lobster Cream Sauce (see permit, page 186)
Sautéed Creolefish with Crabmeat and Butter (see common dolphin, page 90)

Sand Perch

Group: Sea Bass

Other common name(s):
　"Squirrelfish" (sic)

Latin name:
　Diplectrum formosum
　Family Serranidae

Maximum length:
　1 foot

Maximum weight:
　2 pounds

Cuts:
　whole
　fillet

Meat characteristics:
　tender, white
　low oil content

Preferred cooking methods:
　fry
　poach
　sauté

Tomato Butter (recipe follows)   6 6-ounce sand perch fillets
Vegetable oil for grilling

Serves 6

Light the grill or charcoal 1 hour before cooking. Prepare the Tomato Butter, and hold aside warm.

When the grill is ready, brush the rack with oil. Brush one side of the sand perch fillets with oil and place them oil side down on the rack. Grill for 4 minutes, or until they are turning white on the top side. Brush the top of the fillets with oil and carefully turn them over. Cook for another 4 minutes or so, until the flesh is white all the way through when broken with the tines of a fork.

Remove the grilled sand perch fillets to warm plates. Serve with the Tomato Butter on the side.

Tomato Butter

1 1/2 sticks salted butter   2 tablespoons minced French shallot
2 medium ripe tomatoes, roughly chopped   Salt and freshly ground white pepper

In a small sauté pan, heat 2 tablespoons of the butter and sauté the chopped tomato and minced French shallot. Cook until the tomato has released its juices and the liquid has mostly evaporated. Remove from the heat and pass the mixture through a strainer.

In the same saucepan, melt the remaining butter without allowing it to come to a simmer. Add the cooked tomato mixture and heat together gently without letting the sauce come to a simmer. Season with salt and white pepper to taste.

Note: Atlantic spadefish, black sea bass, creolefish, gray triggerfish, lookdown, mutton snapper, queen triggerfish, scamp, and squirrelfish can also be used with this recipe. Use 6 8-ounce black sea bass steaks. Cooking times are approximately the same. For the Atlantic spadefish, lookdowns, and queen triggerfish, use 6 1-pound whole fish, scaled and drawn. Grilling time for these fish is slightly longer, about 7 minutes, or until the tops start to turn white. Brush the tops with oil and turn over to cook through.

Lime and Onion Marinade (recipe follows)
6 1-pound whole sand perch, scaled and
drawn

Hot sauce, preferably Caribbean-style
habañero pepper sauce

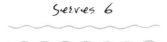

Serves 6

In a skillet or poaching pan large enough to hold all the fish, prepare the Lime and Onion Marinade. Add the fish to the marinade and poach at a simmer for 20 minutes, or until the fish flesh is white all the way through when broken with the tines of a fork.

Transfer the poached fish to wide soup bowls, cutting them in half crosswise if necessary for the fit, and pour the cooking marinade over them. Pass the hot sauce as a condiment.

Lime and Onion Marinade

1 1/2 quarts water
2 cups dry white wine
1/2 cup freshly squeezed lime juice
1 small hot pepper, minced
4 large cloves garlic, minced
1 large onion, chopped

6 green onions, chopped
4 whole cloves
4 whole allspice
4 bay leaves
1 tablespoon salt

Combine all the ingredients and simmer for 10 minutes. Adjust seasonings.

Note: Atlantic threadfin, gaff-topsail catfish, king mackerel, snook, spotted eagle ray, and weakfish are delicious substitutions. Use 6 8-ounce fillet pieces (for the spotted eagle ray, used skinned wing fillet) and cut the simmer time to 10 minutes.

Variations: Small whole sand perch are also excellent poached in Orange-Curry Marinade (page 291) or Sherry Marinade (page 319). Also try (follow recipe exactly except for the following substitutions and additions):

Red Wine Marinade
Substitute red wine for the white and use 1/4 cup fresh lemon juice instead of lime juice. Serve with Louisiana hot sauce.

White Wine Marinade
Replace the lime juice with one lemon, thinly sliced. Use only 2 green onions (chopped), 3 whole cloves, 3 whole allspice, and 3 bay leaves.

Other Delicious Recipes for Sand Perch include:
Fried Sand Perch with Brown Shrimp Sauce (see white mullet, page 245)
Grilled Sand Perch with Criolla Sauce (see black sea bass, page 25)
Grilled Sand Perch with Tomato Sauce (see lookdown, page 179)
Panfried Sand Perch with Lobster Cream Sauce (see permit, page 186)
Poached Sand Perch with Horseradish and Sour Cream Sauce (see Atlantic croaker, page 95)
Sand Perch Fillets with Artichokes and Mushrooms in Brown Lemon-Butter Sauce (see black drum, page 100)
Sand Perch with Oyster and Crabmeat Sauce Gratiné (see pinfish, page 256)
Sautéed Sand Perch with Citrus-Garlic Sauce (see Atlantic threadfin, page 341)
Whole Cracker-Crumb-Coated Panfried Sand Perch with Key Lime Sauce (see white grunt, page 147)
Whole Panfried Sand Perch with Colbert Sauce (see red porgy, page 262)
Whole Panfried Sand Perch with Onion, Garlic, and Red Wine Sauce (see pilot fish, page 190)
Whole Panfried Sand Perch with Salsa Roja (see striped mullet, page 240)

Speckled Hind

Group: Sea Bass

Other common name(s):
Hind

Latin name:
Epinephelus drummondhayi
Family Serranidae

Maximum length:
2 feet 6 inches

Maximum weight:
40 pounds

Cuts:
whole (small)
steak
fillet

Meat characteristics:
white, flaky
low-to-medium oil
content

Preferred cooking methods:
bake
braise
fry
poach
steam

Marquis Sauce (recipe follows)
1 1/2 quarts water, or enough to cover
    fillets (about 1 inch deep in skillet)
1 lemon, thinly sliced
1 medium onion, thinly sliced
2 sprigs fresh parsley
2 bay leaves

1 clove garlic, mashed
6 whole black peppercorns
2 teaspoons salt
1/4 teaspoon cayenne pepper
6 8-ounce pieces speckled hind
    fillet, skinned

Serves 6

Prepare the Marquis Sauce and hold aside warm or tepid.

In a heavy, wide skillet, bring the water to a boil with the lemon, onion, parsley, bay leaves, garlic, peppercorns, salt, and cayenne. Let boil for 3 minutes to allow the water to draw the flavor from the seasoning ingredients. Lower the heat to a simmer. Lay in the fillets and poach for 10 minutes, or until the fish is flaky when broken with a fork.

With a long spatula, carefully remove the fillets from the water, drain, and place on warm dinner plates. Nap the poached speckled hind fillets with the Marquis Sauce, and serve.

Marquis Sauce

6 large egg yolks
3 tablespoons freshly squeezed lemon juice
1 teaspoon salt

1/2 teaspoon cayenne pepper
3 sticks salted butter
2 ounces black caviar, or black fish roe

Put the egg yolks, lemon juice, salt, and cayenne in a blender and blend on low for 5 to 7 seconds. In a small saucepan, melt the butter and heat it until it comes to a simmer. Turn the blender on high and pour the hot butter, in a thin stream, into the egg yolk mixture until all is incorporated. The heat from the butter will cook the Marquis Sauce. Fold in the caviar. Serve warm or tepid.

Note: Other fish excellent with this recipe are black drum, common dolphin, gulf flounder, lookdown, striped bass, and tilefish.

Peanut oil for frying
1 cup all-purpose flour
2 teaspoons salt
1 teaspoon freshly ground white pepper
2 eggs, separated
1 teaspoon Louisiana hot sauce

2 cups beer, at room temperature
2 1/2 pounds speckled hind fillets, skinned
3 lemons, halved
1 1/2 cups Tartar Sauce (page 375) or
   Cocktail Sauce (page 375)

Serves 6

Heat 1 inch oil in a wide, heavy frying pan to 350° to 375°. In a bowl, combine the flour, salt, and white pepper. Beat in the egg yolks and hot sauce. Beat in the beer 1/2 cup at a time, until the batter is smooth. In another bowl, beat the egg whites until they stand in soft peaks, and fold them into the batter. Dip the speckled hind fillets into the batter, turning to be sure they are completely coated, and fry, without crowding the pan, for about 4 minutes a side, or until they are nicely browned on both sides. Drain on absorbent paper.

Serve garnished with lemon halves, and pass the Tartar or Cocktail Sauce, or both.

Note: Many other fish work wonderfully with this recipe, including Atlantic croaker, Atlantic spadefish, bonefish, lookdown, permit, pinfish, red porgy, sailor's-choice, scamp, tripletail, white mullet, and yellowtail snapper. Use 6 8-ounce skinned fillets of tripletail and yellowtail snapper or 6 6-ounce skinned fillets of Atlantic spadefish.

Variations

(follow recipe exactly except for the following substitutions and additions):

Chili Beer Batter

Combine 1 tablespoon chili powder with the flour, salt, and pepper mixture.

Curry Beer Batter

Combine 2 teaspoons curry powder with the flour, salt, and pepper mixture.

Herbed Beer Batter

Combine 1 teaspoon powdered thyme, 1 teaspoon powdered oregano, and 1 teaspoon powdered marjoram with the flour, salt, and pepper mixture. Omit the Louisiana hot sauce.

Pepper Beer Batter

Combine 1 teaspoon black pepper and 1 teaspoon cayenne with the flour, salt, and pepper mixture. Omit the Louisiana hot sauce.

Other Delicious Recipes for Speckled Hind include:

Baked Shrimp-Stuffed Speckled Hind (see black drum, page 98)

Étouffée of Speckled Hind (see blackfin tuna, page 218)

Fillet of Speckled Hind Baked en Papillote with a Shrimp, Crabmeat, and White Wine Sauce (see Florida pompano, page 161)

Fried Whole Speckled Hind with Creole Mustard Sauce (see creolefish, page 29)

Fried Whole Speckled Hind with Sweet Mustard and Egg Sauce (see pinfish, page 254)

Grilled Speckled Hind with Tomato-Red Wine Sauce (see Atlantic spadefish, page 325)

Herbed Garlic Speckled Hind (see yellowtail snapper, page 316)

Poached Speckled Hind Fillets with Hollandaise Sauce (see striped bass, page 63)

Speckled Hind Poached in Orange-Curry Marinade (see shortfin mako shark, page 291)

Whole Cornmeal-Fried Speckled Hind with Mosca Sauce (see Atlantic croaker, page 93)

Whole Steamed Speckled Hind Marinière (see weakfish, page 122)

Spotted Jewfish

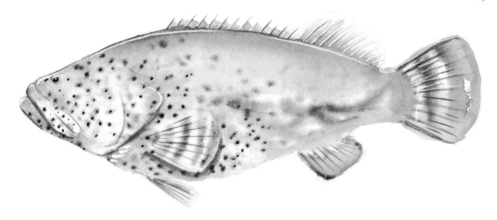

Group: Sea Bass

Other common name(s):
  Jewfish
Latin name:
  Epinephelus itajara
  Family Serranidae
Maximum length:
  8 feet

Maximum weight:
  680 pounds
Cuts:
  whole (small)
  steak
  fillet
Meat characteristics:
  firm, medium-white,
  flaky
  low-to-medium oil
  content

*Preferred cooking
methods:*
  bake
  fry
  grill
  poach
  sauté

Spotted Jewfish Baked with Onion and Lime

1 5-pound whole spotted jewfish, scaled
   and drawn
All-purpose flour
1 stick salted butter, melted

Salt and freshly ground black pepper
3 large onions, thinly sliced
2 limes, thinly sliced
1/2 cup dry white wine

Serves 6 to 8

Preheat the oven to 450°. Rub the spotted jewfish inside and out with flour, brush it with melted butter, and season it with salt and pepper. Put the fish in a buttered baking pan, lay the sliced onions and limes on and around it, and pour in the wine.

Bake for approximately 45 minutes (10 minutes per inch of thickness of the fish). Baste from time to time with the pan juices to keep the fish moist.

When the fish is done, remove it carefully from the pan with a wide spatula to a heated serving platter, or cut it into portions and serve it up onto heated dinner plates right from the pan. Spoon the pan juices over the servings.

Note: Great barracuda, red drum, and spotfin flounder are also excellent baked this way.

Cold Poached Spotted Jewfish Ravigote with Boiled New Potatoes

Ravigote Mayonnaise (recipe follows)
2 quarts water, or enough to cover fish
   (about 2 inches deep in skillet)
1 lemon, thinly sliced
1 medium onion, thinly sliced
2 sprigs fresh parsley
2 bay leaves
1 clove garlic, mashed
6 whole black peppercorns
2 teaspoons salt
1/4 teaspoon cayenne pepper
6 6-ounce pieces spotted jewfish fillet,
   skinned
6 large lettuce leaves
18 cold boiled new potatoes

Serves 6

Begin by making the Ravigote Mayonnaise; refrigerate until ready to use.

In a wide skillet, bring the water to a boil with the lemon, onion, parsley, bay leaves, garlic, peppercorns, salt, and cayenne. Let boil for 3 minutes to allow the water to draw the flavor from the seasoning ingredients. Lower the heat to a simmer and lay in the spotted jewfish fillets. Poach for 10 minutes, or until the fish is flaky when broken with a fork. With a long spatula, carefully remove the fillets from the water and drain. Cover and chill.

In a bowl, break the spotted jewfish meat into pieces the size of crabmeat lumps. With a wooden spoon, fold the Ravigote Mayonnaise into the fish pieces. Work it only enough for the sauce to be well distributed and all the fish well coated. Refrigerate tightly covered for several hours or until well chilled.

To serve: Line 6 chilled plates with lettuce leaves, spoon on the Spotted Jewfish Ravigote, and garnish with three cold boiled new potatoes per plate.

Ravigote Mayonnaise

~~~~~~~~~

3 anchovy fillets, minced
3 green onions (white and green parts),
   minced

2 tablespoons minced red pimiento
2 tablespoons minced green bell pepper
1 1/4 cups Mayonnaise (page 374)

Blend the anchovy fillets, green onions, red pimiento, and green bell pepper into the mayonnaise, and refrigerate for at least an hour before using so that the flavors can meld.

Note: You may also use Atlantic sailfish (2 1/4 lbs.), black drum (1 1/2 lbs.), bluefish (2 1/4 lbs.), hard-tail jack (2 1/4 lbs.), red snapper (2 1/4 lbs.), shortfin mako shark (2 1/2 lbs.), or tarpon (2 1/4 lbs.) in this recipe.

Variations: Also try Cold Poached Spotted Jewfish with Aioli Sauce (page 328), Antiboise Sauce (page 294), Cypriote Sauce (page 284), or Espagnole Mayonnaise (page 303).

Other Delicious Recipes for Spotted Jewfish include:
Baked Crabmeat-Stuffed Spotted Jewfish Fillet (see greater amberjack, page 168)
Fillet of Spotted Jewfish with Browned Butter, Lemon Juice, and Caper Sauce
   (see blacktip shark, page 296)
Hot Spotted Jewfish and Artichoke Salad and Russian Dressing with Caviar
   (see largetooth sawfish, page 279)
Hot Spotted Jewfish and Mushroom Salad with Dijon Mustard Dressing
   (see Snook, page 320)
Poached Spotted Jewfish Fillets with Maltaise Sauce (see common dolphin,
   page 88)

Ragout of Spotted Jewfish au Gratin (see swordfish, page 332)

Soda-Fried Spotted Jewfish "Chips" with Fresh Tomato Catsup (see shortfin mako shark, page 289)

Spotted Jewfish with Creole Sauce Piquante (see wahoo, page 209)

Spotted Jewfish Fillets with Mornay Sauce (see yellowtail snapper, page 314)

Spotted Jewfish Garlic Soup (see skipjack tuna, page 223)

Spotted Jewfish Tamales with Piquant Green Sauce (see Spanish mackerel, page 203)

Tamales with Spotted Jewfish and Roasted Tomato and Chili Sauce (see common jack, page 156)

Whole Baked Spotted Jewfish with Spinach Stuffing (see jolthead porgy, page 250)

Black Grouper (Yellow Phase)

Group: Sea Bass, Grouper

Other common name(s):
  Grouper
  Huachinango
  "Spotted Jewfish"
Latin name:
  Mycteroperca bonaci
  Family Serranidae
Maximum length:
  4 feet

Maximum weight:
  180 pounds
Cuts:
  whole (small)
  steak
  fillet
Meat characteristics:
  firm, white, flaky
  low oil content

Preferred cooking methods:
  bake
  fry
  poach
  sauté

Breaded Black Grouper with Creole Tomato Sauce

Creole Tomato Sauce (recipe follows)
2 eggs
1/2 cup water
6 6-ounce black grouper fillets
Salt and freshly ground black pepper

1 1/2 cups French bread crumbs
4 tablespoons salted butter
1/4 cup peanut oil
2 tablespoons minced fresh parsley

Serves 6

Prepare the Creole Tomato Sauce, and hold aside warm.

Beat the eggs together with the water to make an egg wash. Lightly season the black grouper fillets with salt and black pepper, dip them in the egg wash, and dredge in the bread crumbs. Melt the butter in the peanut oil in a wide, heavy skillet and fry the fillets, without crowding the pan, 4 minutes on each side, or until they are golden brown.

Transfer the cooked black grouper fillets to warm dinner plates, spoon the Creole Tomato Sauce over the top, and sprinkle with the chopped parsley.

Creole Tomato Sauce

1 stick salted butter
1 large green bell pepper, seeded and
  chopped
2 large onions, chopped
2 ribs celery, finely chopped
5 large tomatoes, preferably Creoles,
  chopped

1/2 cup dry white wine
3 bay leaves
1/2 teaspoon dried thyme
Salt, freshly ground black pepper, and
  cayenne pepper

In a sauté pan, melt the butter and sauté the green peppers, onions, and celery for 3 minutes. Add the tomatoes, wine, bay leaves, and thyme, and simmer for 15 minutes. Season to taste with salt, black pepper, and cayenne. Serve warm.

Note: Also delicious in this recipe are Atlantic threadfin, black sea bass, hogfish, ling cobia, mutton snapper, red drum, spotfin flounder, and spotted eagle ray (use skinned wing fillet).

Achiote-Garlic Paste (recipe follows)
6 8-ounce black grouper steaks
Vegetable oil for the grill

1 cup water-soaked wood chips: mesquite,
hickory, pecan, etc.
1/2 cup hot melted salted butter

Serves 6

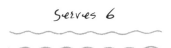

Light the charcoal 1 hour before cooking. Prepare the Achiote-Garlic Paste and paint the black grouper steaks on all sides with it.

When the grill is ready, brush the hot rack with oil and arrange the fish on the rack so that they don't touch each other. Throw in a few water-soaked wood chips and cover the grill. Let cook for 10 minutes, turning once midway and basting with the remaining paste.

Serve the wood-grilled steaks dribbled with melted butter.

Achiote-Garlic Paste

1/2 cup peeled garlic cloves
1/4 cup ground achiote seeds
1 teaspoon ground dried oregano
1 teaspoon ground cumin

1 teaspoon ground allspice
1/2 teaspoon cayenne pepper
1/2 cup freshly squeezed lime juice
1 tablespoon salt

In a blender, blend the paste ingredients on high until smooth.

Note: Atlantic sailfish, blacktip shark, bluefish, great barracuda, greater amberjack, hard-tail jack, king mackerel, and swordfish may also be used with this recipe.

Variations

(follow recipe exactly except for the following substitutions and additions):

Creole Garlic Paste

Use 1 tablespoon ground dried oregano leaves and 1/4 teaspoon ground allspice. Replace the achiote, cumin, and lime juice with 1 tablespoon ground dried marjoram leaves, 1 tablespoon dried thyme leaves, 1 tablespoon ground black pepper, 1 teaspoon mace, and 1/2 cup peanut oil. Add the salt and blend ingredients on high into a smooth paste.

Italian Herb-Garlic Paste

Use 1 tablespoon ground dried oregano leaves. Substitute 1 tablespoon ground dried basil leaves, 1 tablespoon dried ground rosemary leaves, 1 tablespoon ground black pepper, and 1/2 cup olive oil for the achiote seeds, cumin, allspice, cayenne pepper, and lime juice. Add the salt and blend ingredients on high into a smooth paste.

Other Delicious Recipes for Black Grouper include:

Baked Black Grouper in Court-Bouillon (see red drum, page 110)

Baked Crabmeat-Stuffed Black Grouper (see gulf kingfish, page 106)

Baked Shrimp-Stuffed Black Grouper (see black drum, page 98)

Black Grouper in Caribbean "Blaff" (see Spanish mackerel, page 202)

Black Grouper Fillets with Lobster-Browned Butter Sauce (see gulf flounder, page 132)

Black Grouper en Papillote with Fennel (see pigfish, page 139)

Breaded Fillets of Black Grouper with Green Mayonnaise (see red drum, page 109)

Broiled Black Grouper with Poulette Sauce (see red porgy, page 260)

Ceviche of Black Grouper (see creolefish, page 28)

Ragout of Black Grouper au Gratin (see swordfish, page 332)

Steamed Black Grouper Fillets with Espagnole Mayonnaise (see mutton snapper, page 303)

Wood-Grilled Black Grouper Steaks with Mexican Seasonings (see bluefish, page 66)

Red Grouper

Group: Sea Bass, Grouper

Other common name(s):
  Grouper
  Huachinango

Latin name:
  Epinephalus morio
  Family Serranidae

Maximum length:
  3 feet 6 inches

Maximum weight:
  50 pounds

Cuts:
  whole (small)
  steak
  fillet

Meat characteristics:
  firm, white, flaky
  low-to-medium oil
  content

Preferred cooking methods:
  bake
  broil
  grill
  poach
  sauté

1 6-pound whole red grouper, scaled and
    drawn
All-purpose flour
1/2 stick salted butter, melted
Salt and freshly ground black pepper

6 slices bacon
3 large onions, thinly sliced
1/2 cup dry white wine, or fish stock (page 371)

Serves 6–8

Preheat the oven to 450°. Rub the red grouper inside and out with flour, brush it with melted butter, and season it with salt and pepper. Lay it in a buttered baking pan. Lay the bacon slices over the top of the fish. Lay the onions on and around the fish. Pour in the wine or fish stock.

Bake the fish for approximately 45 minutes (10 minutes per inch of thickness of the fish). Baste from time to time with the pan juices to keep the fish moist.

When the fish is done, remove it carefully from the pan with a wide spatula to a heated serving platter, or cut it into portions and place onto heated dinner plates right from the pan. Spoon the bacon and onions over the servings.

Note: Black sea bass, dog snapper, gulf flounder, largetooth sawfish, spot drum, and tripletail are also delicious baked this way.

6 cups fish stock (page 371) or shellfish
   stock (page 372)
6 tomatoes, skinned (see Note), seeded, and
   chopped
1 large onion, chopped
3 tablespoons minced fresh parsley
3 fresh hot red peppers, seeded and minced

4 cloves garlic, minced
3 bay leaves
1 1/2 teaspoons dried thyme
1 1/2 pounds red grouper fillets, skinned
   and diced
Salt

Serves 6

In a saucepan, combine the fish or shellfish stock with the tomatoes, onion, parsley, hot red peppers, garlic, bay leaves, and thyme. Bring to a boil, lower to a simmer, cover, and cook for 20 minutes. Add the red grouper and simmer for ten minutes, or until fish is opaque and tender.

Add salt to taste, and serve.

Notes: To skin the tomatoes, immerse them in boiling water for 1 to 2 minutes, then plunge them into cold water.

Permit, pigfish, squirrelfish, tarpon, and white grunt are also excellent with this recipe.

Other Delicious Recipes for Red Grouper include:

Baked Shrimp-Stuffed Red Grouper (see black drum, page 98)

Broiled Red Grouper (see gulf flounder, page 131)

Caribbean Red Grouper Salad (see mutton snapper, page 305)

"Chops" of Red Grouper (see spotted sea trout, page 118)

Cold Poached Red Grouper Fillets with Spicy Creole Mayonnaise (see red snapper, page 309)

Fillet of Red Grouper Baked en Papillote with a Shrimp, Crabmeat, and White Wine Sauce (see Florida pompano, page 161)

Poached Red Grouper Fillets with Creamy Pimiento-Butter Sauce (see ling cobia, page 85)

Red Grouper Croquettes Meunière (see skipjack tuna, page 221)

Red Grouper Fillets with Artichokes and Mushroons in Brown Lemon-Butter Sauce (see black drum, page 100)

Red Grouper Fillets with Mornay Sauce (see yellowtail snapper, page 314)

Red Grouper with Puerto Rican Sauce (see swordfish, page 333)

Red Grouper with Seafood-White Wine Sauce Gratiné (see white mullet, page 243)

Scamp

Group: Sea Bass, Grouper

Other common name(s):
  none
Latin name:
  Mycteroperca phenax
  Family Serranidae
Maximum length:
  2 feet

Maximum weight:
  12 pounds
Cuts:
  whole
  steak
  fillet
Meat characteristics:
  white, flaky
  low oil content

Preferred cooking methods:
  bake
  fry
  poach
  sauté

Moulin Rouge Sauce (recipe follows)
1 cup milk
1 egg
1 1/2 cups finely ground yellow cornmeal
2 teaspoons salt
1 teaspoon freshly ground black pepper

1/2 teaspoon cayenne pepper
Peanut oil for frying
2 1/4 pounds 1/2-inch-thick scamp fillets,
  skinned
3 lemons, quartered

Serves 6

Prepare the Moulin Rouge Sauce and refrigerate.

Blend the milk and egg in one mixing bowl and the cornmeal, salt, black pepper, and cayenne in another. In a wide, heavy frying pan, heat 1/2 inch oil to 350° to 375°. Dip the scamp fillets in the milk and egg wash and then dredge them in the seasoned cornmeal. Fry on both sides, without crowding the fish in the pan, until they are golden, about 2 1/2 minutes per side. Drain the fish on absorbent paper.

Serve with Moulin Rouge Sauce and lemon quarters.

Moulin Rouge Sauce

1 cup heavy cream, whipped
3/4 cup chili sauce
1/4 cup minced garlic chives
2 tablespoons sour cream

2 tablespoons Worcestershire sauce
2 teaspoons mixed Italian herbs
1 teaspoon Louisiana hot sauce, or to
  taste

In a bowl, combine the whipped heavy cream with the chili sauce, garlic chives, sour cream, Worcestershire sauce, and mixed Italian herbs. Season to taste with Louisiana hot sauce.

Cover and store in the refrigerator for 1 hour before using to allow the herb flavors to infuse into the sauce.

Note:　Common dolphin, gaff-topsail catfish, jolthead porgy, lookdown, permit, pinfish, sheepshead, striped mullet, and weakfish are also excellent fried this way.

Variations:　Fried scamp fillets are also excellent with Spicy Creole Mayonnaise (page 310), Sweet Mustard and Egg Sauce (page 254), or Two Sisters Sauce (page 184).

3 1 1/2-pound whole scamp, filleted and skinned

Sesame-Brandy Marinade (recipe follows)
Vegetable oil for the grill

Serves 6

Light the grill or charcoal 1 hour before cooking. Prepare the Sesame-Brandy Marinade, and hold aside to come to room temperature.

Lay the fillets in a single layer in a dish. Pour the Sesame-Brandy Marinade over the fish and let marinate for 1/2 hour in the refrigerator, basting occasionally.

When the grill is ready, oil the rack and grill the fillets, basting with the sauce, carefully turning only once, for 5 minutes, or until the fillets are nicely browned.

Carefully remove to plates and serve.

Sesame-Brandy Marinade

1 stick salted butter
1/2 cup freshly squeezed lemon juice
1/2 cup sesame seeds

1/4 cup brandy
1/4 cup soy sauce
3 cloves garlic, pressed

In a small saucepan, melt the butter, remove from the heat, and stir in the lemon juice, sesame seeds, brandy, soy sauce, and garlic. Bring to room temperature before marinating fish.

Note: You may also use Atlantic threadfin, red porgy, sailor's-choice, striped bass, or tilefish in this recipe.

Other Delicious Recipes for Scamp include:

Baked Scamp with Apples and Onions (see hogfish, page 368)

Baked Scamp in Creole Court-Bouillon (see red drum, page 110)

Beer-Battered Fried Scamp (see speckled hind, page 39)

Broiled Scamp with Balsamic Vinegar (see Atlantic moonfish, page 153)

Fried Battered Scamp with Two Sisters Sauce (see permit, page 184)

Fried Cornmeal-Battered Scamp Fillets (see striped mullet, page 239)

Fried Whole Scamp with Sweet Mustard and Egg Sauce (see pinfish, page 254)

Grilled Scamp with Tomato Butter (see sand perch, page 32)

Panfried Scamp with Lobster Cream Sauce (see permit, page 186)

Scamp Barbacoa (see great barracuda, page 20)

Sautéed Fillet of Scamp with Crabmeat and Butter (see common dolphin, page 90)

Striped Bass

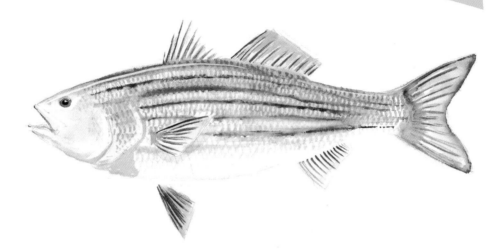

Group: Temperate Bass

Other common name(s):
Bass
Striper
Rockfish

Latin name:
Morone saxatilis
Family Percichthyidae

Maximum size:
6 feet

Maximum weight:
125 pounds

Cuts:
whole (small)
steak
fillet

Meat characteristics:
firm, white
low oil content

Preferred cooking methods:
bake
braise
fry
poach
sauté

2 sticks salted butter
1 1/2 pounds sliced fresh mushrooms
4 French shallots, minced
2 cloves garlic, minced
Salt and freshly ground black pepper
6 large ripe tomatoes, skinned (see Note),
   seeded, and chopped
1/2 cup dry white wine

2 tablespoons freshly squeezed lemon juice
3 dozen black olives, pitted
Salt and freshly ground black pepper
1 5-pound whole striped bass, dressed
Salt and freshly ground black pepper
2 tablespoons olive oil
Heavy-duty aluminum foil

Serves 6

Preheat the oven to 350°. Melt 2 tablespoons of the butter in a saucepan and sauté the mushrooms, shallots, and garlic until all the liquids are evaporated. Season lightly with salt and pepper. Hold aside.

In another saucepan, reduce the chopped tomatoes by half. Add the white wine, lemon juice, and black olives and cook together for about 3 minutes. Add the cooked mushroom mixture, season to taste with salt and pepper, and hold aside.

Rub the striped bass inside and out with salt and pepper.

On the stovetop, melt the remaining butter in a baking pan or ovenproof dish and add the olive oil. Lay the striped bass into the pan and bake for about 30 minutes, or until the fish is golden on the outside and completely opaque. Remove from the oven. Turn the oven up to 400°.

Take a piece of heavy-duty aluminum foil wide enough to fold over the fish and seal closed, or a piece twice the length of the fish that can also fold over and seal closed. Spread some of the sauce over the foil where the fish will be placed. Lay the fish onto the sauced foil and spread the remaining sauce with olives over the fish. Fold up the foil and seal it well.

Carefully place the papillote onto a baking sheet and bake for about 12 minutes, or until the foil has puffed from the escaping steam. Transfer the papillote onto a serving platter.

To serve, bring the platter to the table and tear the foil open in the middle along the length of the fish, folding the foil back as you go. Cut the top fillet into three portions and lift them up to serve with some of the sauce and olives. Remove the fish skeleton and bones and serve three more portions from the bottom fillet with the remaining sauce and olives.

Notes: To skin the tomatoes, immerse them in boiling water for 1 to 2 minutes, then plunge them into cold water. Spot drum and yellowtail snapper are also excellent prepared this way.

Poached Striped Bass Fillets with Hollandaise Sauce

Hollandaise Sauce (recipe follows)
1 1/2 quarts water, or enough to cover
    fillets (about 1 inch deep in skillet)
1 lemon, thinly sliced
1 medium onion, thinly sliced
2 sprigs fresh parsley

2 bay leaves
1 clove garlic, mashed
6 whole black peppercorns
2 teaspoons salt
1/4 teaspoon cayenne pepper
6 8-ounce striped bass fillets, skinned

Serves 6

Prepare the Hollandaise Sauce, and hold aside warm or tepid.

In a heavy, wide skillet, bring the water to a boil with the lemon, onion, parsley, bay leaves, garlic, peppercorns, salt, and cayenne. Let boil for 3 minutes to allow the water to draw the flavor from the seasoning ingredients. Lower the heat to a simmer. Lay in the fillets and poach for 10 minutes, or until the fish is completely cooked and flaky when broken with a fork.

With a long spatula, carefully remove the fillets from the water, drain, and place on warm dinner plates. Nap the poached striped bass fillets with the Hollandaise Sauce and serve.

Hollandaise Sauce

6 large egg yolks
3 tablespoons freshly squeezed lemon juice
1 teaspoon salt

1/2 teaspoon cayenne pepper
3 sticks salted butter

Put the egg yolks, lemon juice, salt, and cayenne in a blender and blend on low for 5 to 7 seconds. In a small saucepan, melt the butter and heat it until it comes to a simmer. Turn the blender on high and pour the hot butter, in a thin stream, into the egg yolk mixture until all is incorporated. The heat from the butter will cook the Hollandaise.

Note: You can also use mutton snapper or speckled hind with this recipe.

Variations: Poached striped bass fillets are also delicious with Colbert Sauce (page 262). Also try (follow recipe exactly except for the following substitutions and additions):

Paloise Sauce
Add 1 tablespoon freshly minced spearmint leaves to the egg yolk mixture.

Other Delicious Recipes for Striped Bass include:
Baked Crabmeat-Stuffed Striped Bass (see gulf kingfish, page 106)
Charcoal-Grilled Butterflied Striped Bass (see great barracuda, page 18)
Cold Poached Striped Bass Fillets with Spicy Creole Mayonnaise (see red snapper, page 309)
Grilled Striped Bass Fillets in Sesame-Brandy Marinade (see scamp, page 58)
Poached Striped Bass Fillets with Maltaise Sauce (see common dolphin, page 88)
Poached Striped Bass with Marquis Sauce (see speckled hind, page 37)
Steamed Striped Bass with Cypriote Sauce (see scalloped hammerhead shark, page 284)
Striped Bass Fillets with Artichokes and Mushrooms in Brown Lemon-Butter Sauce (see black drum, page 100)
Striped Bass Poached in Sherry (see snook, page 319)
Whole Baked Striped Bass with Spinach Stuffing (see jolthead porgy, page 250)
Whole Steamed Striped Bass Marinière (see weakfish, page 122)

Bluefish

Group: Bluefish

Other common name(s):
  Blues

Latin name:
  Pomatomus saltatrix
  Family Pomatomidae

Maximum length:
  3 feet 9 inches

Maximum weight:
  27 pounds

Cuts:
  whole (small)
  steak
  fillet

Meat characteristics:
  dark, rich, tender
  high oil content

Preferred cooking methods:
  bake
  broil
  grill
  poach
  sauté

Mexican Paste (recipe follows)

6 8-ounce bluefish steaks

Vegetable oil for the grill

1 cup water-soaked wood chips: mesquite,
   hickory, pecan, etc.

1/2 cup hot melted salted butter

3 limes, halved

Serves 6

Light the charcoal 1 hour before cooking. Prepare the Mexican Paste and paint the bluefish steaks on all sides with it.

When the grill is ready, brush the rack with oil and arrange the bluefish steaks on the rack so that they don't touch each other. Throw in a few water-soaked wood chips and cover the grill. Cook for 10 minutes, turning once midway, and basting with the remaining seasoning blend.

Serve the bluefish steaks topped with the melted butter and garnished with the lime halves.

Mexican Paste

1/2 cup bacon drippings, or olive oil

1/2 cup chili powder

2 tablespoons ground cumin

1 tablespoon cayenne pepper

1 tablespoon salt

In a blender, combine the bacon drippings with the chili, cumin, cayenne, and salt. Blend on high until you have a smooth paste.

Note: Atlantic moonfish, black grouper, blue marlin, hard-tail jack, king mackerel, and rainbow runner are also excellent prepared this way.

Variations: Wood-grilled bluefish steaks are also delicious served with Achiote-Garlic Paste (page 49), Creole Garlic Paste (page 50), Italian Herb-Garlic Paste (page 50), or Sweet Herbs (page 197).

Dough:
2 cups all-purpose flour
1 cup corn flour (see Note)
1 1/2 teaspoons baking powder
1/2 teaspoon salt
1 1/3 cups warm water

Stuffing:
2 tablespoons olive oil
3 fresh tabasco or cayenne peppers,
 stemmed, seeded, and minced (see
 Note)

1 medium onion, chopped
1 small green bell pepper, stemmed,
 seeded, and chopped
2 medium tomatoes, chopped
2 large cloves garlic, minced
1 teaspoon chili powder
1/4 teaspoon dried oregano
1 teaspoon salt
1 1/2 pounds bluefish fillet, skinned
1 tablespoon chopped fresh cilantro
Peanut oil for frying
Chopped onions and salsa, or hot sauce

Serves 6

Begin by making the dough for the round, puffed tortillas, which will have an end snipped off and then opened up to hold the bluefish stuffing, pita-bread fashion. In a bowl, combine the flour with the corn flour, baking powder, and salt. Slowly stir in the water, working the mixture into a stiff dough. Wrap the dough in plastic wrap and let stand at least 20 minutes to mature.

In a saucepan large enough to hold the fish, heat the olive oil and sauté the hot peppers, onion, and green bell pepper. When the onion begins to brown, add the tomatoes, garlic, chili powder, oregano, and salt. Simmer for 5 minutes to sweat the tomatoes and bring the flavors together.

Add the bluefish and cook together about 10 minutes. Flake the fish apart and work into the vegetables to make a stuffing. Continue simmering to reduce any existing liquids. Test for seasoning and add the chopped cilantro. Hold aside warm.

Now, divide the tortilla dough into six equal portions and roll each portion into a ball. Place the balls on a floured surface and roll them into round flat tortillas, 1/4 inch thick.

Heat 1/4 inch peanut oil in a skillet to 350° and fry the tortillas, without crowding them in the pan, for 1 minute on each side, or until they are puffed and golden brown. Drain on absorbent paper.

When the tortillas are cool enough to handle, cut off a 1-inch strip across the widest side and open them up to make pouches, as in pita bread. Stuff the bluefish and vegetable mixture into the pouches and garnish with chopped onions and salsa or hot sauce. Serve hot or at room temperature.

Notes: Corn flour is often used in the frying of seafood rather than white flour. It can be bought as plain corn flour in specialty stores or as corn masa flour or "masa harina" in stores that sell Mexican or Central and South American food products. It is the flour that corn tortillas are made from. It can also be gotten in the form of "fish-fry," which is corn flour that is already seasoned with salt and pepper.

Other hot peppers can be substituted if you prefer. Check the hotness of the sauce as you add the peppers to meet your own tastes.

American eel, Atlantic bonito, hard-tail jack, scalloped hammerhead shark, and tarpon may be used in place of bluefish.

Other Delicious Recipes for Bluefish include:

Baked Bluefish with Apples and Onions (see hogfish, page 368)
Bluefish Boudin (see Atlantic moonfish, page 152)
Bluefish-Stuffed Bell Peppers (see Atlantic bonito, page 214)
Bluefish Tamales with Piquant Green Sauce (see Spanish mackerel, page 203)
Broiled Bluefish Fillets with Cilantro Butter (see weakfish, page 123)

Cold Poached Bluefish Ravigote with Boiled New Potatoes (see spotted jewfish,
    page 43)

Creole Bisque of Bluefish (see tilefish, page 348)

Étouffée of Bluefish (see blackfin tuna, page 218)

Grilled Bluefish with Tomato-Red Wine Sauce (see Atlantic spadefish, page 325)

Hot Bluefish and Artichoke Salad and Russian Dressing with Caviar (see large
    tooth sawfish, page 279)

Marinated Escabèche of Bluefish (see hard-tail jack, page 176)

Matelote of Bluefish (see American eel, page 126)

Wood-Grilled Bluefish Steaks with Achiote-Garlic Paste (see black grouper,
    page 49)

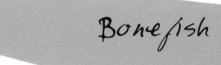

Bonefish

Group: Bonefish

Other common name(s):
none

Latin name:
Albula vulpes
Family Albulidae

Maximum length:
3 feet

Maximum weight:
19 pounds

Cuts:
whole (small)
fillet

Meat characteristics:
firm, white
medium oil content

Preferred cooking methods:
bake
braise
fry
poach
steam

1 4-pound whole bonefish, dressed   Water
Salt and freshly ground white pepper   Chivry Butter (recipe follows)

Serves 6

You will need a fish poacher/steamer or other long or wide pan or Dutch oven with a basket or rack to accommodate the fish for this preparation.

Rub the bonefish inside and out with salt and white pepper. Lay the fish into the basket or onto the rack. Add only enough water to the bottom of the pan so that it does not exceed the level of the basket or rack. Cover the pan, place it on the stovetop, and bring the water to a boil. Place the basket or rack into the pan, cover, and cook with the water steaming for about 30 minutes, or until the fish flakes with the touch of a fork.

Just before the fish is served, make the Chivry Butter.

Carefully transfer the steamed bonefish to a warm serving platter and bring it to the table. Cut the top fillet into three portions, remove the bones, then cut the bottom fillet into three portions. Spoon Chivry Butter over each serving.

Chivry Butter

2 sticks salted butter   1/4 cup minced fresh chives
8 French shallots, minced   1 tablespoon minced fresh tarragon
1/4 cup minced fresh parsley

Melt 2 tablespoons of the butter in a small saucepan. Add the minced shallots and sauté them until translucent, about 2 minutes. Add the parsley, chives, and tarragon. Then add the remaining butter in six pieces, one at a time, adding each piece before the one before has completely melted. Remove the saucepan from the heat before adding the last piece. The purpose here is never to allow the butter to reach a heat high enough for it to separate. This way the sauce will remain fluffy and creamy without adding any thickening agent. Serve immediately.

Note: Jolthead porgy, lookdown, pilot fish, and scalloped hammerhead shark also work well prepared this way.

3 1 1/2-pound whole bonefish, drawn (see
    Note)
Salt and freshly ground white pepper
2 dozen large fresh sorrel leaves (see
    Note), enough to completely wrap the
    fish fillets

1 quart water
Reserved fish heads and bones
1 small onion, sliced
4 green onion tops
1/4 teaspoon dried thyme

1 bay leaf
1/2 teaspoon dried tarragon
1/3 cup dry white wine
1 tablespoon cornstarch
2 tablespoons water

2 tablespoons salted butter
6 green onions, minced
1 French shallot, minced
3 large zucchini, cut in large dice
1 pint fresh mushrooms, sliced
Salt and freshly ground black pepper

Serves 6

Fillet the bonefish and skin the fillets. Cut out the fine lines of bones in the fillets, and reserve. Degill the heads and reserve with the bones. Season the fillets lightly with the salt and white pepper. Wrap them in the sorrel leaves and hold them aside.

In a large saucepan, bring the water to a boil. Add the heads and bones of the fish, and the onion, green onion tops, thyme, and bay leaf. Cover and simmer for 30 minutes. Strain the stock and boil briskly to reduce it to 1 1/2 cups. Add the tarragon and white wine, and simmer for 15 minutes. Mix the cornstarch with the 2 tablespoons water and whisk it into the sauce. Bring to a simmer, stirring to prevent any lumps from forming, and simmer until the sauce thickens. Cover and keep warm.

In a wide, shallow saucepan, melt the butter and sauté the green onions and French shallot just until they are limp. Add the zucchini and mushrooms, season with salt and pepper, and sauté together for 2 minutes. Lay the wrapped fillets over the zucchini and mushrooms in the pan, cover, and simmer for 10 minutes.

Spoon the pan juices out from the fish and vegetables and add them to the sauce. Bring the sauce back to a simmer and season to taste with salt and pepper.

Serve the sorrel-wrapped bonefish fillets over the vegetables and nap with the sauce.

Notes: If you prefer, you can have the fish merchant fillet, skin, and bone the bonefish and degill the heads; you will need to bring home the heads and bones for the sauce.

Spinach can be used in place of the sorrel. Sorrel, however, has a marvelous lemony taste that enhances the flavors of this combination.

Gulf kingfish, permit, and pigfish are delicious substitutions.

Variations
(follow recipe exactly except for the following substitutions and additions):

with Onions and Mushrooms
Use 3 large onions, skinned and roughly chopped, instead of zucchini. The sorrel-leaf wrap is optional.

with Tomatoes and Mushrooms
Substitute 3 large tomatoes, cut into large dice, for the zucchini. The sorrel-leaf wrap is optional.

with Yellow Squash and Mushrooms
Replace the zucchini with 6 small yellow squash, cut into large dice. The sorrel-leaf wrap is optional.

Other Delicious Recipes for Bonefish include:

Beer-Battered Fried Bonefish (see speckled hind, page 39)

Bonefish Fillets with Cucumber and Spinach (see gulf kingfish, page 104)

Bonefish with Pecans (see lookdown, page 181)

Marinated Bonefish Salad with Giardeniera (see squirrelfish, page 329)

Poached Bonefish with Horseradish and Sour Cream Sauce (see Atlantic croaker, page 95)

Gaff-Topsail Catfish

Group: Sea Catfish

Other common name(s):
  Gaff-top
Latin name:
  Bagre marinus
  Family Ariidae
Maximum length:
  2 feet

Maximum weight:
  5 1/2 pounds
Cuts:
  fillet
Meat characteristics:
  tender, white, flaky
  medium oil content

Preferred cooking methods:
  bake
  broil
  fry
  sauté
  steam

Peanut Sauce (recipe follows)
6 3/4- to 1-pound whole gaff-topsail
    catfish, scaled and drawn

Salt and freshly ground white pepper
1/2 cup peanut oil
6 large French bread croutons (page 370)

Serves 6

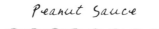

Prepare the Peanut Sauce, and hold aside warm.

Rub the gaff-topsail catfish with salt and white pepper. Heat the oil until hot in a heavy skillet and fry the fish, without crowding the pan, for 5 minutes on each side, until lightly browned. Remove the fish from the oil and drain on absorbent paper. Add the cooked catfish to the sauce in the skillet, cover, and simmer for 5 minutes.

Serve the fish on the croutons with the Peanut Sauce spooned over.

Peanut Sauce

1/4 cup peanut oil
1 small onion, chopped
3 medium tomatoes, diced
1 small eggplant, skinned and diced

3/4 cup roasted shelled peanuts
1/4 cup water
2 teaspoons sugar
Salt and cayenne pepper to taste

In a skillet or sauté pan, heat the peanut oil and sauté the chopped onion until it becomes limp. Add the tomatoes and eggplant and simmer for 10 minutes. Process the peanuts with the water and sugar in a blender into a paste. Add the paste to the pan, and simmer gently for 30 minutes. Season to taste with salt and cayenne.

Note: Permit, sheepshead, spot drum, and spotted eagle ray are also excellent prepared in this recipe. For the spotted eagle ray, use cuts of skinned wing fillet.

Variations: Whole pan-fried gaff-topsail catfish is also excellent with Aurora Sauce (page 114).

Fried Gaff-Topsail Catfish Fingers with Pink Horseradish Mayonnaise

Pink Horseradish Mayonnaise
  (recipe follows)
2 1/4 pounds gaff-topsail catfish fillet,
  skinned
1 egg
1 cup milk
1 cup water

2 cups corn flour (see Note)
2 teaspoons salt
1 teaspoon freshly ground white pepper
1/2 teaspoon cayenne pepper
Peanut oil for frying
3 lemons, halved

Serves 6

Prepare the Pink Horseradish Mayonnaise and hold in the refrigerator.

Slice the catfish fillet into strips, or "fingers," 1/2 inch thick and the length of your own finger.

In a bowl, beat the egg, milk, and water together to make an egg wash. In a separate bowl, combine the corn flour with the salt, white pepper, and cayenne. Heat 1/2 inch oil in a wide, heavy skillet to 350°. Dip the fish fingers into the egg wash, coating completely, then dredge in the seasoned corn flour. Fry, without crowding the pan, for approximately 4 minutes, or until golden brown on all sides. Drain the catfish fingers on absorbent paper.

Serve with lemon halves and individual small dishes of Pink Horseradish Mayonnaise on the side for dipping.

Pink Horseradish Mayonnaise

3/4 cup Mayonnaise (page 374)
3/4 cup catsup
1 teaspoon pressed garlic

2 teaspoons prepared horseradish
3 tablespoons white vinegar

In a small bowl, blend together the five ingredients. Cover tightly and refrigerate until ready to use.

Notes: Some diners may prefer just a sprinkle of lemon or lime juice to finish off the flavors. This preparation also makes a wonderful appetizer for up to 12 people.

Corn flour is often used in the frying of seafood rather than white flour. It can be bought as plain corn flour in specialty stores or as corn masa flour or "masa harina" in stores that sell Mexican or Central and South American food products. It is the flour that corn tortillas are made from. It can also be gotten in the form of "fish-fry," which is corn flour that is already seasoned with salt and pepper.

2 1/4 pounds skinned hogfish, pilot fish, tripletail, or white grunt fillets are delightful substitutions.

Variations: Other cream sauces such as Ravigote Mayonnaise (page 44), Rémoulade Sauce (page 353), and Tartar Sauce (page 375) also make excellent dipping sauces for the "fingers." Or, instead of dipping, try the "fingers" napped with Black Anchovy Butter (page 212), Béarnaise Sauce (page 358), Bourguignonne Sauce (page 366), or Beurre Noir Sauce (page 213).

Other Delicious Recipes for Gaff-Topsail Catfish include:
Fried Battered Gaff-Topsail Catfish with Two Sisters Sauce (see permit, page 184)
Fried Cornmeal-Battered Gaff-Topsail Catfish Fillets (see striped mullet, page 239)
Fried Gaff-Topsail Catfish with Black Anchovy Butter (see Atlantic bonito, page 212)
Fried Gaff-Topsail Catfish Fillets with Bourguignonne Sauce (see hogfish, page 366)
Fried Gaff-Topsail Catfish Fillets with Moulin Rouge Sauce (see scamp, page 56)
Gaff-Topsail Catfish Beignets with Rémoulade Sauce (see gray triggerfish, page 353)

Gaff-Topsail Catfish Fillets Stuffed with Shrimp Soufflé (see spotfin flounder, page 135)

Gaff-Topsail Catfish Poached with Lime and Onion (see sand perch, page 34)

Gaff-Topsail Catfish-Stuffed Bell Peppers (see Atlantic bonito, page 214)

Panfried Gaff-Topsail Catfish Fillets with Algiers Sauce (see spot drum, page 113)

Panfried Gaff-Topsail Catfish with Lobster Cream Sauce (see permit, page 186)

Poached Gaff-Topsail Catfish Fillets with Maltaise Sauce (see common dolphin, page 88)

Ling Cobia

Group: Cobia

Other common name(s):
Ling
Black Bonito
Lemon Fish (for its
"lemony" flavor)

Latin name:
Rachycentron cana-
dum Family Rachy-
centridae

Maximum length
6 feet 7 inches

Maximum weight:
110 pounds

Cuts:
steak
fillet

Meat characteristics:
firm, medium white
low-to-medium oil
content

Preferred cooking
methods:
bake
broil
grill
poach
sauté

Grilled Ling Cobia Steaks with Onions, Green Bell Peppers, and Eggplant

1/4 cup olive oil
4 cloves garlic, chopped
2 large onions, chopped
2 medium green bell peppers, seeded and
    chopped
1 large eggplant, cut into 1/2-inch dice
1 cup dry white wine
1/2 teaspoon dried thyme
Salt, freshly ground white pepper, and
    cayenne pepper

4 tomatoes, skinned (see Note), seeded,
    and chopped
2 tablespoons chopped fresh parsley
6 8- to 10-ounce ling cobia steaks
1 tablespoon melted butter
Salt and freshly ground white pepper
Vegetable oil for grilling
Chopped fresh parsley

Serves 6

Light the grill 1 hour before cooking.

In a sauté pan, heat the olive oil and sauté the garlic until lightly browned. Add the onion and bell pepper, and sauté for 10 minutes. Add the eggplant, white wine, and thyme, season with salt, white pepper, and cayenne, and simmer for 15 minutes. Stir occasionally to prevent sticking and ensure even cooking. Add the tomatoes and chopped parsley, adjust the seasonings, and heat only long enough for all to be good and hot. Hold aside and keep warm.

When the grill is ready, oil the rack. Brush the ling cobia steaks with the melted butter and season lightly with salt and pepper. Grill for 4 minutes on each side, or until cooked to a flaky doneness.

Spoon the eggplant and vegetable mixture onto warm plates and place a grilled ling cobia steak in the center of each. Garnish with chopped parsley.

Note: To skin the tomatoes, immerse them in boiling water for 1 to 2 minutes, then plunge them into cold water.

Black sea bass, great barracuda, red drum and skipjack tuna are also excellent cooked this way. Use 6 6-ounce pieces of red drum fillet.

Poached Ling Cobia Fillets with Creamy Pimiento-Butter Sauce

Creamy Pimiento-Butter Sauce
  (recipe follows)
2 quarts water, or enough to cover fish
  (about 1 inch deep in skillet)
1 lemon, thinly sliced
1 medium onion, thinly sliced
2 sprigs fresh parsley

2 bay leaves
1 clove garlic, mashed
6 whole black peppercorns
2 teaspoons salt
1/4 teaspoon cayenne pepper
6 6-ounce pieces ling cobia fillet, skinned

Serves 6

Prepare the Creamy Pimiento-Butter Sauce, and hold aside warm.

In a wide skillet, bring the water to a boil with the lemon, onion, parsley, bay leaves, garlic, peppercorns, salt, and cayenne. Let boil for 3 minutes to allow the water to draw the flavor from the seasoning ingredients. Lower the heat to a simmer and lay in the ling cobia fillets. Poach for 10 minutes, or until the fish is flaky when broken with a fork.

With a long spatula, carefully remove the fillets from the water, drain, and place on warm plates. Nap with the warm sauce, and serve.

Creamy Pimiento-Butter Sauce

1/2 cup dry white wine
2 tablespoons minced shallots
1/2 cup minced pimiento
1/4 cup heavy cream
1 1/2 sticks cold salted butter, cut into 6
  pieces each

1 tablespoon chopped fresh parsley
Salt, freshly ground white pepper, and
  cayenne pepper

In a saucepan, bring the wine to a boil with the shallots and pimiento. Boil until the mixture is reduced by three-quarters, then add the cream and simmer until thickened. Add a piece of butter and whisk it into the sauce, over low heat, until the butter is incorporated and the sauce is smooth. Continue adding the butter pieces, one at a time, and whisking until they have all been incorporated. Never let the sauce come to a simmer or it will separate and lose its smooth, creamy texture. Add the parsley and season to taste with salt, white pepper, and cayenne. Serve warm.

Note: Atlantic moonfish, common dolphin, dog snapper, greater amberjack, red grouper and swordfish are delicious substitutions.

Other Delicious Recipes for Ling Cobia include:

Baked Crabmeat-Stuffed Ling Cobia Fillet (see greater amberjack, page 168)

Breaded Ling Cobia with Creole Tomato Sauce (see black grouper, page 47)

Caribbean Ling Cobia Salad (see mutton snapper, page 305)

Charcoal-Grilled Ling Cobia with Garlic Sauce (see blue marlin, page 236)

Curried Fillets of Ling Cobia (see sailor's-choice, page 143)

Grilled Ling Cobia Fillets with Tomato-Oyster Sauce (see Florida pompano, page 164)

Grilled Ling Cobia Steaks with Criolla Sauce (see black sea bass, page 25)

Ling Cobia and Potato Salad with Chive Vinaigrette (see yellowfin tuna, page 227)

Panfried Ling Cobia with Bienville Sauce (see wahoo, page 207)

Ragout of Ling Cobia au Gratin (see swordfish, page 332)

Sautéed Battered Ling Cobia Fillets with Lemon-Butter Sauce (see red snapper, page 311)

Tamales with Ling Cobia and Roasted Tomato and Chili Sauce (see common jack, page 156)

Common Dolphin

Group Dolphin

Other common name(s):
  Dolphin
  Mahi Mahi
Latin name:
  Coryphaena hippurus
  Family Coryphaenidae
Maximum length:
  6 feet 6 inches

Maximum weight:
  87 pounds
Cuts:
  whole (small)
  steak
  fillet
Meat characteristics:
  firm, white
  medium oil content

Preferred cooking methods:
  bake
  fry
  grill
  poach
  sauté

Maltaise Sauce (recipe follows)
1 1/2 quarts water, or enough to cover
   fillets (about 1 inch deep in skillet)
1 lemon, thinly sliced
1 medium onion, thinly sliced
2 sprigs fresh parsley
2 bay leaves

1 clove garlic, mashed
6 whole black peppercorns
2 teaspoons salt
1/4 teaspoon cayenne pepper
6 8-ounce pieces common dolphin fillet,
   skinned

Serves 6

Prepare the Maltaise Sauce, and hold aside warm or tepid.

In a heavy, wide skillet, bring the water to a boil with the lemon, onion, parsley, bay leaves, garlic, peppercorns, salt, and cayenne. Let boil for 3 minutes to allow the water to draw the flavor from the seasoning ingredients. Lower the heat to a simmer. Lay in the fillets and poach for 10 minutes, or until the fish is flaky when broken with a fork.

With a long spatula, carefully remove the fillets from the water, drain, and place on warm dinner plates. Top the fillets with the Maltaise Sauce, and serve.

Maltaise Sauce

6 large egg yolks
3 tablespoons freshly squeezed lemon juice
1 teaspoon salt
1/2 teaspoon cayenne pepper

1 teaspoon grated orange zest
3 sticks salted butter
1/4 cup freshly squeezed orange juice

Put the egg yolks, lemon juice, salt, cayenne, and grated orange zest in a blender and blend on low for 5 to 7 seconds. In a small saucepan, melt the butter and heat it until it comes to a simmer. Turn the blender on high and pour the hot butter, in a thin stream, into the egg yolk mixture until all is incorporated. The heat from the butter will cook the sauce. Blend in the orange juice. Serve warm or tepid.

Note: Black drum, black sea bass, Florida pompano, gaff-topsail catfish, spotted jewfish, striped bass, and tripletail are also excellent in this recipe.

1 1/2 sticks salted butter

1 pound crabmeat, picked clean of shell

6 8-ounce common dolphin steaks

1 teaspoon salt

1/4 teaspoon freshly ground white pepper

2 tablespoons light-flavored olive oil

2 tablespoons chopped fresh parsley

3 lemons, halved

Serves 6

Melt the butter in a saucepan and heat the crabmeat. Disturb the crabmeat as little as possible so as not to break up the lumps. Keep warm.

Season the common dolphin steaks lightly with the salt and pepper. Heat the oil in a wide, heavy skillet and sauté the steaks 6 minutes on each side.

Place the cooked fish steaks on warm dinner plates and spoon the hot crabmeat and butter over the top. Sprinkle with the chopped parsley and garnish with lemon halves.

Note: 6 6-ounce creole fish, Florida pompano, or scamp fillets, or 6 8-ounce blackfin tuna, greater amberjack, largetooth sawfish, or wahoo steaks are wonderful substitutions. Cooking time for the fillets is 3 to 4 minutes on each side. The steaks take 6 minutes on each side.

Variations

(follow recipe exactly except for the following substitutions and additions):

with Crawfish and Butter

Use 1 pound crawfish tail meat instead of crabmeat.

with Lobster and Butter

Instead of crabmeat, use 1 pound Florida or Maine lobster tail meat, cut into large dice and cooked in the butter about 2 minutes, or until it becomes opaque.

with Oysters and Butter

Replace the crabmeat with 3 dozen raw oysters, shelled, and cooked in the butter about 2 minutes, until edges of the oysters begin to curl.

with Shrimp and Butter

Instead of crabmeat, use 1 pound small-to-medium peeled raw shrimp (deveined) cooked in the butter only long enough for the shrimp to turn pink but retain a nice crisp bite.

with Soft-Shell Crab and Butter

As an alternative to crabmeat, use 6 small soft-shell crabs (cleaned) cooked in the butter, turning once, about 2 minutes a side.

Other Delicious Recipes for Common Dolphin include:

Broiled Common Dolphin (see gulf flounder, page 131)

Common Dolphin Fillets with Lobster-Browned Butter Sauce (see gulf flounder, page 132)

Common Dolphin with Pecans (see lookdown, page 181)

Fillet of Common Dolphin Baked en Papillote with a Shrimp, Crabmeat, and White Wine Sauce (see Florida pompano, page 161)

Fried Common Dolphin Fillets with Moulin Rouge Sauce (see scamp, page 56)

Hot Common Dolphin and Mushroom Salad with Dijon Mustard Dressing (see snook, page 320)

Panfried Common Dolphin with Lobster Cream Sauce (see permit, page 186)

Poached Common Dolphin Fillets with Creamy Pimiento-Butter Sauce (see ling cobia, page 85)

Poached Common Dolphin Fillets with Marquis Sauce (see speckled hind, page 37)

Ragout of Common Dolphin au Gratin (see swordfish, page 332)

Sautéed Common Dolphin Steaks Marseilles-Style (see rainbow runner, page 194)

Soda-Fried Common Dolphin "Chips" with Fresh Tomato Catsup (see shortfin mako shark, page 289)

91

Atlantic Croaker

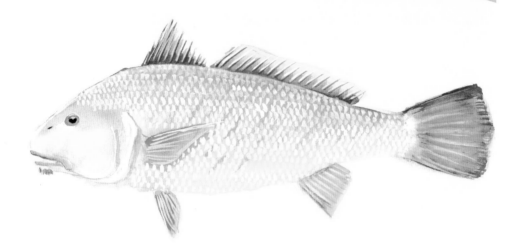

Group: Drum

Other common name(s):
  Croaker
  Bull Croaker
Latin name:
  Micropogon undulatus
  Family Sciaenidae
Maximum length:
  1 foot 8 inches

Maximum weight:
  4 pounds
Cuts:
  whole
  fillet
Meat characteristics:
  firm, white, flaky
  low oil content

Preferred cooking methods:
  bake
  fry
  poach
  sauté
  steam

Mosca Sauce (recipe follows)

6 1-pound whole Atlantic croakers, scaled
    and drawn

Salt, freshly ground black pepper, and
    cayenne pepper

3 cups fine yellow cornmeal

Peanut oil for frying

Serves 6

~~~~~~~~~~~~~~~~~~~~~~~~~~~~

Make the Mosca Sauce before cooking the croakers, and hold it aside warm.

Rub the croakers inside and out with salt, black pepper, and cayenne. Dredge them in the yellow cornmeal.

Add 1/2 inch of peanut oil to a wide, heavy skillet and heat to 375°. Carefully lay the croakers into the oil without crowding the pan. This may have to be done in more than a single batch. Cook them on one side for about 5 minutes, turn them over only once, and complete cooking for 5 minutes or more on the other side. The completely cooked fish will flake at the touch of a fork. Drain the fish on absorbent paper.

Transfer the croakers to warm dinner plates, spoon the Mosca Sauce over the top, and serve.

Mosca Sauce

~~~~~~~~~~~~~~~~~~~~~~~~~~~~

1 cup light-flavored olive oil

1/2 cup chopped garlic

1 tablespoon dried rosemary

1 tablespoon crumbled dried oregano

1 tablespoon whole dried thyme leaves

1/2 cup dry white wine

1 tablespoon salt

1/2 tablespoon freshly ground black
    pepper

In a saucepan, combine the olive oil with the garlic, rosemary, oregano, and thyme. Bring to a boil. Carefully add the white wine, salt, and black pepper and bring to a boil again. Serve warm.

Note: Atlantic threadfin, red porgy, speckled hind, and striped mullet are also excellent in this recipe.

Poached Atlantic Croaker with Horseradish and Sour Cream Sauce

6 1-pound whole Atlantic croakers, scaled
   and drawn
1/2 lemon
Horseradish and Sour Cream Sauce
   (recipe follows)
1 1/2 quarts water, or enough to cover fish
   (about 1 inch deep in skillet)
1 lemon, thinly sliced

1 medium onion, thinly sliced
2 sprigs fresh parsley
2 bay leaves
1 clove garlic, mashed
6 whole black peppercorns
1 tablespoon salt
1/4 teaspoon cayenne pepper

Serves 6

Wash the Atlantic croakers and wipe them dry. Rub them inside and out with the half lemon and hold aside. Prepare the Horseradish and Sour Cream Sauce, cover, and hold aside.

In a wide, heavy skillet, bring the water to a boil with the lemon slices, onion, parsley, bay leaves, garlic, peppercorns, salt, and cayenne. Let boil for 3 minutes to allow the water to draw the flavor from the seasoning ingredients. Lower the heat to a simmer and lay in as many of the Atlantic croakers as will easily fit. You will have to do this in several batches. Bring back to a simmer and poach for 15 minutes, or until the fish are flaky when broken with a fork.

With a long, wide spatula, carefully remove the Atlantic croakers, drain, and serve on warm plates with the Horseradish and Sour Cream Sauce on the side.

Horseradish and Sour Cream Sauce

1 cup sour cream
1/4 cup prepared horseradish

1 teaspoon freshly ground black pepper
1/2 teaspoon salt

In a small bowl, combine the sour cream, horseradish, pepper, and salt. Serve at room temperature.

Note: Other fish to try with recipe are American eel, bonefish, permit, pigfish, pilot fish, pinfish, sailor's-choice, sand perch, and white mullet. For the American eel, use 6 pounds skinned eel divided into 6 portions.

Other Delicious Recipes for Atlantic Croaker include:

Atlantic Croaker Beignets with Rémoulade Sauce (see gray triggerfish, page 353)

Beer-Battered Fried Atlantic Croaker (see speckled hind, page 39)

Breaded Fillets of Atlantic Croaker with Green Mayonnaise (see red drum, page 109)

Fried Atlantic Croaker with Brown Shrimp Sauce (see white mullet, page 245)

Fried Battered Atlantic Croaker with Two Sisters Sauce (see permit, page 184)

Grilled Atlantic Croaker Andalouse (see white grunt, page 149)

Herbed Garlic Atlantic Croaker (see yellowtail snapper, page 316)

Panfried Atlantic Croaker Fillets with Algiers Sauce (see spot drum, page 113)

Panfried Atlantic Croaker with Lobster Cream Sauce (see permit, page 186)

Whole Cracker-Crumb-Coated Panfried Atlantic Croaker with Key Lime Sauce (see white grunt, page 147)

Whole Panfried Atlantic Croaker with Aurora Sauce (see spot drum, page 114)

Whole Panfried Atlantic Croaker with Salsa Roja (see striped mullet, page 240)

Black Drum

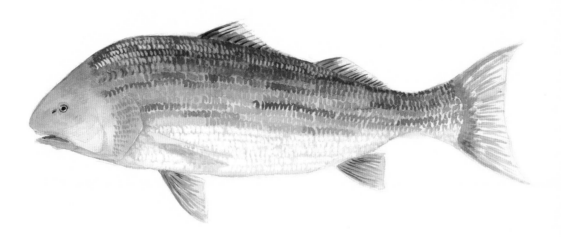

Group: Drum

Other common name(s):	Maximum weight:	Preferred cooking methods:
Drum	113 pounds	bake
Black Sea Drum	Cuts:	braise
Sea Drum	whole (small)	poach
Latin name:	steak	sauté
Pogonias cromis	fillet	steam
Family Sciaenidae	Meat characteristics:	
Maximum length:	firm, white, flaky	
3 feet 3 inches	medium oil content	

Baked Shrimp-Stuffed Black Drum

Shrimp Stuffing:
2 tablespoons olive oil
1 medium onion, chopped
4 green onions, chopped
2 cloves garlic, chopped
1/4 teaspoon dried thyme
2 cups toasted French bread crumbs
Water or fish stock (page 371)
1 pound peeled raw shrimp, deveined and
    chopped
Salt and freshly ground white pepper
1 egg, lightly beaten
1 5- to 6-pound whole black drum, scaled
    and drawn

1 teaspoon salt
1/2 teaspoon freshly ground white pepper
1/2 teaspoon cayenne pepper
1/2 cup all-purpose flour
Skewers or toothpicks
1/4 cup olive oil
6 tomatoes, chopped
2 onions, chopped
1 medium bell pepper, seeded and chopped
2 bay leaves
3 cups boiling water
Salt and freshly ground white pepper

Serves 6

Preheat the oven to 350°. In a skillet, heat the olive oil and sauté the onions, green onions, and garlic just until they begin to color. Add the thyme and bread crumbs, and moisten with a few tablespoons water or fish stock. Add the chopped shrimp and cook for 3 minutes. Season to taste with salt and white pepper. Remove from heat and cool. Blend in the egg.

Wash the black drum and wipe dry. Use a sharp knife to cut three shallow diagonal incisions across each side of the fish. Rub the fish with salt, white pepper, and cayenne, especially in the incisions and the inside cavity. Then rub the fish with flour. Fill the cavity of the fish with the bread crumbs and shrimp stuffing and hold it together with skewers or toothpicks.

In a baking pan large enough to hold the fish, heat 1/4 cup olive oil until it begins to smoke, and quickly sear the fish on both sides to get a pleasing brown color. Add the tomato, onion, bell pepper, bay leaves, and boiling water and sprinkle lightly with salt and pepper. Bake for 45 minutes, or until the fish is flaky all the way through.

Serve with the pan vegetables and liquids spooned over it as a sauce.

Note: This recipe is also delicious with black grouper, hogfish, jolthead porgy, pilot fish, red drum, red grouper, snook, speckled hind, spotfin flounder, and weakfish.

Black Drum Fillets with Artichokes and Mushrooms, in Brown Lemon-Butter Sauce

Brown Lemon-Butter Sauce (recipe
  follows)
6 8-ounce pieces black drum fillets
Salt and freshly ground black pepper
7 tablespoons salted butter

6 cooked artichoke hearts (see Note), cut
  in strips
3 cups sliced fresh mushrooms
Salt and freshly ground white pepper to
  taste

Serves 6

Prepare the Brown Lemon-Butter Sauce, and hold aside warm.

Dry the black drum pieces and season them lightly with salt and pepper. In a wide, heavy skillet, melt the 7 tablespoons butter and sauté the black drum over medium heat for 10 minutes. Remove the fillets from the skillet and place in a warm oven. In the same skillet, sauté the artichoke hearts and mushrooms until they are tender. Season with salt and pepper.

To serve, place the sautéed black drum fillets on six warm plates, top with the sautéed artichoke hearts and mushrooms, and spoon on the sauce.

Brown Lemon-Butter Sauce

1 tablespoon salted butter
1 tablespoon all-purpose flour
3/4 cup beef stock, or beef bouillon

1 stick salted butter, cut into 4 pieces
2 tablespoons freshly squeezed lemon juice
Salt and freshly ground black pepper

In a small saucepan, melt the tablespoon of butter and blend in the flour. Cook while whisking for 7 minutes over a moderate heat until the mixture, a roux, acquires a nut-brown color. Whisk in the stock and simmer for 5 minutes. Add the 1 stick of butter, whisking to incorporate, and the lemon juice, and heat without boiling to retain a fluffy texture from the butter. Season to taste with salt and black pepper.

Notes: You may use artichoke hearts from a jar.

For delicious alternatives, use 6 8-ounce dog snapper, hogfish, Florida pompano, red grouper, weakfish, or yellowtail snapper fillet pieces or 6 6-ounce sand perch, striped bass, or weakfish fillets.

Variations
(follow recipe exactly except for the following substitutions and additions):

with Pearl Onions and Garlic
Use 2 sticks of butter instead of 1, and 3/4 cup fish stock (page 371) or shellfish stock (page 372) instead of beef stock in the sauce. Replace the artichoke and mushrooms with 1 pint cooked pearl onions and 1/3 cup chopped garlic.

with Roma Tomatoes and Red Onion
Use 2 sticks of butter instead of 1, 3/4 cup fish stock (page 371) or shellfish stock (page 372) instead of beef stock, and 1 dozen halved roma tomatoes and 3 cups chopped red onion in place of the artichoke and mushrooms.

with Turnip and Onion
Use 2 sticks of butter instead of 1 and fish stock (page 371) or shellfish stock (page 372) instead of beef stock. Substitute 6 cooked medium turnips cut in strips and 3 cups chopped onions for the artichokes and mushrooms.

Other Delicious Recipes for Black Drum include:

Baked Black Drum in Creole Court-Bouillon (see red drum, page 110)

Black Drum Fillet Marguery (see sheepshead, page 265)

Broiled Black Drum with Poulette Sauce (see red porgy, page 260)

Caribbean Black Drum Salad (see mutton snapper, page 305)

Cold Poached Black Drum Fillets with Green Onion Mayonnaise (see black sea bass, page 23)

Cold Poached Black Drum Fillets with Spicy Creole Mayonnaise (see red snapper, page 309)

Cold Poached Black Drum Ravigote with Boiled New Potatoes (see spotted jewfish, page 43)

Creole Bisque of Black Drum (see tilefish, page 348)

Grilled Black Drum with Béarnaise Sauce (see queen triggerfish, page 358)

Poached Black Drum Fillets with Maltaise Sauce (see common dolphin, page 88)

Poached Black Drum Fillets with Marquis Sauce (see speckled hind, page 37)

Whole Baked Black Drum with Chanterelles (see spotfin flounder, page 136)

Gulf Kingfish

Group: Drum

Other common name(s):
  Whiting
  King Whiting
  Kingfish
Latin name:
  Menticirrhus littoralis
  Family Sciaenidae
Maximum length:
  2 feet

Maximum weight:
  4 pounds
Cuts:
  whole
  fillet
Meat characteristics:
  white, flaky
  low oil content

Preferred cooking methods:
  bake
  fry
  poach
  sauté

3 1 1/2-pound whole gulf kingfish, drawn
  (see Note)
Salt and freshly ground white pepper

1 quart water
Reserved fish heads and bones
1 small onion, sliced
4 green onion tops
1/4 teaspoon dried thyme
1 bay leaf
1/2 teaspoon dried tarragon
1/3 cup dry white wine

1 tablespoon cornstarch
2 tablespoons water

2 tablespoons salted butter
6 green onions, minced
1 French shallot, minced
3 large cucumbers, skinned, seeded, and
  cut in large dice
1 pound fresh spinach, prepped and
  chopped
Salt and freshly ground black pepper

Serves 6

Fillet the gulf kingfish and skin the fillets. Cut out the fine lines of bones in the fillets. Degill the heads and reserve the heads and bones. Season the fillets lightly with salt and white pepper and hold them aside.

Bring the water to a boil in a large saucepan. Add the heads and bones of the fish, and the onion, green onion tops, thyme, and bay leaf. Cover and simmer for 30 minutes. Strain the stock and reduce it to 1 1/2 cups. Add the tarragon and white wine, and simmer 15 minutes. Mix 1 tablespoon cornstarch with the 2 tablespoons water and whisk it into the sauce. Bring to a simmer, stirring to prevent any lumps from forming, and simmer until the sauce thickens. Cover the sauce and keep warm.

In a wide, shallow saucepan, heat the butter and sauté the green onions and French shallot just until they are limp. Add the cucumber and spinach, season with salt and pepper, and sauté together for 2 minutes. Lay the fillets over the cucumber and spinach in the pan, cover, and simmer for 10 minutes.

Spoon the pan juices from the fish and vegetables into the sauce. Bring the sauce back to a simmer and season to taste with salt and pepper.

Serve the gulf kingfish fillets over the vegetables on warm plates, topped with the sauce.

Note: If you prefer, have the fish merchant fillet, skin, and bone the fish and degill the heads; you will need to bring home the heads and bones for the sauce.

You can also use bonefish, permit, pigfish, tile fish, or yellowtail snapper in this recipe.

6 1-pound whole gulf kingfish, scaled and drawn

1 lemon, halved

6 tablespoons softened salted butter

Salt and freshly ground white pepper

Crabmeat Stuffing:

1 stick salted butter

8 green onions, finely chopped

3 ribs celery, minced

1/4 cup all-purpose flour

3 tablespoons chopped fresh parsley

1/4 teaspoon dried thyme

1 teaspoon salt, or to taste

1/2 teaspoon freshly ground white pepper

1/4 teaspoon cayenne pepper

1 1/2 cups fish stock (page 371), or water

3 cups crumbled stale French bread (see Note)

2 tablespoons freshly squeezed lemon juice

2 large eggs, lightly beaten

1 pound crabmeat

3 lemons, halved

Serves 6

Preheat the oven to 400°. Wash the gulf kingfish and wipe dry. Rub the fish inside and out with the lemon halves, then the softened butter. Sprinkle lightly with salt and white pepper.

In a wide, heavy skillet, melt the stick of butter and sauté the chopped green onions and celery until limp, about 2 minutes. Add the flour, stir, and cook for 3 minutes more. Add the parsley, thyme, salt, white pepper, cayenne, and fish stock. Stir and cook for 5 minutes and remove from the heat. Fold in the crumbled French bread. Stir and heat until all is well blended. Remove from the heat. When the mixture has cooled slightly, add the lemon juice and check the seasonings. Blend in the beaten eggs and carefully fold in the crabmeat so it is not broken up too much. Stuff the crabmeat mixture into the gulf kingfish.

Place the stuffed gulf kingfish into a wide baking dish and bake for 20 minutes, basting once or twice with the pan juices, or until the flesh of the fish is flaky all the way through and the stuffing has set.

Serve garnished with lemon halves.

Notes: The bread should be stale. Its staleness and dryness will determine the lightness of the stuffing. If in making the stuffing there is not enough moisture to hold it together, add a little more fish stock or water. Almost any bread can be used, but French bread remains the lightest in this preparation.

Black grouper, black sea bass, creolefish, dog snapper, gulf flounder, red drum, red snapper, spotfin flounder, spotted sea trout, and striped bass are also delicious prepared this way. (In preparing the gulf or spotfin flounder, make a cut down the backbone the full length from head to tail; then, using the cut as a guide, insert your knife under the flesh of the fish along the bones from the middle to the edges near the outer side fins. Do not cut all the way through: you are creating pockets here to hold the stuffing.) Or try 1 5- to 6-pound whole black grouper, red drum, red snapper, or stripped bass, scaled and drawn, and bake for 45 minutes.

Other Delicious Recipes for Gulf Kingfish include:

Baked Gulf Kingfish in Creole Court-Bouillon (see red drum, page 110)

Charcoal-Grilled Butterflied Gulf Kingfish (see great barracuda, page 18)

Creole Étouffée of Gulf Kingfish (see Atlantic sailfish, page 230)

Étouffée of Gulf Kingfish (see blackfin tuna, page 218)

Fried Cornmeal-Battered Gulf Kingfish Fillets (see striped mullet, page 239)

Fried Gulf Kingfish with Brown Shrimp Sauce (see white mullet, page 245)

Gulf Kingfish in Caribbean "Blaff" (see Spanish mackerel, page 202)

Gulf Kingfish Fillets with Sorrel, Zucchini, and Mushrooms (see bonefish, page 74)

Gulf Kingfish with Puerto Rican Sauce (see swordfish, page 333)

Panfried Gulf Kingfish Fillets with Algiers Sauce (see spot drum, page 113)

Panfried Gulf Kingfish with Lobster Cream Sauce (see permit, page 186)

Red Drum

Group: Drum

Other common name(s):	Maximum weight:	Preferred cooking methods:
Redfish	90 pounds	bake
Rat Red	*Cuts:*	fry
Channel Drum	whole (small)	poach
Bull Red	steak	sauté
Latin name:	fillet	steam
Sciaenops ocellatus	*Meat characteristics:*	
Family Sciaenidae	firm, white, flaky	
Maximum length:	low-to-medium oil	
5 feet	content	

Breaded Fillets of Red Drum with Green Mayonnaise

Green Mayonnaise (recipe follows)
2 eggs
1/2 cup water
6 6-ounce red drum fillets
Salt and freshly ground black pepper

1 1/2 cups French bread crumbs
4 tablespoons salted butter
1/4 cup peanut oil
2 tablespoons minced fresh parsley

Serves 6

Prepare the Green Mayonnaise, and refrigerate until ready to serve.

Beat the eggs together with the water. Lightly season the red drum fillets with salt and black pepper, dip them in the egg wash, and dredge in the bread crumbs. Melt the butter in the peanut oil in a wide, heavy skillet and fry the fillets 4 minutes on each side, or until they are golden brown.

Transfer the cooked red drum fillets to warm dinner plates, sprinkle with the chopped parsley, and serve with the Green Mayonnaise.

Green Mayonnaise

1 cup Mayonnaise (page 374)
2 tablespoons minced cooked spinach
2 tablespoons minced fresh parsley
2 tablespoons minced fresh watercress

1 tablespoon minced fresh tarragon
1 teaspoon freshly squeezed lemon juice
1/2 teaspoon salt
1/4 teaspoon freshly ground white pepper

Into the mayonnaise, blend all the other ingredients. Cover tightly and keep refrigerated.

Note: Atlantic croaker, Atlantic threadfin, black grouper, dog snapper, hogfish, spot drum, spotfin flounder, spotted sea trout, and weakfish are excellent prepared this way.

109

1 5- to 6-pound whole red drum, scaled and drawn
Salt and freshly ground black pepper
1 tablespoon salted butter

Creole Court-Bouillon:
1 stick salted butter
4 tablespoons all-purpose flour
2 large yellow onions, chopped
8 green onions, chopped
1 rib celery, chopped
2 cloves garlic, minced

4 large tomatoes, chopped
2 cups water, or fish stock (page 371)
1/2 cup red wine
1 tablespoon freshly squeezed lemon juice
1/2 teaspoon dried thyme
1/2 teaspoon dried marjoram
3 bay leaves
1/4 teaspoon ground allspice
2 tablespoons salt
1 teaspoon freshly ground black pepper
1/2 teaspoon cayenne pepper

Serves 6

Preheat the oven to 350°. Wash the red drum, pat it dry, and rub it inside and out with salt, black pepper, and the 1 tablespoon butter. Hold aside.

Melt the stick of butter in a wide, deep, ovenproof pan and add the flour. Cook together, stirring, until the flour browns lightly. Add the yellow onions, green onions, celery, and garlic, and continue cooking until the onions are limp. Add all the remaining ingredients and simmer together for 15 minutes.

Lay the red drum into the pan with the sauce and baste. Cover the pan and bake for 1 hour, or until the flesh of the fish flakes when broken with a fork. Baste several times during cooking.

With a long spatula, transfer the fillets to a warm serving platter or warm plates, spoon the sauce over the fish, and serve.

> *Note*: Black drum, black grouper, gulf kingfish, rainbow runner, red snapper, scamp, sheepshead, or Spanish mackerel also work well in this recipe.

Other Delicious Recipes for Red Drum include:

Baked Crabmeat-Stuffed Red Drum (see gulf kingfish, page 106)

Baked Shrimp-Stuffed Red Drum (see black drum, page 98)

Breaded Red Drum with Creole Tomato Sauce (see black grouper, page 47)

Grilled Red Drum Steaks with Onions, Green Bell Peppers, and Eggplant (see ling cobia, page 84)

Panfried Red Drum Fillets with Shrimp Creole Sauce (see Atlantic threadfin, page 342)

Poached Red Drum Fillets with Rockefeller Sauce (see tripletail, page 363)

Poached Red Drum with Parsley-Lemon Butter (see sheepshead, page 267)

Red Drum Baked with Onion and Lime (see spotted jewfish, page 42)

Sautéed Red Drum with Crabmeat and Butter (see common dolphin, page 90)

Skillet-Grilled Red Drum Fillets Pontchartrain (see dog snapper, page 299)

Whole Baked Red Drum with Chanterelles (see spotfin flounder, page 136)

Whole Baked Red Drum with Spinach Stuffing (see jolthead porgy, page 250)

Spot Drum

Group: Drum

Other common name(s):	Maximum weight:	Preferred cooking methods:
Spot	2 pounds	bake
Latin name:	Cuts:	fry
Leiostomus xanthurus	whole	sauté
Family Sciaenidae	fillet	steam
Maximum length:	Meat characteristics:	
1 foot 2 inches	white, flaky	
	low oil content	

Panfried Spot Drum Fillets with Algiers Sauce

Algiers Sauce (recipe follows)   Salt and freshly ground black pepper
6 8-ounce spot drum fillets   1/4 cup light-flavored olive oil

Serves 6

Prepare the Algiers Sauce, cover, and hold aside warm.

Season the spot drum fillets with salt and black pepper. Heat the olive oil in a skillet and cook the fillets, without crowding the pan, for 4 minutes on each side, turning only once during the cooking. Transfer the fillets to warm plates and nap with the warm Algiers Sauce.

Algiers Sauce

8 large tomatoes, chopped   1/2 teaspoon cayenne pepper, or to taste
1 cup minced stemmed fresh parsley   Salt, freshly ground black pepper, and
4 cloves garlic, pressed or finely minced   cayenne pepper
1 tablespoon Hungarian paprika   1/2 teaspoon freshly ground black pepper,
1 teaspoon ground cumin   or to taste

Combine the chopped tomatoes in a saucepan with the parsley, garlic, paprika, cumin, black pepper, and cayenne. Bring to a simmer and cook uncovered until the tomato liquids have reduced and the ingredients have become a thick sauce, about 30 minutes. Season with salt and adjust peppers if desired. Serve warm.

Note: Atlantic croaker, gaff-topsail catfish, gulf flounder, and gulf kingfish also work well in this recipe.

Aurora Sauce (recipe follows)
6 3/4-to-1-pound whole spot drums, scaled
    and drawn
Salt and freshly ground black pepper

1/2 cup peanut oil
6 large French bread croutons (page 370)
1 tablespoon chopped fresh parsley

Serves 6

Prepare the Aurora Sauce, and hold aside warm. Wash and dry the spot drums and rub them with salt and pepper. Heat the oil until hot in a heavy skillet and fry the fish, without crowding the pan, for 5 minutes on each side, until lightly browned. Drain the fish on absorbent paper.

To serve, place the fish on the croutons on warm dinner plates, nap with the Aurora Sauce, and garnish with the chopped parsley.

Aurora Sauce

6 tablespoons butter
3 tablespoons all-purpose flour
1/2 cup hot fish stock (page 371), or
    shellfish stock (page 372)

1 cup canned tomato puree
Salt, freshly ground white pepper, and
    cayenne pepper to taste

In a small saucepan, melt the butter and stir in the flour. Stir and cook until the mixture becomes foamy, about 2 minutes. Whisk in the hot stock and bring to a boil. Add the tomato puree and season to taste with salt, white pepper, and cayenne. Simmer for 15 to 20 minutes. Serve warm.

Note: Atlantic croaker, pinfish, sailor's-choice, white grunt, and white mullet are also excellent prepared this way.

Other Delicious Recipes for Spot Drum include:

Baked Spot Drum with Bacon and Onion (see red grouper, page 52)

Breaded Fillets of Spot Drum with Green Mayonnaise (see red drum, page 109)

Fried Cornmeal-Battered Spot Drum Fillets (see striped mullet, page 239)

Fried Spot Drum with Black Anchovy Butter (see Atlantic bonito, page 212)

Fried Spot Drum Fillets with Bourguignonne Sauce (see hogfish, page 366)

Marinated Spot Drum Salad Giardeniera (see squirrelfish, page 329)

Panfried Spot Drum with Lobster Cream Sauce (see permit, page 186)

Spot Drum Fillets with Lobster-Browned Butter Sauce (see gulf flounder, page 132)

Spot Drum en Papillote with Black Olives (see striped bass, page 61)

Spot Drum with Pecans (see lookdown, page 181)

Whole Panfried Spot Drum with Onion, Garlic, and Red Wine Sauce (see pilot fish, page 190)

Whole Panfried Spot Drum with Peanut Sauce (see gaff-topsail catfish, page 78)

Spotted Sea Trout

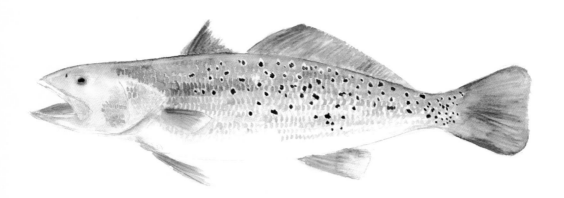

Group: Drum

Other common name(s):
   "Speckled Trout" (sic)
   Speckled Sea Trout
Latin name:
   Cynoscion nebulosus
   Family Sciaenidae
Maximum length:
   3 feet

Maximum weight:
   15 pounds
Cuts:
   whole (smal)
   steak
   fillet
Meat characteristics:
   tender, white, flaky
   low oil content

*Preferred cooking
methods:*
   braise
   fry
   poach
   sauté
   steam

1 4-pound whole spotted sea trout, scaled
   and drawn
Salt and freshly ground black pepper
4 tablespoons salted butter
3 large carrots, roughly chopped
2 large onions, roughly chopped
1 pint fresh mushrooms, roughly chopped
2 ribs celery, roughly chopped

1/2 cup chopped fresh parsley
1 teaspoon dried thyme
2 bay leaves
3 dozen pearl onions, skinned
1/5 to 1 liter red burgundy wine
4 tablespoons salted butter
2 tablespoons all-purpose flour
Salt and freshly ground black pepper

Serves 6

Preheat the oven to 400°. Wash and dry the spotted sea trout and rub it inside and out with salt and black pepper. Hold aside.

Melt the butter in the bottom of a braising pan or Dutch oven on the stovetop and lightly sauté the carrots, onions, mushrooms, and celery until they just begin to brown. Add the parsley, thyme, and bay leaves.

Lay the sea trout into the pan on top of the sautéed vegetables. Add the pearl onions and enough wine to just barely cover the fish. Bring the liquids to a boil on the stovetop, cover the pan, and bake in the oven for 30 minutes. Carefully transfer the fish and pearl onions to a serving platter and hold in a warm oven. Strain the pan liquids into a saucepan.

Knead 2 tablespoons of the butter together with the flour to make a *beurre manié*. Add the *beurre manié* to the pan liquids and simmer together until the liquids have thickened, about 3 minutes. Season to taste with salt and pepper, if desired. Remove the sauce from the heat and whisk in the remaining butter.

Cut the spotted sea trout at the table into fillet portions, and serve with the sauce spooned over.

Note: Red snapper and sheepshead are also delicious prepared this way.

1 stick salted butter

8 green onions, chopped

2 ribs celery, chopped

1 large clove garlic, minced

1/4 cup all-purpose flour

4 medium tomatoes, skinned (see Note), seeded, and chopped

3 cups crumbled stale French bread

2 tablespoons chopped fresh parsley

1/2 teaspoon dried thyme

1 teaspoon salt, or to taste

1/2 teaspoon freshly ground white pepper

1/4 teaspoon cayenne pepper

2 tablespoons freshly squeezed lemon juice

2 large eggs, beaten

1 1/2 pounds spotted sea trout fillet, finely chopped

1 1/2 cups cracker crumbs (see Note)

Peanut oil for frying

1 1/2 cups Tartar Sauce (page 375)

3 lemons, halved

Serves 6

In a sauté pan, melt the butter, add the chopped green onions, celery, and garlic, and sauté for 2 minutes, or until the vegetables are limp. Add the flour, stir, and cook for 2 minutes more. Add the tomatoes and cook until they have released their liquids, about 2 minutes. Add the crumbled French bread, parsley, thyme, salt, white pepper, and cayenne. Stir and cook about 3 minutes, until the bread crumbs have absorbed the liquids from the pan. Remove from the heat and allow to cool slightly.

When the mixture has cooled, add the lemon juice and blend in the beaten eggs. Carefully fold in the chopped spotted sea trout and check the seasonings.

Divide the mixture into 12 portions and shape each of these portions into "chops," as in the shape of a lamb or pork chop. Roll the "chops" in the cracker crumbs.

In a wide, heavy skillet, heat about 1/2 inch oil to 350° and fry the "chops," without crowding the pan, for 3 to 4 minutes on each side, or until nicely golden. Drain on absorbent paper.

Serve with Tartar Sauce and half a lemon.

118

Notes: To skin the tomatoes, immerse them in boiling water for 1 to 2 minutes, then plunge them into cold water.

Cracker crumbs are made by crushing crackers with a rolling pin, or using a food processor.

American eel, gray triggerfish, red grouper, skipjack tuna, squirrelfish, and tarpon also make delicious "chops." For the American eel, use 1 1/2 pounds skinned fillet.

Variations: "Chops" of spotted sea trout are also excellent served with Brown Lemon-Butter Sauce (page 100) or Green Mayonnaise (page 109).

The shape does not have to be "chops"; balls or croquettes (football shapes) also work well. Make twelve croquettes or two dozen balls. Fry the balls for 6 minutes, turning as they fry to brown all over.

Other Delicious Recipes for Spotted Sea Trout include:

Baked Crabmeat-Stuffed Spotted Sea Trout (see gulf kingfish, page 106)

Breaded Fillets of Spotted Sea Trout with Green Mayonnaise (see red drum, page 109)

Charcoal-Grilled Butterflied Spotted Sea Trout (see great barracuda, page 18)

Cold Poached Spotted Sea Trout Fillets with Spicy Creole Mayonnaise (see red snapper, page 309)

Fillet of Spotted Sea Trout Baked en Papillote with a Shrimp, Crabmeat, and White Wine Sauce (see Florida pompano, page 161)

Fried Cornmeal-Battered Spotted Sea Trout Fillets (see striped mullet, page 239)

Sautéed Battered Spotted Sea Trout Fillets with Lemon-Butter Sauce (see red snapper, page 311)

Skillet-Grilled Spotted Sea Trout Fillets Pontchartrain (see dog snapper, page 299)

Spotted Sea Trout Croquettes Meunière (see skipjack tuna, page 221)

Spotted Sea Trout Fillet Marguery (see sheepshead, page 265)

Spotted Sea Trout Fillets Florentine (see tilefish, page 346)

Spotted Sea Trout with Seafood-White Wine Sauce Gratiné (see white mullet, page 243)

Weakfish

Group: Drum

Other common name(s):	Maximum weight:	Preferred cooking methods:
Grey Trout	6 pounds	bake
Sea Trout	*Cuts:*	fry
Latin name:	whole	poach
Cynoscion regalis	steak	sauté
Family Sciaenidae	fillet	steam
Maximum length:	*Meat characteristics:*	
2 feet 4 inches	white, tender, flaky	
	low oil content	

1 large yellow onion, minced
4 French shallots, minced
4 large cloves garlic, pressed or finely
   minced
1 750-ml bottle dry white wine
1/4 cup chopped fresh parsley

2 bay leaves
1/2 teaspoon dried thyme
Juice of 2 lemons
1 4-pound whole weakfish, scaled and
   drawn
Salt and freshly ground white pepper

Serves 6

You will need a fish poacher/steamer or other long or wide covered pan or Dutch oven with a basket or rack to accommodate the fish for this preparation.

Preheat the oven to 375°. In the fish poacher, combine the minced onion, shallots, pressed garlic, white wine, parsley, bay leaves, thyme, and lemon juice. Bring to a boil to allow the flavors of the seasoning vegetables and herbs to be released into the liquid.

Wash and dry the weakfish and rub it inside and out with salt and white pepper. Place the seasoned fish in the basket or on the rack in the pot, making sure it is high enough that the fish does not lie in the liquid. Cover the pan and bring the liquid back to a boil on the stovetop, then bake in the oven for 30 minutes. Carefully transfer the fish to a warm platter and hold in a warm oven.

On the stovetop, bring the pan liquids to a brisk boil and reduce by half. Adjust the seasonings if desired.

Serve out the weakfish at the table. Fillet into six portions and spoon the reduced pan liquids over the top as a sauce.

Note: Mutton snapper, snook, speckled hind, striped bass, and tilefish are also excellent in this recipe.

Cilantro Butter (recipe follows)   Salt and freshly ground black pepper
6 6- to 8-ounce weakfish fillets

Serves 6

Preheat the broiler. Prepare the Cilantro Butter, brush the weakfish fillets with it, and sprinkle lightly with salt and pepper. Place the fillets in a baking dish and broil for about 7 minutes, basting regularly.

When the flesh is flaky all the way through, remove the weakfish from the broiler onto warm dinner plates. Spoon the remaining Cilantro Butter over the cooked fillets and serve.

Cilantro Butter

1 stick salted butter   2 tablespoons minced fresh cilantro leaves
2 teaspoons chili powder   2 tablespoons white vinegar

In a small saucepan, melt the butter, remove from the heat, and stir in the chili powder, minced cilantro leaves, and vinegar.

Note: Bluefish, great barracuda, red porgy, sailor's-choice, southern stingray, and spotfin flounder are delicious alternatives to weakfish. For the southern stingray, use skinned wing fillets.

Variations

(follow recipe exactly except for the following substitutions and additions):

with Garlic-Chive Butter
Use 2 tablespoons minced fresh garlic chives in place of the chili powder and cilantro.

with Rosemary Butter
Replace the chili powder and cilantro with 2 tablespoons fresh rosemary leaves. Use 1 1/2 sticks of butter rather than just 1.

with Tarragon Butter
Use 1 1/2 sticks of butter and substitute 2 tablespoons of minced fresh tarragon leaves for the chili powder and cilantro.

Other Delicious Recipes for Weakfish include:

Baked Shrimp-Stuffed Weakfish (see black drum, page 98)
Breaded Fillets of Weakfish with Green Mayonnaise (see red drum, page 109)
Charcoal-Grilled Butterflied Weakfish (see great barracuda, page 18)
Cold Poached Weakfish Fillets with Green Basil Mayonnaise (see queen triggerfish, page 356)
Fried Weakfish Fillets with Moulin Rouge Sauce (see scamp, page 56)
New Orleans-Style Deep-Fried Weakfish Fillets Meunière (see jolthead porgy, page 249)
Weakfish Fillets with Artichokes and Mushrooms in Brown Lemon-Butter Sauce (see black drum, page 100)
Weakfish Fillet Marguery (see sheepshead, page 265)
Weakfish Fillets with Lobster-Browned Butter Sauce (see gulf flounder, page 132)
Weakfish Poached with Lime and Onion (see sand perch, page 34)
Weakfish with Seafood-White Wine Sauce Gratiné (see white mullet, page 243)
Whole Baked Weakfish with Spinach Stuffing (see jolthead porgy, page 250)

American Eel

Group: Eels, Freshwater

Other common name(s):
Eel

Latin name:
Anguilla rostrata
Family Anguillidae

Maximum length:
4 feet 11 inches

Maximum weight:
2 pounds

Cuts:
whole
steak (small)
fillet

Meat characteristics:
firm, white
high oil content

Preferred cooking methods:
fry
grill
poach
steam
stew

2 cups red wine
1 quart fish stock (page 371)
2 pounds American eel fillet, skinned and
   cut into 1 x 2-inch lengths
4 whole cloves
2 whole allspice
2 bay leaves
1/4 teaspoon dried thyme
1/4 teaspoon dried marjoram

1 stick salted butter
2 large onions, chopped
2 cloves garlic, minced
4 tablespoons all-purpose flour
Salt, freshly ground black pepper, and
   cayenne pepper
2 tablespoons minced fresh parsley
12 French bread croutons (page 370)

Serves 6

In a wide, heavy skillet, bring the red wine and fish stock to a boil. Boil for 5 minutes, turn down to a simmer, and poach the eel for 8 minutes. Remove the poached eel with a slotted spoon and hold aside warm, first trimming off and discarding any trailing pieces. Add the cloves, allspice, bay leaves, thyme, and marjoram to the cooking liquid, bring to a boil, and reduce by half.

In another saucepan, melt the butter and sauté the onions and garlic until they begin to color. Stir in the flour and continue cooking until lightly browned. Whisk 1 cup of the reduced red wine and fish stock into the flour mixture, then add remaining liquid. Bring to a boil and let thicken. Season to taste with salt, black pepper, and cayenne, and add the minced parsley.

Place two croutons each in warm soup bowls, spoon the hot American eel over them, and top with the Matelote Sauce as a stew.

Note: 2-inch strips of skinned fillet of blackfin tuna, bluefish, common jack, or Spanish mackerel, or 2-inch lengths of skinned spotted eagle ray wings can also be used in this recipe.

Variations
(follow recipe exactly except for the following substitutions and additions):

Stew with Sherry
Replace the red wine with 1 cup dry sherry. Use 1 1/2 quarts fish stock (page 371) or shellfish stock (page 372), omit the allspice and marjoram, and increase the thyme to 1/2 teaspoon.

1/4 cup olive oil

2 pounds American eel fillet, skinned and boned

4 green onions, chopped

4 large cloves garlic, minced

1 fresh habanero (Scotch bonnet) pepper, stemmed, seeded, and minced (see Note)

1/2 teaspoon dried thyme

2 bay leaves

2 tablespoons chopped fresh parsley

1/4 cup freshly squeezed lime juice

1 tablespoon salt, or to taste

1/2 teaspoon freshly ground white pepper

2 cups raw white rice

4 cups fish stock (page 371)

3 limes, halved

Habañero pepper sauce (bottled Caribbean-style pepper sauce)

Serves 6

In a heavy casserole or saucepan, heat the olive oil and sauté the American eel fillet for 2 minutes on each side. Remove the fish and set aside to cool.

Add the green onions, garlic, and hot pepper to the pan, and sauté them until they become limp. Add the thyme, bay leaves, parsley, lime juice, salt, white pepper, and rice. Stir in the fish stock and bring to a boil.

While the liquids are coming to a boil, shred the cooked American eel fillet apart into small lumps using two forks. Stir the lumps into the other ingredients. When the stock comes to a boil, turn down the heat, cover, and simmer gently for approximately 20 minutes, or until all the liquids have been absorbed by the rice.

Serve with the limes on warm plates and pass the habañero pepper sauce.

Notes: Any hot pepper may be used, but if habañero pepper is available, it is the best for this recipe.

Atlantic bonito, blue marlin, hard-tail jack, rainbow runner, skipjack tuna, tripletail, or wahoo are also delicious prepared this way. Use 2 pounds fish fillet, skinned and boned.

Other Delicious Recipes for American Eel include:

American Eel Chowder with Potatoes and Tomatoes (see greater amberjack, page 170)

American Eel with Creole Sauce Piquante (see wahoo, page 209)

American Eel Stew with White Wine (see spotted eagle ray, page 275)

American Eel-Stuffed Hand Tortillas (see bluefish, page 68)

Caribbean-Style American Eel Stew (see pilot fish, page 189)

"Chops" of American Eel (see spotted sea trout, page 118)

Creole-Style American Eel Pot-au-Feu (see tarpon, page 336)

Fried American Eel with Black Anchovy Butter (see Atlantic bonito, page 212)

Marinated Escabèche of American Eel (see hard-tail jack, page 176)

Poached American Eel with Horseradish and Sour Cream Sauce (see Atlantic croaker, page 95)

Poached American Eel with Parsley-Lemon Butter (see sheepshead, page 267)

Steamed American Eel with Aioli Sauce (see squirrelfish, page 328)

Gulf Flounder

Group: Flounder, Lefteye Family

Other common name(s):
Flounder

Latin name:
Paralichthys albigutta
Family Bothidae

Maximum length:
1 foot 6 inches

Maximum weight:
5 pounds

Cuts:
whole
fillet

Meat characteristics:
tender, white, flaky
low-to-medium oil
content

Preferred cooking methods:
bake
braise
sauté
steam

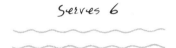

Broiled Gulf Flounder

6 1-pound whole gulf flounder, scaled and
    drawn
1/2 cup melted salted butter
Juice of 2 lemons

Salt and freshly ground white pepper
2 tablespoons chopped fresh
    parsley

Serves 6

Preheat the broiler. Combine the melted butter with the lemon juice and brush a large baking pan with some of the mixture. Wash and dry the flounder and arrange them in the pan. Score the tops of the fish three times each diagonally, brush with the butter-lemon mixture, and season with salt and white pepper.

Place the pan about 3 inches from the broiler element. Broil 7 minutes or so, without turning, or until opaque completely through. Baste the fish several times during the broiling with the pan drippings and butter-lemon mixture.

Carefully transfer the broiled gulf flounder to warm plates. Combine any pan drippings with the remaining butter-lemon mixture and dribble over the fish. Garnish with the chopped parsley.

Note: Black sea bass, common dolphin, gray triggerfish, Florida pompano, and red grouper are also excellent prepared this way.

6 6-ounce gulf flounder fillets
Salt, freshly ground black pepper, and
   Hungarian paprika
3 sticks salted butter
Juice of 3 lemons
1/4 cup water

Hungarian paprika
1/2 cup dry white wine
1 pound Florida or Maine lobster tail
   meat, diced
2 tablespoons chopped fresh parsley

Serves 6

Dry the gulf flounder fillets and sprinkle both sides with salt, pepper, and paprika.

Melt 2 sticks of the butter in a large, heavy skillet, and heat until it begins to color. Lay the seasoned gulf flounder fillets in the skillet flesh side down, and cook for 2 minutes over medium heat. Add the lemon juice, turn the fish over, and add the water. Lightly sprinkle the fish again with paprika. Cover the pan and cook 6 minutes more. Carefully transfer the fish from the skillet to warmed plates and hold in a warm oven.

Add the wine to the skillet and boil for 1 minute. Add the diced lobster and cook for 2 minutes, just until it is opaque and still tender. Add the remaining stick butter, cut into four pieces and whisk until it is incorporated. Keep the sauce warm without letting it come to a boil, or it will separate and lose its fluffy texture. Add the parsley.

To serve, spoon the sauce over the fish fillets.

Note: Black grouper, common dolphin, pinfish, red snapper, spot drum, weakfish, and white grunt are delicious alternatives to gulf flounder. Cook the second side, covered, for 6 minutes.

Variations
(follow recipe exactly except for the following substitutions and additions):

with Anchovy-Browned Butter Sauce
Substitute 1 tin anchovies, chopped, for the lobster.

with Crabmeat-Browned Butter Sauce
In place of the lobster, use 1 pound lump crabmeat.

with Crawfish-Browned Butter Sauce
Use 1 pound crawfish tail meat instead of lobster.

with Shrimp-Browned Butter Sauce
Replace the lobster with 1 pound small peeled and deveined raw shrimp.

Other Delicious Recipes for Gulf Flounder include:
Baked Crabmeat-Stuffed Gulf Flounder (see gulf kingfish, page 104)
Baked Gulf Flounder with Bacon and Onion (see red grouper, page 52)
Broiled Gulf Flounder with Balsamic Vinegar (see Atlantic moonfish, page 153)
Charcoal-Grilled Gulf Flounder with Plantation Groundnut Sauce (see southern
    stingray, page 270)
Fillet of Gulf Flounder Baked en Papillote with a Shrimp, Crabmeat, and White
    Wine Sauce (see Florida pompano, page 161)
Gulf Flounder Fillets Florentine (see tilefish, page 346)
Gulf Flounder with Pecans (see lookdown, page 181)
New Orleans-Style Deep-Fried Gulf Flounder Fillets Meunière (see jolthead porgy,
    page 249)
Panfried Gulf Flounder Fillets with Algiers Sauce (see spot drum, page 113)
Panfried Gulf Flounder with Lobster Cream Sauce (see permit, page 186)
Poached Gulf Flounder with Marquis Sauce (see speckled hind, page 37)
Whole Panfried Gulf Flounder with Colbert Sauce (see red porgy, page 262)

Spotfin Flounder

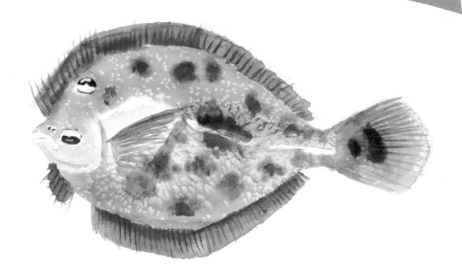

Group: Flounder, Lefteye Family

Other common name(s):
Spotfin
Flounder

Latin name:
Cyclopsetta fimbriatta
Family Bothidae

Maximum length:
1 foot 3 inches

Maximum weight:
4 pounds

Cuts:
whole
fillet

Meat characteristics:
tender, white, flaky
low oil content

Preferred cooking methods:
bake
fry
poach
sauté
steam

Shrimp Soufflé:

1/2 pound raw shrimp, shelled, deveined, and diced
3 egg whites
1 teaspoon salt
1/4 teaspoon freshly ground white pepper
1/4 teaspoon grated nutmeg
1/2 cup heavy cream

3 tablespoons salted butter
6 6-ounce spotfin flounder fillets
Cotton string
1 cup dry white wine
2 cups heavy cream
Juice of 1 lemon
Salt and freshly ground white pepper
2 tablespoons minced fresh parsley

Serves 6

Preheat the oven to 400°. In a food processor, grind the shrimp very fine, then gradually add the egg whites. When well blended, add the salt, white pepper, and nutmeg. Then while mixing, add the 1/2 cup of heavy cream and continue to mix thoroughly until well blended. Chill.

Butter a shallow baking pan with 1 tablespoon of the butter. Lay the spotfin flounder fillets out flat and spoon some of the shrimp soufflé on top of each fillet. Roll up the fillets around the shrimp filling and tie the rolls closed with cotton string.

Pour the white wine into the baking pan, add the stuffed fillets, loosely cover with foil, and bake about 12 to 15 minutes, or until the shrimp mixture is firm, but fluffy to the touch. Remove the fish to warm plates. On the stovetop, reduce the cooking liquid by half, add the 2 cups of cream, and reduce to desired consistency. Add the lemon juice and salt and white pepper to taste, and finish with the remaining 2 tablespoons butter.

Spoon the sauce over each portion of spotfin flounder, garnish with the chopped parsley, and serve.

Note: Gaff-topsail catfish and red snapper are also delicious prepared this way.

1 5-pound whole spotfin flounder, scaled
   and drawn
3 tablespoons light-flavored olive oil
Salt and freshly ground black pepper
1/4 cup chopped garlic
1/2 cup chopped green onions
1 pound fresh chanterelles, or other fresh
   mushrooms, brushed clean

1/3 cup chopped fresh parsley
1 teaspoon dried thyme
1 teaspoon dried rosemary
1 cup dry white wine
1 cup fish stock (page 371)
1/2 cup freshly squeezed lemon juice
Salt and freshly ground black pepper

Serves 6

Preheat the oven to 375°. Wash and dry the spotfin flounder, brush it with a little of the olive oil, and season inside and out with salt and black pepper. Lay the fish into a baking pan or Dutch oven with a cover.

Heat the remaining olive oil in a skillet or sauté pan, add the garlic and green onions, and sauté until they begin to color. Add the chanterelles, half of the parsley, and the thyme and rosemary. Stir around and cook for only about a minute. Add the white wine and fish stock and reduce to half. Remove from the heat.

Sprinkle about 2 tablespoons of the lemon juice over the fish. Spoon the chanterelle mixture onto the top of the fish. Cover and bake for 35 minutes, or until the flesh flakes easily all the way through. Carefully transfer the flounder to a warm platter and hold warm in the oven.

Deglaze the pan on the stovetop with the remaining lemon juice. Season the pan liquids to taste with salt and pepper.

Serve up the spotfin flounder at the table. Cut the top fillet into three serving pieces, remove the bones, then cut the bottom fillet into three pieces. Spoon the chanterelles and pan liquids over the fish, sprinkle with the remaining parsley, and serve.

> *Note*: Black drum, mutton snapper, red drum, and sheepshead are also excellent baked this way.

Other Delicious Recipes for Spotfin Flounder include:

Baked Crabmeat-Stuffed Spotfin Flounder (see gulf kingfish, page 106)

Baked Shrimp-Stuffed Spotfin Flounder (see black drum, page 98)

Breaded Fillets of Spotfin Flounder with Green Mayonnaise (see red drum, page 109)

Breaded Spotfin Flounder with Creole Tomato Sauce (see black grouper, page 47)

Broiled Spotfin Flounder Fillets with Cilantro Butter (see weakfish, page 123)

Creole Étouffée of Spotfin Flounder (see Atlantic sailfish, page 230)

Fried Cornmeal-Battered Spotfin Flounder Fillets (see striped mullet, page 239)

Panfried Spotfin Flounder Fillets with Shrimp Creole Sauce (see Atlantic threadfin, page 342)

Poached Spotfin Flounder with Parsley-Lemon Butter (see sheepshead, page 267)

Spotfin Flounder Baked with Onion and Lime (see spotted jewfish, page 42)

Spotfin Flounder Boudin (see Atlantic moonfish, page 152)

Spotfin Flounder with Pecans (see lookdown, page 181)

Pigfish

Group: Grunt

Other common name(s):	Maximum weight:	Preferred cooking methods:
Grunt	2 pounds	bake
Pig Grunt	*Cuts:*	fry
Latin name:	whole	poach
Orthopristis	fillet	sauté
chrysoptera	*Meat characteristics:*	
Family Haemulidae	tender, white, flaky	
Maximum length:	low-to-medium oil	
1 foot	content	

4 tablespoons salted butter

2 fennel bulbs, julienned

2 leeks (white part only), julienned

2 ribs celery, stringed and julienned

1 white onion, julienned

4 cloves garlic, minced

2 French shallots, minced

1 tablespoon Herbsaint or Pernod

Salt and freshly ground white pepper

6 1-pound whole pigfish, scaled and drawn

Salt and freshly ground white pepper

Heavy-duty aluminum foil

Juice of 2 lemons

1/4 cup chopped fresh parsley

Serves 6

Preheat the oven to 400°. Melt 2 tablespoons of the butter in a sauté pan and sweat the fennel, leeks, celery, onion, garlic, and shallots just until limp. Add the Herbsaint or Pernod. Season lightly with salt and white pepper and hold aside.

Wash and dry the pigfish and rub inside and out with salt and white pepper.

Tear off six pieces of heavy-duty aluminum foil wide enough to fold over one fish and seal closed, or a piece twice the length of the fish that can also fold over and be sealed closed. Use the remaining 2 tablespoons butter to butter the foil pieces and place a pigfish in the center of each. Stuff the sautéed vegetables into each fish, then sprinkle with the lemon juice and the chopped parsley. Fold the foil over the fish and seal closed with small pinched folds.

Arrange the papillotes on a baking sheet and bake for about 30 minutes, or until the flesh is opaque all the way through. You will have to unfold the foil of one papillote to test for doneness.

Transfer the papillotes onto warm plates. Bring the plates to the table and have everyone tear the foil open in the middle along the length of their fish, folding the foil back as they go. Provide bone plates for each diner.

Note: Black grouper, white grunt, and yellowtail snapper are also excellent in this recipe.

4 tablespoons salted butter

2 medium carrots, sliced thin

1 medium onion, chopped

2 ribs celery, finely chopped

1 tablespoon tomato paste

1/2 cup brandy

1 cup dry white wine

3 medium tomatoes, skinned (see Note), seeded, and chopped

4 cloves garlic, minced

4 bay leaves

1/8 teaspoon crumbled saffron, or to taste

1 1/2 quarts fish stock (page 371), shellfish stock (page 372), or water

4 tablespoons salted butter

1 pound raw shrimp, peeled and deveined

1 1/2 pounds pigfish fillets, skinned and cut into 1-inch pieces

1 dozen freshly shucked oysters

2 medium-sized Florida or Maine lobster tails, cut into 1-inch dice

Salt, freshly ground white pepper, and cayenne pepper

1 cup fresh lump crabmeat, warm

3 tablespoons chopped fresh parsley

6 French bread croutons (page 370), rubbed with cut garlic

Serves 6

In a soup pot, melt the butter and sauté the carrots, onion, and celery for 3 minutes. Add tomato paste and brandy, and ignite. Add the wine, tomatoes, garlic, bay leaves, and saffron. Stir in the stock and simmer gently for 20 minutes.

In a sauté pan, melt the butter and sauté the shrimp, pigfish, oysters, and lobster for 3 minutes. Add the sautéed seafood to the soup pot, and cook for 10 minutes over medium heat. Season to taste with salt, white pepper, and cayenne.

Serve the bouillabaisse topped with the crabmeat and chopped parsley. Garnish each serving with a garlic crouton.

Notes: To skin the tomatoes, immerse them in boiling water for 1 to 2 minutes, then plunge them into cold water.

Try Atlantic bonito, Atlantic moonfish, queen triggerfish, skipjack tuna, triple-tail, or yellowtail snapper with this recipe.

Other Delicious Recipes for Pigfish include:

Broiled Pigfish with Balsamic Vinegar (see Atlantic moonfish, page 153)

Pigfish Boudin (see Atlantic moonfish, page 152)

Pigfish Fillets with Cucumber and Spinach (see gulf kingfish, page 104)

Pigfish Fillets with Sorrel, Zucchini, and Mushrooms (see bonefish, page 74)

Pigfish with Oyster and Crabmeat Sauce Gratiné (see pinfish, page 256)

Pigfish with Pecans (see lookdown, page 181)

Pigfish, Tomato, and Pepper Soup (see red grouper, page 53)

Poached Pigfish with Horseradish and Sour Cream Sauce (see Atlantic croaker, page 95)

Sautééd Pigfish with Citrus-Garlic Sauce (see Atlantic threadfin, page 341)

Sailor's-Choice

Group: Grunt

Other common name(s):
Grunt

Latin name:
Haemulon parra
Family Haemulidae

Maximum length:
1 foot 4 inches

Maximum weight:
2 pounds

Cuts:
whole
fillet

Meat characteristics:
tender, white
medium oil content

Preferred cooking methods:
bake
broil
fry
poach
sauté

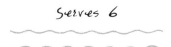

1 1/2 sticks salted butter
2 teaspoons curry powder
2 tablespoons white vinegar

6 6- to 8-ounce sailor's-choice fillets
Salt and freshly ground black pepper

Serves 6

Preheat the broiler. In a small saucepan, melt the butter, remove from the heat, and add the curry powder and vinegar. Brush the sailor's-choice fillets with the mixture and sprinkle lightly with salt and pepper. Place the fillets in a baking dish and broil for about 7 minutes, basting regularly. Do not turn.

When the flesh is flaky all the way through, remove the sailor's-choice from the broiler onto warm dinner plates. Spoon the remaining curry butter over the cooked fillets and serve.

Note: Ling cobia, king mackerel, pilot fish, red porgy, southern stingray, and white grunt are also delicious prepared this way. For the southern stingray, use skinned wing fillets.

1/2 cup peanut oil
1/2 cup all-purpose flour
1 large white onion, chopped
8 green onions, chopped
2 cups sliced okra
2 ribs celery, chopped
1/4 cup chopped fresh parsley
1 1/2 quarts shellfish stock (page 372), or fish stock (page 371), oyster water, or water
1 cup chopped tomato pulp
2 bay leaves
3 crabs, top shell and lungs discarded, quartered
Salt, freshly ground black pepper, and cayenne pepper to taste
2 cups raw shrimp, peeled and deveined
2 cups raw oysters
6 4-ounce pieces sailor's-choice fillet
2 tablespoons filé powder (see Note), optional
3 cups cooked rice

Serves 6

In a large saucepan or soup pot, heat the oil. Add the flour and cook together, while stirring, until it becomes a mahogany-brown color, about 10 minutes. This is a brown roux. Add the white onion, green onions, okra, celery, and parsley and continue cooking until all is browned. Whisk in the stock, and add the tomato pulp, bay leaves, and crabs. Season to taste with salt, pepper, and cayenne, and simmer for 1 hour.

Before serving, add the shrimp, oysters, and sailor's-choice fillets, and simmer for 5 minutes more, or until the fish and seafood are opaque. Add the filé powder and check seasonings.

Serve in large bowls with 1/2 cup rice scooped onto the middle of each serving.

Notes: Filé powder is powdered sassafras leaves, used as a thickening, flavoring, and coloring (darkening) agent. It comes to New Orleans Creole cuisine from the Louisiana Indians.

Try this recipe with Atlantic spadefish, pinfish, southern stingray, and Spanish mackerel. For the southern stingray, use skinned wing fillets.

Other Delicious Recipes for Sailor's-Choice include:

Baked Canapé of Sailor's-Choice (see Atlantic spadefish, page 323)
Beer-Battered Fried Sailor's-Choice (see speckled hind, page 39)
Broiled Sailor's-Choice Fillets with Cilantro Butter (see weakfish, page 123)
Broiled Sailor's-Choice with Poulette Sauce (see red porgy, page 260)
Cold Poached Sailor's-Choice Fillets with Green Basil Mayonnaise (see queen triggerfish, page 356)
Fried Battered Sailor's-Choice with Two Sisters Sauce (see permit, page 184)
Grilled Sailor's-Choice Fillets in Sesame-Brandy Marinade (see scamp, page 58)
Poached Sailor's-Choice with Horseradish and Sour Cream Sauce (see Atlantic croaker, page 95)
Sautéed Sailor's-Choice wtih Citrus-Garlic Sauce (see Atlantic threadfin, page 341)
Steamed Sailor's-Choice Fillets with Espagnole Mayonnaise (see mutton snapper, page 303)
Whole Cracker-Crumb-Coated Panfried Sailor's-Choice with Key Lime Sauce (see white grunt, page 147)
Whole Panfried Sailor's-Choice with Aurora Sauce (see spot drum, page 114)

White Grunt

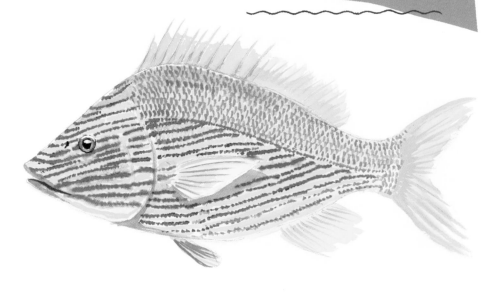

Group: Grunt

Other common name(s):
Grunt

Latin name:
Haemulon plumieri
Family Haemulidae

Maximum length:
1 foot 6 inches

Maximum weight:
2 pounds 6 ounces

Cuts:
whole
steak
fillet

Meat characteristics:
firm, white, flaky
low oil content

Preferred cooking methods:
bake
fry
poach
sauté

Whole Cracker-Crumb-Coated Panfried White Grunt with Key Lime Sauce

Key Lime Sauce (recipe follows)
1 sleeve of saltine crackers (1/4 of a 15- to 16-ounce box), about 40 crackers
Peanut oil for frying
1 1/2 cups milk
2 eggs

6 1-pound whole white grunts, pan-dressed
Salt and freshly ground black pepper
1 1/2 cups all-purpose flour
3 limes, halved

Serves 6

Make the Key Lime Sauce first to allow the flavors to meld. Cover and hold at room temperature while you prepare the fish.

Roll the saltines into crumbs with a rolling pin on a flat surface, or pulse them in a food processor. Heat 1/2 inch of oil in a wide, heavy skillet to 375°. Beat the milk and eggs together in a flat pan to make an egg wash.

Wash and dry the grunts and rub them inside and out with salt and black pepper. Dredge them in the flour, shaking off any excess. Then dip them in the egg wash and dredge in the rolled cracker crumbs. Arrange as many at a time in the frying pan as you can without crowding. The temperature of the oil must not be allowed to dip too far below 350° or the coating will absorb oil before being properly sealed by the heat. Cook the grunt on one side for about 5 minutes, turn, and cook 3 minutes more, or until they are opaque completely through. The cracker crumb coating should be golden brown. Transfer the fish to absorbent paper to drain.

Serve the fish immediately, accompanied with the Key Lime Sauce and a half lime for additional lime flavor.

Key Lime Sauce

1 3/4 cups Mayonnaise (page 374)
1/2 cup freshly squeezed lime juice, from
   Florida Key limes if available
1/4 cup Dijon mustard
1/4 cup soy sauce

1 teaspoon grated lime zest
3 tablespoons habanero pepper sauce
   (bottled Caribbean-style pepper sauce),
   or to taste
Salt

Combine the mayonnaise and lime juice in a bowl with the Dijon mustard, soy sauce, lime zest, and habañero pepper sauce. You can alter the amount of habañero pepper sauce to suit your own taste. Season to taste with salt. Serve at room temperature.

Note: Atlantic croaker, pinfish, sailor's-choice, and sand perch are also excellent prepared this way.

1/4 cup olive oil

4 cloves garlic, chopped

2 large onions, chopped

2 medium bell peppers, seeded, and chopped

1 large eggplant, cut into 1/2-inch dice

1 cup dry white wine

1/2 teaspoon dried thyme

Salt, freshly ground white pepper, and cayenne pepper

4 tomatoes, skinned (see Note), seeded, and chopped

1/4 cup chopped fresh parsley

Vegetable oil for grilling

6 1-pound whole white grunts, dressed and butterflied (see Note)

1/4 cup melted salted butter

Salt and freshly ground white pepper

2 tablespoons chopped fresh parsley

Serves 6

Light the grill or charcoal 1 hour before cooking. In a sauté pan, heat the olive oil and sauté the garlic until lightly browned. Add the onion and bell pepper, and sauté for 10 minutes. Add the eggplant, white wine, and thyme, season with salt, white pepper, and cayenne, and simmer for 15 minutes. Stir occasionally to prevent sticking and ensure even cooking. Add the tomatoes and chopped parsley, adjust the seasonings, and heat only long enough for all to be hot.

When the grill is ready, brush the rack with oil. Brush the white grunts with butter, season lightly with salt and pepper, and grill for 4 minutes on each side, or to desired doneness.

Spoon the Andalouse vegetable mixture in a circle on warm dinner plates and place a grilled white grunt in the center of each. Garnish with the chopped parsley, and serve.

149

Notes: To skin the tomatoes, immerse them in boiling water for 1 to 2 minutes, then plunge them in cold water.

Have the fish merchant do the butterflying, or follow instructions on page 18. Try this recipe with Atlantic bonito, Atlantic croaker, Atlantic moonfish, queen triggerfish, red porgy, red snapper, squirrelfish, or white mullet.

Other Delicious Recipes for White Grunt include:

Cold Poached White Grunt with Green Onion Mayonnaise (see black sea bass, page 23)

Corn-Flour-Fried White Grunt Fillets (see dog snapper, page 300)

Curried Fillets of White Grunt (see sailor's-choice, page 143)

Fried White Grunt Fingers with Pink Horseradish Mayonnaise (see gaff-topsail catfish, page 80)

White Grunt with Creole Sauce Piquante (see wahoo, page 209)

White Grunt Fillets with Lobster-Browned Butter Sauce (see gulf flounder, page 132)

White Grunt Fillets Simmered in Leek and Tomato Sauce (see hard-tail jack, page 174)

White Grunt en Papillote with Fennel (see pigfish, page 139)

White Grunt, Tomato, and Pepper Soup (see red grouper, page 53)

Whole Panfried White Grunt with Aurora Sauce (see spot drum, page 114)

Whole Panfried White Grunt with Espagnole Sauce (see tripletail, page 361)

Whole Panfried White Grunt with Salsa Roja (see striped mullet, page 240)

Atlantic Moonfish

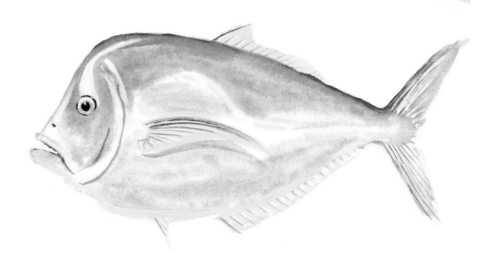

Group: Jack

Other common name(s):
Moonfish

Latin name:
Selene setapinnis
Family Carangidae

Maximum length:
1 foot 3 inches

Maximum weight:
3 pounds

Cuts:
whole
fillet

Meat characteristics:
firm, medium-white
medium oil content

Preferred cooking methods:
bake
broil
grill
poach
sauté

2 pounds Atlantic moonfish fillets, skinned
4 tablespoons salted butter
2 onions, chopped
6 green onions, chopped
4 cloves garlic, minced
1/2 cup chopped fresh parsley
1/2 teaspoon dried thyme

1 1/2 teaspoons salt
1 teaspoon freshly ground white pepper
1/2 teaspoon cayenne pepper
2 cups water
3 cups cooked white rice
4 20-inch-long cleaned sausage casings (see Note)

Serves 6

Grind the Atlantic moonfish fillets in a food processor or food mill, or chop them finely; hold aside.

In a large, heavy skillet, heat the butter and sauté the chopped onions, green onions, and garlic until the onions are wilted. Add the ground Atlantic moonfish, parsley, thyme, salt, pepper, and cayenne. Stir in the water and the cooked rice. Bring to a boil and cook at a medium heat for 10 minutes, or until most of the water is reduced. It is okay to stir the ingredients, even though there is rice, because you want the final stuffing mixture to have a somewhat sticky texture. Adjust the seasonings if necessary. Let cool enough to handle.

Tie the four sausage casings at one end and stuff them with the mixture. Twist each 20-inch length into three equal lengths. Tie the open ends.

The boudin can be cooked in a covered pan with 1/2 inch water for 12 minutes, grilled for 8 minutes, or panfried in a little oil for 4 minutes. Cut the cooked sausages apart and serve two per person.

Notes: Sausage casings are available from grocery butchers or meat markets.

Bluefish, blue marlin, hard-tail jack, king mackerel, pigfish, rainbow runner, red porgy, or spotfin flounder are delicious alternatives.

Broiled Atlantic Moonfish with Balsamic Vinegar

6 1-pound whole Atlantic moonfish, scaled
  and drawn
Salt and freshly ground white pepper

1 1/2 cups melted salted butter, hot
3 tablespoons minced fresh parsley
1/4 cup balsamic vinegar

Serves 6

Preheat the broiler. Dry the Atlantic moonfish and score them several times shallowly across each side in a criss-cross pattern. Season the fish lightly with salt and white pepper.

Place the moonfish on a buttered broiler pan or baking sheet, paint them with melted butter, and broil for 5 minutes on each side, basting several times with the butter, or until the fish is opaque all the way through. Transfer the fish to warm plates and hold in a warm oven.

Add the minced parsley and balsamic vinegar to the remaining melted butter, heat together for a minute or so, spoon the sauce over the broiled fish, and serve.

Note: Atlantic threadfin, creolefish, gulf flounder, lookdown, pigfish, queen triggerfish, red porgy, scamp, and Atlantic spadefish are delicious alternatives with this recipe. Use 6 1 1/2-pound gulf flounders, scaled and drawn, and broil 7 minutes or until done. Use 12 8-ounce Atlantic threadfins and broil for 3 minutes each side or until done.

Variations: Broiled Atlantic moonfish is also excellent served with a seasoned butter (see list page 388) or with Achiote-Garlic Paste (page 49), Creole Garlic Paste (page 50), Italian Herb-Garlic Paste (page 50), Mexican Paste (page 66), or Sweet Herb Paste (page 197).

Other Delicious Recipes for Atlantic Moonfish include:

Baked Canapé of Atlantic Moonfish (see Atlantic spadefish, page 323)

Caribbean Atlantic Moonfish Salad (see mutton snapper, page 305)

Charcoal-Grilled Atlantic Moonfish with Plantation Groundnut Sauce (see southern stingray, page 270)

Charcoal-Grilled Atlantic Moonfish with Tomatillo-Habañero Salsa (see gray triggerfish, page 351)

Grilled Atlantic Moonfish Andalouse (see white grunt, page 149)

Grilled Atlantic Moonfish with Tomato-Red Wine Sauce (see Atlantic spadefish, page 325)

Gulf Coast Bouillabaisse with Atlantic Moonfish (see pigfish, page 140)

New Orleans-Style Deep-Fried Atlantic Moonfish Fillets Meunière (see jolthead porgy, page 249)

Poached Atlantic Moonfish Fillets with Creamy Pimiento-Butter Sauce (see ling cobia, page 85)

Sautéed Atlantic Moonfish with Citrus-Garlic Sauce (see Atlantic threadfin, page 341)

Whole Panfried Atlantic Moonfish with Colbert Sauce (see red porgy, page 262)

Wood-Grilled Atlantic Moonfish Steaks with Mexican Seasonings (see bluefish, page 66)

Common Jack

Group: Jack

Other common name(s):
  Cavalla
  Jack Cravalle
  Jack

Latin name:
  Caranx hippos
  Family Carangidae

Maximum length:
  3 feet 4 inches

Maximum weight:
  54 pounds

Cuts:
  whole (small)
  steak
  fillet

Meat characteristics:
  dark, rich, firm
  medium-to-high oil
  content

Preferred cooking methods:
  bake
  braise
  broil
  grill
  sauté
  steam

Roasted Tomato and Chili Sauce (recipe
    follows)

Corn Masa Dough:
2 cups corn masa flour (see Note)
1 2/3 cups fish stock (page 371)
2 tablespoons peanut oil
1 1/2 teaspoons salt

24 tamale husks, or parchment paper cut
    into 7 × 9-inch rectangles
1 pound common jack fillet, skinned and
    cut into 2 1/2 × 2 1/2 × 1-inch-thick
    squares
Water

Serves 6

Prepare the Roasted Tomato and Chili Sauce, and hold aside warm. In a bowl, combine the corn masa flour with the fish stock, oil, and salt. Work into a solid, yet not too stiff dough. Cover the dough with plastic wrap or a damp kitchen towel and let mature for 15 minutes.

To assemble the tamales, take a heaping tablespoon of the corn masa dough and spread it into a 4-inch square onto each of the 24 tamale husks. Top each tamale with a square of common jack, and top each piece of fish with a tablespoon of the Roasted Tomato and Chili Sauce. Carefully roll or fold the packets into square tamale shapes, seam on top, tucking the ends underneath.

Place the assembled tamales in a steamer basket, or a colander that can be fitted into a large covered pot. Pour 2 inches of water into the bottom of the steamer or pot, without letting the water touch the tamales. Cover the pot and steam the tamales for 45 minutes to an hour, or until the dough has set and separates easily from the husk. To test, partially unwrap one tamale; if not done, rewrap and continue cooking.

Serve four tamales per person, for them to unfold themselves and enjoy, with additional Roasted Tomato and Chili Sauce on the side.

4 medium roasted tomatoes (page 370),
    seeded
4 serrano chilies (see Note), stemmed and
    seeded
1 medium onion, chopped

3 cloves garlic, chopped
2 tablespoons bacon drippings, or peanut
    oil
Salt

    Process the tomatoes, chilies, onion, and garlic in a blender or food processor into a rough puree. Heat the bacon drippings in a skillet until fairly hot, then add the vegetable puree. Cook while stirring constantly for about 10 minutes, or until the sauce colors and thickens. Season with salt to taste. Serve warm.

Notes: If serrano chilies are unavailable, red bell peppers can be used, though the sauce will have a much milder flavor.

Corn flour is often used in the frying of seafood rather than white flour. It can be bought as plain corn flour in specialty stores or as corn masa flour or "masa harina" in stores that sell Mexican or Central and South American food products. It is the flour that corn tortillas are made from. It can also be gotten in the form of "fish-fry," which is corn flour that is already seasoned with salt and pepper.

Atlantic bonito, blacktip shark, great barracuda, largetooth sawfish, ling cobia, pilot fish, Spanish mackerel, and spotted jewfish also work well prepared this way.

Variations: The tamales are also excellent prepared with Espagnole Sauce (page 361), Piquant Green Sauce (page 204), Salsa Roja (page 240), or Tomato-Oyster Sauce (page 164).

Common Jack Smothered in Jalapeño-Tequila Sauce

Jalapeño-Tequila Sauce (recipe follows)
Salt
3/4 cup all-purpose flour
1 teaspoon salt

6 6-ounce pieces common jack fillet
1/2 stick salted butter
3 limes, halved

Serves 6

Prepare the Jalapeño-Tequila Sauce in a large saucepan, and hold aside warm.

In a bowl, combine the flour and salt and dredge the fish fillets in the mixture. Heat the butter in a heavy, wide skillet and fry the fillets until they are golden brown on all sides. Transfer the fish to the pan with the sauce, cover, and simmer together for 5 minutes to 7 minutes.

Carefully lift the fillets out of the pan onto warm serving plates and spoon the sauce over. Garnish with fresh lime halves.

Jalapeño-Tequila Sauce

1/4 cup olive oil
2 jalapeños, stemmed, seeded, and minced
  (see Note)
2 large onions, chopped
4 cloves garlic, minced
4 large tomatoes, chopped

2 tablespoons chopped fresh basil
4 tablespoons chopped fresh cilantro
1/4 cup tequila (see Note)
2 teaspoons cornstarch
1 tablespoon water

In a saucepan, heat the olive oil and sauté the peppers, onions, and garlic until they begin to color. Add the tomatoes, basil, cilantro, and tequila. Season with salt to taste. Cover and simmer for 15 minutes, stirring occasionally. Blend the cornstarch with the water and stir it into the sauce. Adjust the seasonings.

Notes: Use more or less jalapeño to suit your own pepper heat tolerance. Other fresh peppers can be used in place of jalapeños.

The tequila can be replaced with brandy.

Atlantic sailfish, scalloped hammerhead shark, shortfin mako shark, skipjack tuna, and white mullet are delicious substitutions for common jack. For the skipjack tuna and yellowfin tuna, use 6 8-ounce steaks.

Other Delicious Recipes for Common Jack include:

Bahamian Common Jack Chowder (see southern stingray, page 272)

Common Jack in Caribbean "Blaff" (see Spanish mackerel, page 202)

Common Jack with Creole Sauce Piquante (see wahoo, page 209)

Common Jack-Stuffed Bell Peppers (see Atlantic bonito, page 214)

Common Jack Tamales with Piquant Green Sauce (see Spanish mackerel, page 203)

Common Jack and Tomato Bisque (see yellowfin tuna, page 226)

Étouffée of Common Jack (see blackfin tuna, page 218)

Fried Skewered Common Jack (see spotted eagle ray, page 276)

Grilled Common Jack with Criolla Sauce (see black sea bass, page 25)

Herbed Garlic Common Jack (see yellowtail snapper, page 316)

Matelote of Common Jack (see American eel, page 126)

White Bisque of Common Jack with Sherry (see largetooth sawfish, page 281)

Florida Pompano

Group: Jack

Other common name(s):
Pompano

Latin name:
Trachinotus carolinus
Family Carangidae

Maximum length:
2 feet 1 inch

Maximum weight:
8 pounds

Cuts:
whole
fillet

Meat characteristics:
tender, white, delicate
medium-to-high oil
content

Preferred cooking methods:
bake
grill
poach
sauté
steam

Fillet of Florida Pompano Baked en Papillote with a Shrimp, Crabmeat, and White Wine Sauce

Shrimp, Crabmeat, and White Wine Sauce
  (recipe follows)
Cooking parchment, unwaxed freezer
  paper, or aluminum foil

Salted butter
6 6-ounce Florida pompano fillets,
  skinned

Serves 6

Preheat the oven to 425°. Prepare the Shrimp, Crabmeat, and White Wine Sauce, and set aside to cool.

Cut six heart shapes from the parchment paper, 10 inches high and 14 inches wide. Lay them out flat and butter them. When the sauce is cool and not too liquid, spoon it onto one side of each heart. Top with a pompano fillet. Fold the other side of the heart over and crimp the edges together in several small folds all the way around the open side. Place the papillotes on a greased baking pan and bake for 20 minutes, or until the paper browns and the sauce inside is bubbly hot.

Remove to warm dinner plates and bring to the table. Using two forks, tear and fold open the papillotes across the length of the top.

Shrimp, Crabmeat, and White Wine Sauce

6 tablespoons salted butter
6 tablespoons all-purpose flour
8 green onions, chopped
1 cup dry white wine
2 cups rich fish stock (page 372),
  or shellfish stock (page 372)
1/4 teaspoon dried thyme

1 teaspoon salt, or to taste
1/2 teaspoon freshly ground white pepper,
  or to taste
1 pound small raw shrimp, peeled and
  deveined
1 pound lump crabmeat

In a saucepan, melt the butter and blend in the flour. Cook together for 3 minutes, then add the chopped green onions. Cook for another 3 minutes, or until the green onions become limp. Whisk in the white wine and stock, then add the thyme, salt, and pepper. Bring to a boil, turn down to a simmer, and cook 10 minutes, or until the sauce reaches a fairly thick consistency. Carefully fold in the shrimp and simmer for 1 minute more, or just long enough for the shrimp to turn pink. Remove from the heat and fold in the crabmeat.

Notes: When all the seafood is perfectly fresh and delicious, the marvelous perfumes that escape from the papillote on tearing them open at the table are reward enough for having made such an effort.

Common dolphin, gulf flounder, red grouper, speckled hind, spotted sea trout, or yellowtail snapper may be used instead of Florida pompano.

Variations
(follow recipe exactly except for the following substitutions and additions):

with Crawfish and White Wine Sauce
Replace the shrimp and crabmeat with 1 pound crawfish tail meat and fat, diced. Fold the crawfish into the cooked sauce and simmer for 2 minutes, or until crawfish becomes opaque.

with Lobster and White Wine Sauce
Use 3 small Florida or Maine lobster tails, diced, in place of the shrimp and crabmeat. Fold the lobster into the cooked sauce and simmer about 2 minutes, only long enough for the lobster to become opaque.

with Oyster and White Wine Sauce
Oyster water may be used instead of fish stock. Replace the shrimp and crabmeat with 3 dozen shucked raw oysters. Fold the oysters into the cooked sauce and simmer about 2 minutes, just until the edges of the oysters begin to curl.

with Scallops and White Wine Sauce
Use 1 pound small bay or calico scallops instead of shrimp and crabmeat. Fold the scallops into the cooked sauce and simmer about 2 minutes, only long enough for them to become opaque.

Grilled Florida Pompano Fillets with Tomato-Oyster Sauce

Tomato-Oyster Sauce (recipe follows)
Vegetable oil for grilling

6 8-ounce Florida pompano fillets

Serves 6

Light the grill or charcoal 1 hour before cooking. Prepare the Tomato-Oyster Sauce, and hold aside warm.

When the grill is ready, brush the rack with oil. Brush one side of the pompano fillets with oil and place them on the rack oil side down. Grill for 4 minutes, or until the fillets are turning white even on the top side. Brush the top of the fillets with oil and carefully turn them over. Cook for another 4 minutes or so, until they are opaque all the way through.

Remove the grilled Florida pompano fillets to warm plates and serve with the warm Tomato-Oyster Sauce spooned over.

Tomato-Oyster Sauce

2 tablespoons olive oil
1 large onion, finely chopped
1 tablespoon all-purpose flour
3 medium tomatoes, skinned (see Note), seeded, and finely chopped
4 large cloves garlic, minced

1/2 teaspoon dried oregano
1 tablespoon minced fresh basil
1 cup chopped fresh raw oysters
Salt and freshly ground black pepper
2 tablespoons chopped fresh parsley

In a skillet, heat the olive oil and sauté the onion until lightly browned. Blend in the flour, stir, and cook for 1 minute, then add the tomatoes, garlic, oregano, and basil. Cover and simmer for 15 minutes, or until the tomatoes are cooked into the sauce.

Just before serving, add the oysters and season with salt and black pepper. Cook about 1 minute more, just long enough for the oyster pieces to be cooked but not yet tough. Blend in the parsley. Serve warm.

Notes: To skin the tomatoes, immerse them in boiling water for 1 to 2 minutes, then plunge them into cold water.

Atlantic spadefish, ling cobia, lookdown, queen triggerfish, and yellowfin tuna can also be used with this recipe. Cooking times are approximately the same. For the Atlantic spadefish, lookdowns, and queen triggerfish, use 6 1-pound whole fish, scaled and drawn. Grilling time for these fish is slightly longer, about 7 minutes, or until the tops start to turn white, then brush the top with oil and turn over to cook through.

Variations: The grilled fillets are also excellent with Espagnole Sauce (page 361), Piquant Green Sauce (page 204), or Roasted Tomato and Chili Sauce (page 157).

Other Delicious Recipes for Florida Pompano include:

Broiled Florida Pompano (see gulf flounder, page 131)

Cold Poached Florida Pompano Fillets with Green Basil Mayonnaise (see queen triggerfish, page 356)

Florida Pompano Fillets with Artichokes and Mushrooms in Brown Lemon-Butter Sauce (see black drum, page 100)

Florida Pompano Fillets Florentine (see tilefish, page 346)

Florida Pompano Fillet Marguery (see sheepshead, page 265)

Florida Pompano with Pecans (see lookdown, page 181)

Florida Pompano with Seafood-White Wine Sauce Gratiné (see white mullet, page 243)

Grilled Florida Pompano Fillets with Criolla Sauce (see black sea bass, page 25)

New Orleans-Style Deep-Fried Florida Pompano Fillets Meunière (see jolthead porgy, page 249)

Poached Florida Pompano Fillets with Maltaise Sauce (see common dolphin, page 88)

Sautéed Fillet of Florida Pompano with Crabmeat and Butter (see common dolphin, page 90)

Skillet-Grilled Florida Pompano Fillets Pontchartrain (see dog snapper, page 299)

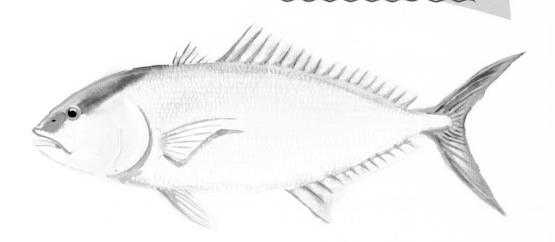

Greater Amberjack

Group: Jack

Other common name(s):
Amberjack
Jack
Latin name:
Seriola dumerili
Family Carangidae
Maximum length:
5 feet

Maximum weight:
176 pounds
Cuts:
whole (small)
steak
fillet
Meat characteristics:
firm, medium-white
medium oil content

Preferred cooking methods:
bake
broil
grill
poach
steam
stew

1 2 1/2- to 3-pound greater amberjack
   fillet, thick piece if possible
2 tablespoons softened salted butter
Salt and freshly ground white pepper

Crabmeat Stuffing:
3 tablespoons salted butter
4 French shallots, finely chopped
2 cloves garlic, finely chopped
1 cup sliced fresh mushrooms
2 cups heavy cream

1/4 cup chopped fresh chives
1 tablespoon minced fresh basil
1 teaspoon dried tarragon
Juice of 1 lemon
1 pound crabmeat

Salted butter
All-purpose flour
2 tablespoons melted butter
1 tablespoon chopped fresh parsley
2 lemons, quartered

Serves 6

In this preparation, the crabmeat is stuffed into the Greater Amberjack fillet after you have sliced a pocket into the fillet to hold it.

Lay the thick fillet piece on a flat surface. Using a very sharp filleting or paring knife, cut into it halfway through its thickness the length of the piece. Do not cut all the way through to the ends of the fillet. The ends should remain closed to hold any liquids that may otherwise drain out. After you have made the first cut halfway through the thickness of the fillet, turn your knife from straight up and down to an horizontal position and make a cut from the bottom of the first cut into the inside side of the fillet. Make this cut twice, once into each side of the inside of the fillet. Again, do not cut all the way through the fish. What you are doing here is making a pocket to hold the stuffing. Rub the fillet inside and out with the softened butter, salt, and white pepper. Hold aside.

Preheat the oven to 350°. Make the crabmeat stuffing. Melt the 3 tablespoons butter in a saucepan. Add the shallots, garlic, and mushrooms and sauté for a single minute. Add the heavy cream, chives, basil, tarragon, and lemon juice. Simmer until the sauce is thickened and then fold in the crabmeat without breaking it up.

Season with salt and white pepper. Continue cooking only long enough to thoroughly heat the crabmeat. Remove from the stove.

Butter a baking dish and place the amberjack fillet into it. Hold the pocket of the fillet open and spoon in the crabmeat mixture, pressing it into the sides of the pocket. Dust the top of the stuffed fillet with a little flour and bake for 30 minutes, or until the fish is opaque throughout. Baste it several times during the cooking with the pan drippings and the melted butter.

Transfer the cooked crabmeat-stuffed greater amberjack fillet to a warm platter and sprinkle with the chopped parsley. Serve out cut straight through into six equal portions, garnished with chopped parsley and a lemon wedge.

Note: Blackfin tuna, largetooth sawfish, ling cobia, and spotted jewfish also work well baked this way.

1 2- to 3-pound whole greater amberjack, drawn (see Note)
2 quarts fish stock (page 371), or water
6 whole black peppercorns
4 bay leaves
1/2 teaspoon dried thyme
1/2 teaspoon dried marjoram
1/2 teaspoon dried oregano
1/4 cup olive oil
4 medium unpeeled potatoes, scrubbed and chopped

2 medium onions, chopped
2 leeks (white and tender part of green only) thinly sliced
2 medium carrots, thinly sliced
4 cloves garlic, minced
4 large ripe tomatoes, skinned (see Note), seeded, and chopped
Salt, freshly ground black pepper, and cayenne pepper

Serves 6

Fillet and skin the greater amberjack and put the meat aside. Degill the head. Put the fish stock in a saucepan with the greater amberjack head and bones, whole black peppercorns, bay leaves, thyme, marjoram, and oregano. Bring to a boil, cover, and boil gently for 1 hour to make a stock.

In a soup pot, heat the olive oil and sauté the potatoes, onions, leeks, carrots, and garlic until they begin to color. Stir in the chopped tomatoes. Strain the stock into the pot. Season with salt, black pepper, and cayenne, cover, and simmer for 30 minutes.

About 10 minutes before serving, cut the greater amberjack meat into bite-sized pieces and add to the soup. Add more water if too much of the liquid has evaporated (though remember, this is a chowder and should be very thick and hearty), and adjust the seasoning if necessary.

Notes: If you prefer, have the fish merchant fillet, skin, and bone the fish and degill the head; you will need to bring home the head and bones for the stock. To skin the tomatoes, immerse them in boiling water for 1 to 2 minutes, then plunge them into cold water.

American eel, blacktip shark, red snapper, and wahoo may also be used with this recipe. Use 1 2- to 3-pound scaled, skinned, and drawn fish, or 2 to 3 pounds skinned eel.

Variations
(follow recipe exactly except for the following substitutions and additions):

Chowder with Chayote and Potatoes
In place of the leeks and tomatoes, use 4 green onions, chopped, and 4 large chayote (mirliton), skinned, seeded, and chopped. (If chayote are not available, you can use yellow squash.) After the stock is prepared, heat the olive oil in a soup pot and sauté the potatoes, onions, green onions, carrots, and garlic until they begin to color. Stir in the chopped chayote.

Chowder with Eggplant and Tomatoes
Instead of potatoes, leeks, and carrots, use 2 medium eggplants, skinned and chopped, and 4 green onions, chopped. After the stock is prepared, heat the olive oil in a soup pot and sauté the eggplant, onions, green onions, and garlic until they begin to color.

Chowder with Yucca and Yellow Squash
Replace the potatoes, leeks, carrots, and tomatoes with 4 cups yucca chopped into small dice, 6 chopped green onions, and 4 chopped medium yellow squash. After the stock is prepared, heat the olive oil in a soup pot and sauté the yucca, onions, green onions, and garlic until they begin to color. Stir in the squash dice.

Other Delicious Recipes for Greater Amberjack include:

Broiled Greater Amberjack Steaks with Creole Mustard and Chive Cream Sauce (see Atlantic sailfish, page 232)

Creole-Style Greater Amberjack Pot-au-Feu (see tarpon, page 336)

Greater Amberjack Croquettes Meunière (see skipjack tuna, page 221)

Panfried Greater Amberjack with Antiboise Sauce (see blacktip shark, page 294)

Panfried Greater Amberjack with Bienville Sauce (see wahoo, page 207)

Poached Greater Amberjack Fillets with Creamy Pimiento-Butter Sauce (see ling cobia, page 85)

Ragout of Greater Amberjack au Gratin (see swordfish, page 332)

Sautéed Battered Greater Amberjack Fillets with Lemon-Butter Sauce (see red snapper, page 311)

Sautéed Greater Amberjack Steaks Marseilles-Style (see rainbow runner, page 194)

Sautéed Steak of Greater Amberjack with Crabmeat and Butter (see common dolphin, page 90)

White Bisque of Greater Amberjack with Sherry (see largetooth sawfish, page 281)

Wood-Grilled Greater Amberjack Steaks with Achiote-Garlic Paste (see black grouper, page 49)

Hard-Tail Jack

Group: Jack

Other common name(s):	Maximum weight:	Preferred cooking methods:
Hardtail	4 pounds	braise
Runner	*Cuts:*	broil
Blue Runner	whole	grill
Latin name:	steak	poach
Caranx crysos	fillet	sauté
Family Carangidae	*Meat characteristics:*	steam
Maximum length:	dark, rich, firm	
1 foot 8 inches	high oil content	

Leek and Tomato Sauce (recipe follows)
6 6- to 8-ounce hard-tail jack fillets, skinned

2 tablespoons salted butter
18 medium fresh mushroom caps

Serves 6

Prepare the Leek and Tomato Sauce, pour into a wide sauté pan, and add the hard-tail jack fillets. Cover and simmer gently for 12 minutes, or until the fish is completely opaque.

While simmering the fish, heat the 2 tablespoons butter in a sauté pan and quickly sauté the mushroom caps. Keep warm.

When the fish are cooked, carefully lift the fillets onto warmed dishes, spoon the sauce over the top, and top with the sautéed mushroom caps.

Leek and Tomato Sauce

1 stick salted butter, melted
1 large leek (white part only), chopped
1 large onion, chopped
1 large tomato, skinned (see Note), seeded, and chopped
1 clove garlic, minced
1/4 teaspoon dried oregano

1/4 teaspoon dried thyme
1/4 teaspoon Hungarian paprika
1 1/2 cups dry white wine
1 1/2 cups fish stock (page 371)
1 1/2 cups heavy cream
Salt, freshly ground white pepper, and cayenne

In a saucepan, combine the butter, leek, onion, tomato, garlic, and seasonings with the white wine and fish stock. Bring to a boil and reduce to half. Add the heavy cream, and reduce until the sauce has reached a relatively thick consistency. Season to taste with salt, white pepper, and cayenne.

Notes:　To skin the tomato, immerse in boiling water for 1 to 2 minutes, then plunge into cold water.

Black sea bass, creolefish, hogfish, squirrelfish, and white grunt are also excellent in this recipe.

Marinade:

2 large green bell peppers, stemmed,
    seeded, and sliced into thin strips
2 medium onions, sliced thinly
2 large carrots, scraped and thinly sliced
2 bay leaves
1 teaspoon minced fresh ginger
12 black peppercorns

1/4 teaspoon freshly ground nutmeg
1 teaspoon salt, or to taste
1 1/2 cups water
1/2 cup wine vinegar

1/4 cup olive oil
2 pounds hard-tail jack fillets, sliced into
    thin pieces

Serves 6

In a saucepan, combine all the marinade ingredients except the vinegar. Bring to a simmer, cover, and cook for 10 minutes. Add the vinegar, bring back to a simmer, lower the heat so it no longer simmers, and keep warm. Adjust the seasonings if necessary.

In a wide, heavy skillet, heat the olive oil and sauté the hard-tail jack fillets for 5 minutes, until lightly browned on both sides and opaque completely through. Pour the marinade over the hard-tail jack and bring to a simmer.

Serve immediately, or transfer the escabèche to a serving platter, cover, refrigerate until chilled, and serve cold.

Note: Try this recipe with Atlantic bonito, American eel, bluefish, pilot fish, Spanish mackerel, swordfish, and yellowfin tuna. For the American eel, use 2 pounds skinned steaks cut into 1-inch-thick pieces.

Other Delicious Recipes for Hard-Tail Jack include:

Caribbean Hard-Tail Jack with Rice (see American eel, page 128)

Cold Poached Hard-Tail Jack Ravigote with Boiled New Potatoes (see spotted jewfish, page 43)

Creole-Style Hard-Tail Jack Pot-au-Feu (see tarpon, page 336)

Fillet of Hard-Tail Jack with Browned Butter, Lemon Juice, and Caper Sauce (see blacktip shark, page 296)

Hard-Tail Jack Barbacoa (see great barracuda, page 20)

Hard-Tail Jack Boudin (see Atlantic moonfish, page 152)

Hard-Tail Jack with Potatoes, Bacon, and Garlic (see scalloped hammerhead shark, page 286)

Hard-Tail Jack-Stuffed Bell Peppers (see Atlantic bonito, page 214)

Hard-Tail Jack-Stuffed Hand Tortillas (see bluefish, page 68)

Wood-Grilled Hard-Tail Jack Steaks with Achiote-Garlic Paste (see black grouper, page 49)

Wood-Grilled Hard-Tail Jack Steaks with Mexican Seasonings (see bluefish, page 66)

Wood-Grilled Hard-Tail Jack Steaks with Sweet Herbs (see king mackerel, page 197)

Lookdown

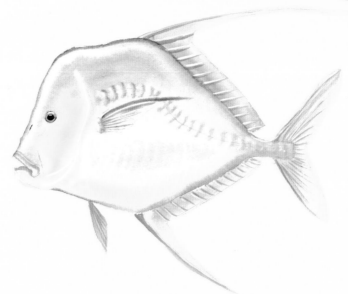

Group: Jack

Other common name(s):
none

Latin name:
Selene vomer
Family Carangidae

Maximum length:
1 foot 6 inches

Maximum weight:
3 pounds

Cuts:
whole
fillet

Meat characteristics:
firm, white
medium oil content

Preferred cooking methods:
broil
fry
grill
poach
steam

Grilled Lookdown with Tomato Sauce

Tomato Sauce (recipe follows)

6 1-pound whole lookdowns, scaled and drawn

Vegetable oil for grilling

Serves 6

Light the grill or charcoal 1 hour before cooking. Prepare the Tomato Sauce, and hold aside warm.

When the grill is ready, brush the rack with oil. Brush the lookdowns on both sides with the vegetable oil and grill for about 7 minutes, or until they are turning white even on the top side. Brush the top of the fish with oil and carefully turn them over. Cook for another 7 minutes or so, until they are opaque all the way through.

Transfer the grilled lookdowns to warm plates and serve with the warm Tomato Sauce spooned over.

Tomato Sauce

2 tablespoons olive oil

1 small onion, chopped

2 cloves garlic, chopped

1/2 rib celery, chopped

4 medium tomatoes, chopped

1 tablespoon minced fresh basil

1 tablespoon minced fresh parsley

Salt and freshly ground black pepper

In a saucepan, heat the olive oil and sauté the onion, garlic, and celery until they become translucent. Add the chopped tomatoes and the herbs. Cook only long enough for the tomatoes to collapse into a thick yet liquid state. Strain the sauce through a sieve and season to taste with salt and pepper. Serve warm.

Note: Atlantic spadefish, great barracuda, jolthead porgy, queen triggerfish, and sand perch can also be used with this recipe. Use 6 6-ounce sand perch fillets.

1 1/2 cups pecan halves or pieces

2 sticks salted butter

2 whole eggs

1 cup milk

2 teaspoons salt

1 teaspoon freshly ground black pepper

1 cup all-purpose flour

6 1-pound whole lookdowns, scaled and
drawn

Peanut oil for frying

Serves 6

In a small saucepan, sauté the pecans in the butter until they become golden brown. Set aside and keep hot.

Combine the eggs and milk in one mixing bowl, and the salt, pepper and flour in another. Heat 1/2 inch oil in a wide, heavy frying pan until it is hot but not smoking, about 375°. Dredge the lookdowns in the seasoned flour, dip in the egg wash, and dredge again in the flour. Shake off any excess flour and lay the fish into hot oil without crowding the pan. Fry the fish to a golden brown on one side and then the other—this will take about 10 minutes. Drain the lookdowns on absorbent paper.

Place each lookdown on a warm plate and spoon on the hot pecans and butter.

Note: Atlantic spadefish, black sea bass, bonefish, common dolphin, dog snapper, Florida pompano, gulf flounder, jolthead porgy, pigfish, spot drum, and spotfin flounder are wonderful alternatives for this recipe. The gulf and spotfin flounder and pigfish should be fried for 10 minutes, while the Atlantic spadefish, bonefish, jolthead porgy, and spot drum require an approximately 15 minute frying time.

Variations: Try using 1 1/2 cups halves or pieces of almonds, cashews, hazelnuts, peanuts, pine nuts, pistachios, or walnuts or 1/2 cup shelled roasted pumpkin seeds instead of pecans.

Other Delicious Recipes for Lookdown include:

Beer-Battered Fried Lookdown (see speckled hind, page 39)

Broiled Lookdown with Balsamic Vinegar (see Atlantic moonfish, page 153)

Charcoal-Grilled Lookdown with Tomatillo-Habañero Salsa (see gray triggerfish, page 351)

Creole Bisque of Lookdown (see tilefish, page 348)

Fried Lookdown Fillets with Moulin Rouge Sauce (see scamp, page 56)

Grilled Lookdown with Criolla Sauce (see black sea bass, page 25)

Grilled Lookdown with Tomato-Oyster Sauce (see Florida pompano, page 164)

Hot Lookdown and Mushroom Salad with Dijon Mustard Dressing (see snook, page 320)

Lookdown Beignets with Rémoulade Sauce (see gray triggerfish, page 353)

Poached Lookdown with Marquis Sauce (see speckled hind, page 37)

Poached Lookdown with Parsley-Lemon Butter (see sheepshead, page 267)

Steamed Whole Lookdown with Chivry Butter (see bonefish, page 72)

Permit

Group: Jack

Other common name(s):	*Maximum weight:*	*Preferred cooking*
"Pompano" (sic)	50 pounds	*methods:*
Jack	*Cuts:*	bake
Latin name:	whole (small)	broil
Trachinotus falcatus	steak	fry
Family Carangidae	fillet	grill
Maximum length:	*Meat characteristics:*	poach
3 feet	tender, white, flaky	
	medium oil content	

Two Sisters Sauce (recipe follows)
1 cup milk
1 egg
1 1/2 cups finely ground yellow cornmeal
2 teaspoons salt
1 teaspoon freshly ground black pepper

1/2 teaspoon cayenne pepper
Peanut oil for frying
2 1/4 pounds 1/2-inch-thick permit fillets,
    skinned
3 lemons, halved

Serves 6

Prepare the Two Sisters Sauce and refrigerate. Blend in the milk and egg in one mixing bowl and the cornmeal, salt, black pepper, and cayenne in another. Pour enough oil to get a depth of 1/2 inch in a large heavy frying pan and heat to 350° to 375°. Dip the permit fillets in the milk and egg wash and then dredge them in the seasoned cornmeal. Fry on both sides, without crowding the fish in the pan, until they are golden, about 2 1/2 minutes per side.

Drain the cooked permit fillets on absorbent paper, and serve with Two Sisters Sauce.

Two Sisters Sauce

1/2 cup Mayonnaise (page 374)
1/4 cup Dijon mustard
1/2 cup sour cream

1/4 cup prepared horseradish
Salt to taste

In a bowl, combine the mayonnaise with the Dijon mustard, sour cream, and horseradish. Season to taste with salt. Cover and store in the refrigerator until ready for use.

Note: This recipe is also excellent with Atlantic croaker, Atlantic threadfin, gaff-topsail catfish, sailor's-choice, scamp, or striped mullet.

Variations: Fried battered permit fillets are also excellent served with Cocktail Sauce (page 375), Moulin Rouge Sauce (page 56), Spicy Creole Mayonnaise (page 310), Sweet Mustard-Egg Sauce (page 254), or Tartar Sauce (page 375).

4 green onions, chopped
2 cloves garlic, minced
1/4 teaspoon dried marjoram
1/2 cup dry white wine
1 1/2 quarts shellfish stock (page 372), or fish stock (page 371)
3 pints heavy cream
1/4 cup peanut oil

All-purpose flour
6 6- to 8-ounce pieces permit fillet
1 pound Florida or Maine lobster tail meat, diced
Salt, freshly ground white pepper, and cayenne pepper to taste
Chopped fresh parsley

Serves 6

In a saucepan, combine the green onions, garlic, marjoram, and white wine, and boil briskly until reduced by half. Add the fish stock and heavy cream, and simmer for 45 minutes, or until the sauce has thickened. Hold aside warm.

In a sauté pan, heat the oil. Lightly flour the permit fillets and sauté them for 7 minutes, or until they are almost cooked. Hold in a warm oven.

Add the lobster to the sauce, season to taste with salt, white pepper, and cayenne. Add the permit fillets and simmer for 5 minutes, or until the fish is completely opaque.

Serve the fillets on warm plates with the sauce spooned over, and garnished with the chopped parsley.

Note: Try this recipe with Atlantic croaker, common dolphin, creolefish, gaff-topsail catfish, gray triggerfish, gulf flounder, gulf kingfish, jolthead porgy, sand perch, scamp, spot drum, or white mullet. For the gaff-topsail catfish, gray triggerfish, gulf flounder, gulf kingfish, and white mullet, use 6 6-ounce fillets and cook for 4 minutes.

Variations

(follow recipe exactly except for the following substitutions and additions):

with Crabmeat Cream Sauce

Use 1 pound lump crabmeat in place of lobster.

with Crawfish Cream Sauce

Replace the lobster meat with 1 pound crawfish tails.

with Oyster Cream Sauce

Replace the lobster with 3 dozen shucked raw oysters.

with Scallop Cream Sauce

Replace the lobster with 1 pound small raw bay scallops.

with Shrimp Cream Sauce

Use 1 pound small peeled and deveined raw shrimp in place of lobster meat.

cccccccccccccccccccccccccccccccccccccccccccc

Other Delicious Recipes for Permit include:

Beer-Battered Fried Permit (see speckled hind, page 39)

Corn-Flour-Fried Permit Fillets (see dog snapper, page 300)

Fried Cornmeal-Battered Permit Fillets (see striped mullet, page 239)

Fried Permit Fillets with Moulin Rouge Sauce (see scamp, page 56)

New Orleans-Style Deep-Fried Permit Fillets Meunière (see jolthead porgy, page 249)

Permit Fillets with Cucumber and Spinach (see gulf kingfish, page 104)

Permit Fillets in Saffron-White Wine Sauce (see tarpon, page 338)

Permit Fillets with Sorrel, Zucchini, and Mushrooms (see bonefish, page 74)

Permit, Tomato, and Pepper Soup (see red grouper, page 53)

Poached Permit with Horseradish and Sour Cream Sauce (see Atlantic croaker, page 95)

Whole Panfried Permit with Peanut Sauce (see gaff-topsail catfish, page 78)

Pilot Fish

Group: Jack

Other common name(s):
Pilot

Latin name:
Naucrates ductor
Family Carangidae

Maximum length:
2 feet 3 inches

Maximum weight:
7 pounds

Cuts:
whole
steak
fillet

Meat characteristics:
firm, white
medium oil content

Preferred cooking methods:
bake
braise
fry
steam
stew

6 tomatoes, chopped

2 onions, chopped

6 cloves garlic, chopped

1 teaspoon dried oregano

2 cups fish stock (page 371)

4 carrots, scraped and diced

4 ribs celery, stringed and diced

1 tablespoon hot Hungarian paprika

1/2 cup dry sherry

Salt and freshly ground black pepper

2 pounds pilot fish, pan-dressed, skinned, and cut into 1-inch-thick steaks

Juice of 1 lime

Serves 6

Combine the chopped tomatoes in a large saucepan or soup pot with the onions, garlic, oregano, and fish stock. Cover, bring to a simmer, and cook for about 15 minutes.

Add the carrots, celery, paprika, and sherry. Cover and simmer for another 5 minutes or so, until the carrots begin to tenderize. Season with salt and black pepper. Add the pilot fish steaks and simmer for 10 minutes, or until they are completely opaque. Adjust seasonings if desired, and stir in the lime juice.

Serve the Caribbean Pilot Fish Stew in large bowls with side plates for each diner to use in boning the steaks as they go.

Note: American eel, swordfish, and tarpon also work well in this stew. For the American eel, use 2 pounds skinned steaks cut 1 inch thick.

Whole Panfried Pilot Fish with Onion, Garlic, and Red Wine Sauce

6 3/4- to 1-pound whole pilot fish, scaled
   and drawn
Salt and freshly ground black pepper
1 cup peanut oil
1 large onion, chopped
2 tablespoons all-purpose flour
1 1/2 cups dry red wine

2 tablespoons chopped garlic
2 tablespoons chopped fresh parsley
3 bay leaves
1/2 teaspoon dried thyme
1/2 teaspoon cayenne pepper
6 large French bread croutons (page 370)

Serves 6

Rub the pilot fish with salt and pepper. Heat the oil until hot in a wide, heavy skillet and fry the fish about 5 minutes on each side, until lightly browned. Remove the fish from the oil and set aside.

In the same oil, sauté the onion and flour together until browned. Add the red wine, garlic, parsley, bay leaves, thyme, and cayenne pepper. Cover and simmer for 15 minutes. Skim off the fat.

Return the cooked pilot fish to the sauce in the skillet, cover, and simmer for 10 minutes more. Serve the fish on the croutons with the sauce spooned over.

Note: This recipe is also excellent prepared with great barracuda, red porgy, sand perch, spot drum, striped mullet, and tripletail.

Other Delicious Recipes for Pilot Fish include:

Bahamian Pilot Fish Chowder (see southern stingray, page 272)

Baked Pilot Fish with Apples and Onions (see hogfish, page 368)

Baked Shrimp-Stuffed Pilot Fish (see black drum, page 98)

Creole Bisque of Pilot Fish (see tilefish, page 348)

Curried Fillets of Pilot Fish (see sailor's-choice, page 143)

Fried Pilot Fish Fingers with Pink Horseradish Mayonnaise (see gaff-topsail catfish, page 80)

Hot Pilot Fish and Mushroom Salad with Dijon Mustard Dressing (see snook, page 320)

Marinated Escabèche of Pilot Fish (see hard-tail jack, page 176)

Pilot Fish and Tomato Soup (see rainbow runner, page 193)

Poached Pilot Fish with Horseradish and Sour Cream Sauce (see Atlantic croaker, page 95)

Steamed Whole Pilot Fish with Chivry Butter (see bonefish, page 72)

Tamales with Pilot Fish and Roasted Tomato and Chili Sauce (see common jack, page 156)

Rainbow Runner

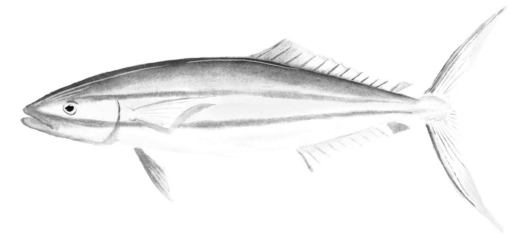

Group: Jack

Other common name(s):
  Rainbow Jack
  Rainbow
Latin name:
  Elagatis bipinnulata
  Family Carangidae
Maximum length:
  3 feet 6 inches

Maximum weight:
  22 pounds
Cuts:
  whole (small)
  steak
  fillet
Meat characteristics:
  dark, rich, firm
  high oil content

Preferred cooking
methods:
  braise
  broil
  grill
  poach
  sauté
  stew

2 1/2 quarts fish stock (page 371), shellfish
   stock (page 372), or water
6 medium tomatoes, skinned (see Note),
   seeded, and chopped
1 medium onion, chopped
1 rib celery, minced
1 large clove garlic, minced
2 tablespoons minced fresh parsley

1 tablespoon minced fresh cilantro
2 bay leaves
1/2 cup raw white rice
2 large carrots, cut into 1/2-inch dice
Salt and freshly ground black pepper
1 1/2 pounds rainbow runner fillet pieces,
   skinned and diced

Serves 6

Pour the stock into a soup pot, and add the tomatoes, onion, celery, garlic, parsley, cilantro, and bay leaves. Bring to a boil, cover, and simmer for 1 hour.

Remove the bay leaves and pass the soup and the vegetables through a strainer or process in batches in a blender or food processor. The vegetables should be completely pureed into the soup liquid.

Return the soup to the pot, add the rice and carrots, and season to taste with salt and black pepper. Bring to a gentle boil, cover, and simmer for 30 minutes more, or until the rice is cooked and tender. Add the diced rainbow runner and simmer for 7 minutes more. Serve immediately.

Notes: To skin the tomatoes, immerse in boiling water for 1 to 2 minutes, then plunge into cold water.

Pilot fish is also excellent in this soup.

Marseilles Sauce (recipe follows)   6 8-ounce rainbow runner steaks
2 tablespoons olive oil

Serves 6

Prepare the Marseilles Sauce, and hold aside warm. Heat a sauté pan or iron skillet very hot and add the olive oil, turning the pan around to coat the bottom. Sauté the rainbow runner steaks for about 8 minutes, turning once halfway through the cooking.

Transfer the steaks to warm plates, nap with the warm Marseilles Sauce, and serve.

Marseilles Sauce

1 tablespoon light-flavored olive oil   3/4 cup capers, mashed
1 medium yellow onion, finely chopped   10 large tomatoes, chopped
1 head garlic, cloves peeled and pressed   Freshly ground black pepper and salt

Heat the olive oil in a wide sauté pan or skillet and sauté the onion until all released liquids have completely reduced. Add the garlic and capers and continue sautéing for another 2 minutes. Add the chopped tomatoes and cook uncovered at a low simmer for about 25 minutes, or until the sauce has thickened, stirring regularly to prevent any sticking and burning. Season to taste with black pepper, and salt if desired (remembering that the capers are highly salted and may lend sufficient saltiness to the sauce). Serve warm.

Other Delicious Recipes for Rainbow Runner include:

Bahamian Rainbow Runner Chowder (see southern stingray, page 272)

Baked Rainbow Runner in Creole Court-Bouillon (see red drum, page 110)

Caribbean Rainbow Runner with Rice (see American eel, page 128)

Cold Poached Rainbow Runner Fillets with Green Basil Mayonnaise (see queen triggerfish, page 356)

Fillet of Rainbow Runner with Browned Butter, Lemon Juice, and Caper Sauce (see blacktip shark, page 296)

Herbed Garlic Rainbow Runner (see yellowtail snapper, page 316)

Rainbow Runner Boudin (see Atlantic moonfish, page 152)

Rainbow Runner with Creole Sauce Piquante (see wahoo, page 209)

Rainbow Runner Garlic Soup (see skipjack tuna, page 223)

Rainbow Runner and Potato Salad with Chive Vinaigrette (see yellowfin tuna, page 227)

Rainbow Runner Tamales with Piquant Green Sauce (see Spanish mackerel, page 203)

Wood-Grilled Rainbow Runner Steaks with Mexican Seasonings (see bluefish, page 66)

King Mackerel

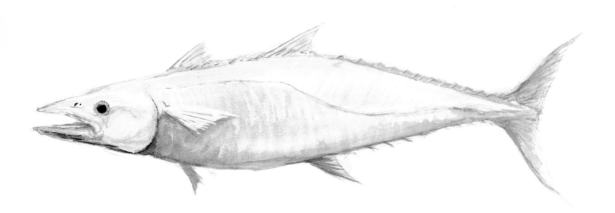

Group: Mackerel

Other common name(s):
  Mackerel
  King
  Kingfish
Latin name:
  Scomboromorus
  cavalla
  Family Scombridae
Maximum length:
  5 feet

Maximum weight:
  90 pounds
Cuts:
  whole (small)
  steak
  fillet
Meat characteristics:
  dark, firm, rich
  high oil content

Preferred cooking
methods:
  bake
  braise
  broil
  grill
  poach
  sauté

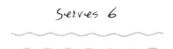
Wood-Grilled King Mackerel Steaks with Sweet Herbs

Sweet Herb Paste (recipe follows)
6 8-ounce king mackerel steaks
Vegetable oil for grilling

1 cup water-soaked wood chips: mesquite, hickory, pecan, etc.
1/2 cup hot melted salted butter

Serves 6

Light the charcoal 1 hour before cooking. Prepare the Sweet Herb Paste and paint the king mackerel steaks on all sides with it.

When the grill is ready, brush the rack with oil and arrange the king mackerel steaks on it so that they don't touch each other. Throw in a few water-soaked wood chips and cover the grill. Cook for 10 minutes, turning once midway and basting with the remaining Sweet Herb Paste.

Serve the wood-grilled king mackerel steaks with the melted butter dribbled over.

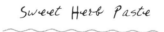
Sweet Herb Paste

3/4 cup light olive oil
1 tablespoon ground dried tarragon
1 tablespoon ground dried thyme

1 tablespoon ground dried oregano
1 tablespoon salt
2 teaspoons freshly ground white pepper

In a blender, combine the olive oil, tarragon, thyme, oregano, salt, and white pepper. Blend on high until you have processed the ingredients into a smooth paste.

Note: Atlantic sailfish, hard-tail jack, and scalloped hammerhead shark also work well grilled this way.

Variations: Wood-grilled king mackerel steaks are also excellent grilled with Achiote-Garlic Paste (page 49) or Mexican Seasonings (page 66).

Drawn Butter (recipe follows)

1 1/2 quarts water, or enough to cover fish
   (about 1 inch deep in skillet)

1 lemon, thinly sliced

1 medium onion, thinly sliced

2 sprigs fresh parsley

2 bay leaves

1 clove garlic, mashed

6 whole black peppercorns

2 teaspoon salt

1/4 teaspoon cayenne pepper

6 6-ounce pieces king mackerel fillet,
   skinned

2 tablespoons chopped fresh parsley

3 lemons, halved

Serves 6

In a wide, heavy skillet, bring the water to a boil with the lemon, onion, parsley, bay leaves, garlic, peppercorns, salt, and cayenne. Let boil for 3 minutes to allow the water to draw the flavor from the seasoning ingredients. Lower the heat to a simmer and poach the fillets for 10 minutes, or until the fish is completely cooked and flaky when broken with a fork.

With a long spatula, carefully remove the king mackerel fillets from the poaching liquor, drain, and place on warm dinner plates. Serve with Drawn Butter spooned over the top and a sprinkling of chopped parsley, garnished with a half lemon.

Drawn Butter

2 sticks salted butter

To "draw" butter is to separate the rich butter oil from the water and milk solids. Place the cold butter in a pan on low heat until it is completely melted. Do not stir! You don't want the water and milk solids to be incorporated back into the butter oil. When the butter is liquid, the milk solids will float to the surface where they can be spooned off and discarded. Then the butter oil, which is now floating on the water that has separated at the bottom of the pan, can be carefully poured off the top. Discard the water and the drawn butter is ready for use.

Note: Blacktip shark, blue marlin, and Spanish mackerel may also be used with this recipe. For the blacktip shark and blue marlin, use 6 6- to 8-ounce fillet pieces. Cooking times are the same.

Other Delicious Recipes for King Mackerel include:

Bahamian King Mackerel Chowder (see southern stingray, page 272)

Curried Fillets of King Mackerel (see sailor's-choice, page 143)

Grilled King Mackerel with Criolla Sauce (see black sea bass, page 25)

King Mackerel Boudin (see Atlantic moonfish, page 152)

King Mackerel Fillets in Saffron-White Wine Sauce (see tarpon, page 338)

King Mackerel Poached with Lime and Onion (see sand perch, page 34)

King Mackerel Poached in Orange-Curry Marinade (see shortfin mako shark, page 291)

King Mackerel Poached in Sherry (see snook, page 319)

King Mackerel with Potatoes, Bacon, and Garlic (see scalloped hammerhead shark, page 286)

King Mackerel Stew with White Wine (see spotted eagle ray, page 275)

Wood-Grilled King Mackerel Steaks with Achiote-Garlic Paste (see black grouper, page 49)

Wood-Grilled King Mackerel Steaks with Mexican Seasonings (see bluefish, page 66)

Spanish Mackerel

Group: Mackerel

Other common name(s):
  Mackerel

Latin name:
  Scomboromorus
  maculatus
  Family Scombridae

Maximum length:
  3 feet 1 inch

Maximum weight:
  11 pounds

Cuts:
  whole
  steak
  fillet

Meat characteristics:
  firm, dark, rich
  high oil content

Preferred cooking
methods:
  bake
  broil
  grill
  poach
  steam
  stew

2 quarts fish stock (page 371), or enough to cover the fish
6 carrots, sliced into 2-inch lengths
3 onions, quartered
2 ribs celery, rough chopped
Juice of 4 limes
1 head garlic, cloves separated, peeled, and lightly crushed
4 sprigs fresh parsley
2 bay leaves
8 whole cloves
1/2 teaspoon dried thyme
2 habañero (Scotch bonnet) peppers, seeded and chopped
Salt
6 small-to-medium green or unripe bananas, peeled & left whole
1 4-pound Spanish mackerel, scaled and drawn

Serves 6

This dish is common to Creole Caribbean cookery. "Blaff" is an onomatopoetic word used to describe the sound that the fish makes when splashed into water.

Make a poaching liquor in a pan that will easily accommodate the whole Spanish mackerel along with the seasoning and garnish ingredients. Pour the fish stock into the pan and add the carrots, onions, celery, lime juice, garlic, parsley, bay leaves, cloves, thyme, and habañero peppers. Bring to a boil and cook for 1 minute. Season to taste with salt.

Add the bananas and the Spanish mackerel and poach at a simmer for 20 minutes, or until the mackerel is completely opaque. Carefully lift the fish out of the poaching liquor onto a warm platter and cut the top and bottom fillets into three portions each.

Serve the "Blaff" in large soup bowls. Place a portion of mackerel into each bowl, cover each portion with the vegetables and a banana, and ladle the poaching liquids over the fish to fill each bowl.

Note: Black grouper, common jack, and gulf kingfish also excellent in this recipe.

Piquant Green Sauce (recipe follows)

Corn Masa Dough:
2 cups corn masa flour (see Note)
1 2/3 cups fish stock (page 371)
2 tablespoons peanut oil
1 1/2 teaspoons salt

24 tamale husks, or parchment paper cut
    into 7 × 9-inch rectangles
1 pound Spanish mackerel fillet, skinned
    and cut into 2 1/2 × 2 1/2 × 1-inch-
    thick squares
Water

Serves 6

Prepare the Piquant Green Sauce, transfer to a small bowl, cover, and let cool.

In a bowl, combine the corn masa flour with the fish stock, oil, and salt. Work into a solid, yet not too stiff dough. Cover the dough with plastic wrap or a damp kitchen towel and let mature for 15 minutes.

To assemble the tamales, take a heaping tablespoon of the corn masa dough and spread it into a 4-inch square onto each of the 24 tamale husks. Place a square of Spanish mackerel on each square of dough, and top each piece of fish with a tablespoon of the Piquant Green Sauce. Carefully roll or fold the packets into square tamale shapes, seam on top, tucking the ends underneath.

Place the assembled tamales into a steamer basket, or a colander that can be fitted into a large covered pot. Pour 2 inches of water into the bottom of the steamer or pot, without letting the water touch the tamales. Cover the pot and steam the tamales for 45 minutes to an hour, or until the dough has set and separates easily from the husk. To test, partially unwrap one tamale; if not done, rewrap and continue cooking.

Serve four tamales per person, for them to unfold themselves, with additional Piquant Green Sauce on the side.

Piquant Green Sauce

2 tablespoons peanut oil
4 green serrano chilies, stemmed, seeded, and chopped
1 large onion, chopped

1 pound green tomatillos, husked, stemmed, and chopped
2 tablespoons minced fresh cilantro
1 teaspoon salt, or to taste

In a saucepan, heat the peanut oil and sauté the chopped chilies and onion until the onion becomes translucent. Add the chopped green tomatillos, cover, and simmer gently for 10 minutes. Add the contents of the pan to a blender container and process into a thick puree, or pass the mixture through a strainer. Stir in the cilantro and salt.

Notes: Corn flour is often used in the frying of seafood rather than white flour. It can be bought as plain corn flour in specialty stores or as corn masa flour or "masa harina" in stores that sell Mexican or Central and South American food products. It is the flour that corn tortillas are made from. It can also be gotten in the form of "fish-fry," which is corn flour that is already seasoned with salt and pepper.

Try bluefish, common jack, rainbow runner, spotted jewfish, and tarpon with this recipe.

Variations: The tamales are also excellent with Espagnole Sauce (page 361), Salsa Roja (page 240), or Tomato-Oyster Sauce (page 164).

Other Delicious Recipes for Spanish Mackerel include:

Baked Spanish Mackerel in Creole Court-Bouillon (see red drum, page 110)

Charcoal-Grilled Butterflied Spanish Mackerel (see great barracuda, page 18)

Marinated Escabèche of Spanish Mackerel (see hard-tail jack, page 176)

Matelote of Spanish Mackerel (see American eel, page 126)

Poached Spanish Mackerel Fillets with Drawn Butter (see king mackerel, page 199)

Soda-Fried Spanish Mackerel "Chips" with Fresh Tomato Catsup (see shortfin mako shark 289)

Spanish Mackerel Barbacoa (see great barracuda, page 20)

Spanish Mackerel with Creole Sauce Piquante (see wahoo, page 209)

Spanish Mackerel with Puerto Rican Sauce (see swordfish, page 333)

Spanish Mackerel-Stuffed Bell Peppers (see Atlantic bonito, page 214)

Steamed Spanish Mackerel Fillets with Espagnole Mayonnaise (see mutton snapper, page 303)

Tamales with Spanish Mackerel and Roasted Tomato and Chili Sauce (see common jack, page 156)

Wahoo

Group: Mackerel

Other common name(s):
Mackerel

Latin name:
Acanthocybium
solanderi
Family Scombridae

Maximum length:
6 feet

Maximum weight:
100 pounds

Cuts:
whole (small)
steak
fillet

Meat characteristics:
firm, medium-white
medium oil content

**Preferred cooking
methods:**
bake
fry
grill
sauté
stew

Bienville Sauce (recipe follows)
6 6- to 8-ounce wahoo fillets or steaks
Salt and freshly ground white pepper

1/2 cup peanut oil
6 large French bread croutons (page 370)
1 tablespoon chopped fresh parsley

Serves 6

Prepare the Bienville Sauce and hold aside warm.

Dry the wahoo fillets and rub them lightly with salt and white pepper. In a heavy, wide skillet, heat the oil until hot and fry the fillets for about 4 minutes on each side, or until lightly browned. Drain on absorbent paper.

Serve the wahoo fillets on the croutons with the Bienville Sauce spooned over, garnished with the chopped parsley.

Bienville Sauce

1 stick salted butter
1 small green or red bell pepper, seeded
  and minced
4 green onions, chopped
2 cloves garlic, minced
1 small jar pimiento, minced
4 tablespoons all-purpose flour

1/2 cup white wine, not too dry
1 1/2 cups fish stock (page 371), shellfish
  stock (page 372), or water
1 teaspoon salt
1/2 teaspoon freshly ground white pepper
1/2 cup grated Swiss cheese
1/2 cup bread crumbs

In a saucepan, melt the butter and sauté the bell pepper, green onions, garlic, and pimiento until limp. Add the flour, stir, and cook together for 3 minutes. Carefully blend the wine into the sauce. Whisk in the stock or water. Season with salt and pepper and simmer for 15 minutes, or until the sauce thickens. Fold in the grated Swiss cheese and bread crumbs and simmer, while stirring, until the cheese is completely melted. Serve warm.

Note: Great barracuda, greater amberjack, ling cobia, and snook are also delicious fried this way.

6 6- to 8-ounce wahoo fillets or steaks,
   skinned
Salt and ground white pepper
1/2 cup all-purpose flour
1/2 cup peanut oil
1/4 cup all-purpose flour
2 large onions, finely chopped
6 cloves garlic, minced
2 large tomatoes, skinned (see Note),
   seeded, and chopped

1/4 cup red wine vinegar
2 1/2 cups fish stock (page 371)
1/2 teaspoon cayenne pepper
1/4 teaspoon ground white pepper
1/4 teaspoon freshly ground black pepper
1 teaspoon salt
2 bay leaves
1/4 teaspoon dried thyme
4 green onions, chopped

Serves 6

Dry the wahoo fillets and rub them with salt and white pepper and flour. In a wide, heavy skillet, heat the peanut oil and fry the fish fillets until nicely golden on all sides. Transfer the fillets to a warm plate.

Add the 1/4 cup flour to the pan, stir, and cook until it becomes a wood-brown color. Add the onions and continue cooking until browned. Add all remaining ingredients, except the green onions and the cooked fish, bring to a boil, and turn down to a simmer. Simmer gently for 30 minutes, until the sauce acquires a semi-thick consistency. Return the fish to the sauce and simmer together for 5 minutes.

Serve the fish and sauce out onto warm dinner plates and garnish with the chopped green onions.

Notes: To skin the tomatoes, immerse them in boiling water for 1 to 2 minutes, then plunge them into cold water.

American eel, common jack, mutton snapper, rainbow runner, Spanish mackerel, spotted jewfish, or white grunt may also be used with this recipe.

Other Delicious Recipes for Wahoo include:

Caribbean Wahoo with Rice (see American eel, page 128)

Creole Étouffée of Wahoo (see Atlantic sailfish, page 230)

Creole-Style Wahoo Pot-au-Feu (see tarpon, page 336)

Étouffée of Wahoo (see blackfin tuna, page 218)

Fried Skewered Wahoo (see spotted eagle ray, page 276)

Sautéed Steak of Wahoo with Crabmeat and Butter (see common dolphin, page 90)

Wahoo Chowder with Potatoes and Tomatoes (see greater amberjack, page 170)

Wahoo Garlic Soup (see skipjack tuna, page 223)

Wahoo Poached in Orange-Curry Marinade (see shortfin mako shark, page 291)

Wahoo with Potatoes, Bacon, and Garlic (see scalloped hammerhead shark, page 286)

Wahoo-Stuffed Bell Peppers (see Atantic bonito, page 214)

Wahoo and Tomato Bisque (see yellowfin tuna, page 226)

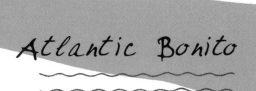

Atlantic Bonito

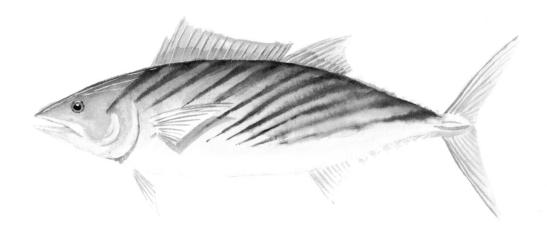

Group: Mackerel, Tuna

Other common name(s):
  Bonito
Latin name:
  Sarda sarda
  Family Scombridae
Maximum length:
  4 feet

Maximum weight:
  27 pounds
Cuts:
  whole (small)
  steak
  fillet
Meat characteristics:
  dark, firm, rich
  high oil content

Preferred cooking methods:
  bake
  broil
  fry
  grill
  poach
  steam

Black Anchovy Butter (recipe follows)

2 1/4 pounds Atlantic bonito fillets, skinned

1 egg

1 cup milk

1 cup water

2 cups corn flour (see Note)

2 teaspoons salt

1 teaspoon freshly ground white pepper

1/2 teaspoon cayenne pepper

Peanut oil for frying

Serves 6

Prepare the Black Anchovy Butter, and hold aside warm. Slice the Atlantic bonito fillets into strips 1/2 inch thick and the length of your own finger.

In bowl, beat the egg, milk, and water together to make an egg wash. In a separate bowl, combine the corn flour with the salt, white pepper, and cayenne. Preheat 1/2 inch oil in a wide, heavy skillet to 350°. Dip the fish fingers into the egg wash, coating completely, then dredge in the seasoned corn flour. Deep-fry, without crowding the pan, for approximately 4 minutes, or until golden brown on all sides. Drain on absorbent paper.

Transfer the fish to warm plates and serve with the Black Anchovy Butter spooned over.

Black Anchovy Butter

2 sticks salted butter

4 green onions, chopped

4 anchovies, minced

1 tablespoon red wine vinegar

1/2 teaspoon freshly ground black pepper

In a skillet, heat the butter until it browns. Add the green onions and anchovies, and sauté until the green onions brown. Add the red wine vinegar and pepper, let sizzle for 30 seconds, and remove from the heat.

Notes: Corn flour is often used in the frying of seafood rather than white flour. It can be bought as plain corn flour in specialty stores or as corn masa flour or "masa harina" in stores that sell Mexican or Central and South American food products. It is the flour that corn tortillas are made from. It can also be gotten in the form of "fish-fry," which is corn flour that is already seasoned with salt and pepper.

American eel, gaff-topsail catfish, hogfish, spot drum, and spotted eagle ray are also delicious fried this way. For the American eel, use 2 1/4 pounds skinned steaks.

Variations: Fried Atlantic bonito is also excellent served with Béarnaise Sauce (page 358) or Bourguignonne Sauce (page 366), and with creamy sauces such as Ravigote Mayonnaise (page 44), Rémoulade Sauce (page 353), and Tartar Sauce (page 375).

For a variation on the Black Anchovy Butter, try (follow recipe exactly except for the following substitutions):

Beurre Noir Sauce
Substitute 1/2 teaspoon salt for the anchovies.

1/2 cup olive oil

2 pounds Atlantic bonito fillets, skinned

1 large onion, chopped

2 ribs celery, chopped

4 cloves garlic, minced

2 large tomatoes, chopped

3 tablespoons minced fresh parsley

1 teaspoon dried oregano

2 teaspoons salt, or to taste

1/2 teaspoon freshly ground black pepper

3/4 cup grated Parmesan cheese (optional)

4 cups bread crumbs

3 eggs, lightly beaten

6 large bell peppers (see Note), left whole
    but stems and seeds removed

1/2 cup water

Serves 6

Preheat the oven to 400°. Heat the olive oil in a wide, heavy skillet and sauté the Atlantic bonito fillets about 5 minutes, until the flesh whitens. Remove them to a plate and, using two forks, shred the meat apart. Hold aside.

To the skillet, add the onion, celery, and garlic and sauté until they become limp. Add the tomatoes, parsley, oregano, salt, and pepper. Simmer for 10 minutes. Add 1/2 cup of the grated Parmesan, the bread crumbs, and the cooked shredded Atlantic bonito. Stir to combine thoroughly. Remove from heat and let cool slightly.

Work the eggs into the mixture. Spoon the mixture into the prepared bell peppers and stand them in a baking dish. Pour the water into the dish and cover with foil.

Bake for 30 minutes, or until the pepper shells are tender. Remove the foil, sprinkle the tops of the stuffed peppers with the remaining cheese, and cook for another 5 minutes, or until the tops have browned slightly.

Notes: Any color bell pepper can be used.

Other fish that work well with this recipes are bluefish, gaff-topsail catfish, hard-tail jack, Spanish mackerel, and wahoo.

214

Other Delicious Recipes for Atlantic Bonito include:

Atlantic Bonito Barbacoa (see great barracuda, page 20)

Atlantic Bonito Croquettes Meunière (see skipjack tuna, page 221)

Atlantic Bonito-Stuffed Hand Tortillas (see bluefish, page 68)

Caribbean Atlantic Bonito with Rice (see American eel, page 128)

Creole Bisque of Atlantic Bonito (see tilefish, page 348)

Creole-Style Atlantic Bonito Pot-au-Feu (see tarpon, page 336)

Fried Atlantic Bonito Fillets with Bourguignonne Sauce (see hogfish, page 366)

Grilled Atlantic Bonito Andalouse (see white grunt, page 149)

Gulf Coast Bouillabaisse with Atlantic Bonito (see pigfish, page 140)

Herbed Garlic Atlantic Bonito (see yellowtail snapper, page 316)

Marinated Escabèche of Atlantic Bonito (see hard-tail jack, page 176)

Tamales with Atlantic Bonito and Roasted Tomato and Chili Sauce (see common jack, page 156)

Blackfin Tuna

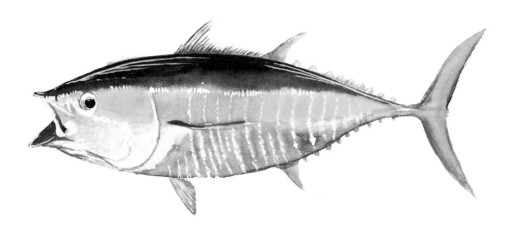

Group: Mackerel, Tuna

Other common name(s):
  Blackfin
  Tuna
Latin name:
  Thunnus atlanticus
  Family Scombridae
Maximum length:
  3 feet 3 inches

Maximum weight:
  42 pounds
Cuts:
  steak
  fillet
Meat characteristics:
  dark, firm, rich
  high oil content

Preferred cooking
methods:
  bake
  broil
  grill
  sauté
  stew

6 6- to 8-ounce blackfin tuna steaks
1/3 cup olive oil
Salt and freshly ground white pepper

1 1/2 cups Italian-style bread crumbs
3 lemons, halved

Serves 6

Lay the blackfin tuna steaks in a baking pan or dish and brush them on all sides with the olive oil. Season lightly with salt and white pepper. Pour the bread crumbs over the fish steaks, turning the steaks until they are completely covered on all sides. Cover the pan with plastic wrap or foil and refrigerate for an hour to set the breading.

Preheat the broiler. Broil the fish steaks 3 inches from the flame for about 4 minutes on each side, or until the breading is browned and the fish is opaque all through.

Serve with lemon halves.

Note: Atlantic sailfish and swordfish also work well in this recipe.

2 pounds blackfin tuna fillets, skinned and cut into 1-inch-square pieces

1 pound small raw shrimp, peeled and deveined

Salt and freshly ground white pepper

Juice of 1/2 lemon

1 stick salted butter

1/2 cup all-purpose flour

8 green onions, chopped

1 large onion, chopped

2 ribs celery, minced

1 small bell pepper, seeded and chopped

3 cups fish stock (page 371), or shellfish stock (page 372)

1/2 teaspoon dried thyme

1/2 teaspoon Hungarian paprika

3 bay leaves

1/4 teaspoon cayenne pepper

4 cloves garlic, minced

1 tablespoon tomato paste

1 1/2 teaspoons salt, or to taste

1 teaspoon freshly ground black pepper

4 cups hot cooked rice

2 tablespoons chopped fresh parsley

Serves 6

In a bowl, combine the blackfin tuna pieces and the shrimp, and season lightly with salt, pepper, and lemon juice. Cover and hold aside.

Heat the butter in a heavy skillet and blend in the flour. Cook together, stirring constantly, until the roux has browned. Add the green onions, onion, celery, and bell pepper and cook together for 5 to 7 minutes. Add the stock, thyme, paprika, bay leaves, cayenne, garlic, and tomato paste. Season with the salt and black pepper. Bring to a boil, turn down to a simmer, and continue cooking for 30 minutes, or until it has acquired a thick, saucy texture. Add the blackfin tuna and shrimp and simmer together for 8 minutes. Check seasonings.

Serve in individual serving bowls, ladled over the hot cooked rice and garnished with the chopped parsley.

Variations

(follow recipe exactly except for the following substitutions and additions):

with Crabmeat
Substitute 1 pound crabmeat for the shrimp.

with Crawfish
Replace the shrimp with 1 pound crawfish tail meat and fat (if available).

with Lobster
Use 1 pound Florida or Maine lobster tail meat, diced, instead of shrimp.

Other Delicious Recipes for Blackfin Tuna include:

Baked Crabmeat-Stuffed Blackfin Tuna Fillet (see greater amberjack, page 168)

Blackfin Tuna with Potatoes, Bacon, and Garlic (see scalloped hammerhead shark, page 286)

Blackfin Tuna with Puerto Rican Sauce (see swordfish, page 333)

Broiled Blackfin Tuna Steaks with Creole Mustard and Chive Cream Sauce (see Atlantic sailfish, page 232)

Creole Étouffée of Blackfin Tuna (see Atlantic sailfish, page 230)

Fried Skewered Blackfin Tuna (see spotted eagle ray, page 276)

Marinated Blackfin Tuna Salad with Giardeniera (see squirrelfish, page 329)

Matelote of Blackfin Tuna (see American eel, page 126)

Sautéed Steak of Blackfin Tuna with Crabmeat and Butter (see common dolphin, page 90)

White Bisque of Blackfin Tuna with Sherry (see largetooth sawfish, page 281)

Skipjack Tuna

Group: Mackerel, Tuna

Other common name(s):
  Skipjack
  Tuna
Latin name:
  Euthynnus pelanis
  Family Scombridae
Maximum length:
  3 feet 3 inches

Maximum weight:
  77 pounds
Cuts:
  steak
  fillet
Meat characteristics:
  dark, firm, rich
  high oil content

*Preferred cooking
methods:*
  bake
  broil
  fry
  grill
  poach
  sauté
  stew

1 stick salted butter
8 green onions, chopped
2 ribs celery, chopped
1/4 cup all-purpose flour
3 cups stale French bread crumbs
2 tablespoons chopped fresh parsley
1/4 teaspoon dried thyme
1 teaspoon salt, or to taste
1/2 teaspoon freshly ground white pepper
1/4 teaspoon cayenne pepper

1 tablespoon freshly squeezed lemon juice
2 large eggs
2 pounds skipjack tuna fillets, skinned
    and finely chopped
1 cup all-purpose flour
1 stick salted butter
1/2 cup corn oil
1/2 cup freshly squeezed lemon juice
2 tablespoons chopped fresh parsley

Serves 6

In a sauté pan, melt the butter and add the chopped green onions and celery. Sauté for 2 minutes, or until they are limp. Add the flour, stir, and cook for 2 minutes more. Add the bread crumbs, parsley, thyme, salt, white pepper, and cayenne. Stir and cook for 2 minutes, then remove from the heat.

When the mixture has cooled slightly, add the lemon juice and blend in the beaten eggs. Carefully fold in the chopped skipjack tuna and check the seasonings.

Divide the mixture into twelve portions and shape each of these portions into ovals, or elongated football shapes, with your hands. Dredge the croquettes in flour.

In a wide, heavy skillet, heat the butter and corn oil and sauté the skipjack tuna croquettes for 3 to 4 minutes on each side, or until nicely golden. Transfer the croquettes to dinner plates and hold warm in the oven.

Add the lemon juice to the cooking liquids in the skillet and heat briefly. Spoon the pan sauce over the croquettes, garnish with the chopped parsley, and serve.

Note: Atlantic bonito, Atlantic sailfish, gray triggerfish, greater amberjack, red grouper, spotted sea trout, and squirrelfish are also excellent in this recipe.

Variation: Instead of croquettes, you can shape the fish into twelve "cakes," like hamburger patties.

1 pound skipjack tuna fillet, skinned
Juice of 1 lemon
4 tablespoons salted butter
4 tablespoons all-purpose flour
1 large onion, finely chopped
1/4 cup minced garlic

1 quart fish stock (page 371), or water
1 pint heavy cream
Salt, freshly ground white pepper, and
    cayenne pepper
1 tablespoon minced fresh parsley

Serves 6

Cut the skipjack tuna fillet into 1/2-inch dice, sprinkle with the lemon juice, and set aside.

In a saucepan, make a roux: Heat the butter, stir in the flour, and cook together without coloring for 2 minutes, or until the flour gives off a cooked, bready aroma. Add the onion and garlic and continue cooking, without coloring, for 3 minutes. Whisk in the fish stock and heavy cream, and bring to a simmer. Season to taste with salt, white pepper, and cayenne. Cover and simmer gently for 15 minutes. Add the skipjack tuna pieces and simmer for 10 minutes more. Adjust the seasonings.

Serve this thick, rich, flavored soup with a little minced parsley sprinkled on top.

Note: Atlantic spadefish, blacktip shark, hogfish, rainbow runner, sheepshead, shortfin mako shark, spotted jewfish, squirrelfish, tarpon, and wahoo are wonderful alternatives to skipjack tuna.

Other Delicious Recipes for Skipjack Tuna include:

Blackened Skipjack Tuna Steaks (see blue marlin, page 235)

Caribbean Skipjack Tuna with Rice (see American eel, page 128)

Caribbean Skipjack Tuna Salad (see mutton snapper, page 305)

Charcoal-Grilled Skipjack Tuna with Tomatillo-Habañero Salsa (see gray triggerfish, page 351)

"Chops" of Skipjack Tuna (see spotted sea trout, page 118)

Grilled Skipjack Tuna Steaks with Onions, Green Bell Peppers, and Eggplant (see ling cobia, page 84)

Gulf Coast Bouillabaisse with Skipjack Tuna (see pigfish, page 140)

Sautéed Skipjack Tuna Steaks Marseilles-Style (see rainbow runner, page 194)

Skipjack Tuna Fillets in Saffron-White Wine Sauce (see tarpon, page 338)

Skipjack Tuna Smothered in Jalapeño-Tequila Sauce (see common jack, page 158)

Steamed Skipjack Tuna with Aioli Sauce (see squirrelfish, page 328)

White Bisque of Skipjack Tuna with Sherry (see largetooth sawfish, page 281)

Yellowfin Tuna

Group: Mackerel, Tuna

Other common name(s):
Yellowfin

Latin name:
Thunnus albacares
(not same as Albacore
Tuna)
Family Scombridae

Maximum length:
6 feet 10 inches

Maximum weight:
365 pounds

Cuts:
steak
fillet

Meat characteristics:
dark, firm, rich
high oil content

*Preferred cooking
methods:*
bake
broil
fry
grill
sauté
stew

6 ripe medium tomatoes
1/2 cup salted butter
1/2 cup all-purpose flour
4 green onions, minced
1 quart hot fish stock (page 371), or
    shellfish stock (page 372)
1 quart half-and-half

Salt and freshly ground white pepper to
    taste
1/4 teaspoon cayenne pepper
1 1/2 pounds yellowfin tuna fillet, skinned
    and diced
2 tablespoons chopped fresh parsley

Serves 6

Immerse the tomatoes in boiling water for 2 minutes, then plunge into cold water. Remove the skin and seeds, reserving any juice and jelly resulting from the process. Discard the skin and seeds. Chop up the tomato pulp and hold aside with the tomato juice.

In a saucepan, make a roux: Melt the butter, whisk in the flour, and cook together stirring, for 3 minutes, or until the mixture comes to a boil and gives off a cooked, bready aroma. Do not let the roux get any darker than a pale buttery color.

Fold in the green onions and stir while cooking for about 2 minutes, or until the green onions are softened but not yet beginning to brown. Slowly whisk in the hot stock, being very sure that there are no lumps in the texture of the soup. Bring to a boil. Add the half-and-half and the reserved tomato pulp, jelly, and juice. Bring the soup to a boil and turn down to a low simmer. Season to taste with salt and white pepper, and add the cayenne. Simmer, uncovered, for 30 minutes. Add the yellowfin tuna dice, and simmer for 10 minutes more. Adjust seasonings to taste.

Serve the bisque out into warm bowls and garnish with the chopped parsley.

Note: Blacktip shark, blue marlin, common jack, and wahoo are also excellent in this bisque.

Yellowfin Tuna and Potato Salad with Chive Vinaigrette

Chive Vinaigrette (recipe follows)
1/2 cup pecan pieces
2 1/2 pounds yellowfin tuna fillet, skinned
1 tablespoon salt
1 teaspoon freshly ground black pepper
1 teaspoon cayenne pepper
2 cloves garlic, pressed

2 cups diced cooked unpeeled new
  potatoes
6 large lettuce leaves
2 cups shredded Romaine or Boston
  lettuce
3 lemons, halved
2 tablespoons chopped fresh parsley

Serves 6

Preheat the oven to 400°. Prepare the Chive Vinaigrette and hold aside. Spread the pecans on a baking sheet in a single layer and toast in the oven for 5 minutes, or until the nuts darken just slightly. Hold aside.

Cut the yellowfin tuna fillet into strips the size of your finger and season them with the salt, black pepper, cayenne, and pressed garlic. In a wide, heavy skillet, combine the yellowfin tuna strips, diced potatoes, and Chive Vinaigrette. Cook the mixture over medium heat for 4 minutes, or until the fish strips are completely opaque.

Place a lettuce leaf on each of six plates, fill the leaves with shredded lettuce, and spoon the hot fish mixture over the lettuce mounds. Sprinkle with the pecan pieces. Garnish the salads with the half lemons and chopped parsley.

Chive Vinaigrette

1 egg
2 tablespoons minced onion
1/4 cup white vinegar
1/2 teaspoon sugar

2 teaspoons salt
2 teaspoons freshly ground white pepper
1 cup virgin olive oil, or vegetable oil
1/2 cup chopped fresh chives

227

In a bowl, combine the egg, onion, vinegar, sugar, salt, and white pepper. Gradually whisk in the oil, making sure that it emulsifies. Stir in the chives.

Note: Largetooth sawfish, ling cobia, mutton snapper, rainbow runner, red snapper, and snook are also excellent in this recipe.

Other Delicious Recipes for Yellowfin Tuna include:

Charcoal-Grilled Yellowfin Tuna with Plantation Groundnut Sauce (see southern stingray, page 270)

Creole Étouffée of Yellowfin Tuna (see Atlantic sailfish, page 230)

Fillets of Yellowfin Tuna with Browned-Butter, Lemon Juice, and Caper Sauce (see blacktip shark, page 296)

Fried Skewered Yellowfin Tuna (see spotted eagle ray, page 276)

Grilled Yellowfin Tuna Fillets with Tomato-Oyster Sauce (see Florida pompano, page 164)

Grilled Yellowfin Tuna Steaks with Criolla Sauce (see black sea bass, page 25)

Hot Yellowfin Tuna and Artichoke Salad and Russian Dressing with Caviar (see largetooth sawfish, page 279)

Hot Yellowfin Tuna and Mushroom Salad with Dijon Mustard Dressing (see snook, page 320)

Marinated Escabèche of Yellowfin Tuna (see hard-tail jack, page 176)

Matelote of Yellowfin Tuna (see American eel, page 126)

Panfried Yellowfin Tuna with Antiboise Sauce (see blacktip shark, page 294)

Yellowfin Tuna Fillets in Saffron-White Wine Sauce (see tarpon, page 338)

Atlantic Sailfish

Group: Marlin

Other common name(s):
Sailfish

Latin name:
Istiophorus
platypterus
Family Istiophoridae

Maximum length:
10 feet 9 inches

Maximum weight:
182 pounds

Cuts:
steak
fillet

Meat characteristics:
firm, dark, rich
high oil content

Preferred cooking methods:
bake
broil
fry
grill
stew

2 1/4 pounds Atlantic sailfish fillets, skinned and cut into 1-inch-square pieces

Salt and freshly ground white pepper

Juice of 1/2 lemon

1 stick salted butter

1/2 cup all-purpose flour

3 large ripe tomatoes, skinned (see Note), seeded, and chopped

1 large onion, chopped

1 rib celery, minced

1 small bell pepper, seeded and chopped

4 green onions, chopped

3 cups fish stock (page 371), or shellfish stock (page 372)

1/2 teaspoon dried marjoram

1/2 teaspoon Hungarian paprika

1/4 teaspoon cayenne pepper

3 bay leaves

4 cloves garlic, minced

1 tablespoon tomato paste

1 1/2 teaspoons salt, or to taste

1 teaspoon freshly ground black pepper

4 cups hot cooked white rice

2 tablespoons chopped fresh parsley

Serves 6

Season the Atlantic sailfish squares lightly with salt, pepper, and lemon juice, cover, and hold aside.

Melt the butter in a wide, heavy skillet and make a roux: Whisk in the flour and cook, whisking constantly, for 2 to 3 minutes, until the mixture is lightly browned and gives off a bready aroma. Add the tomatoes, onion, celery, bell pepper, and green onions and cook together for 5 to 7 minutes. Add the stock, marjoram, paprika, cayenne, bay leaves, garlic, and tomato paste. Season with the salt and black pepper. Bring to a boil, turn down to a simmer, and continue cooking for 30 minutes, or until it has acquired a thick, saucy texture. Add the Atlantic sailfish and simmer together for 8 minutes. Check the seasonings.

Serve in individual serving bowls, ladled over the hot cooked rice and garnished with the chopped parsley.

Notes: To skin the tomatoes, immerse them in boiling water for 1 to 2 minutes, then plunge them into cold water.

Other fish that work well in this recipe are blackfin tuna, gulf kingfish, shortfin mako shark, spotfin flounder, wahoo, and yellowfin tuna.

Broiled Atlantic Sailfish Steaks with Creole Mustard and Chive Cream Sauce

Creole Mustard and Chive Cream Sauce
  (recipe follows)
6 6- to 8-ounce Atlantic sailfish steaks

Juice of 1 lemon
3 tablespoons melted salted butter
Salt and freshly ground black pepper

Serves 6

Preheat the broiler. Prepare the Creole Mustard and Chive Cream Sauce, and hold aside warm. Place the Atlantic sailfish steaks on a broiler pan or in a baking pan and brush them with the lemon juice and melted butter. Season lightly with salt and freshly ground black pepper. Broil for 4 minutes on each side, or until the steaks are opaque all the way through.

Transfer the Atlantic sailfish steaks to warm dinner plates and spoon the warm Creole Mustard and Chive Cream Sauce over each.

Creole Mustard and Chive Cream Sauce

2 tablespoons salted butter
4 green onions, minced
1 small clove garlic, minced
1/2 cup dry white wine
1 cup heavy cream
1/4 cup Creole mustard (see Note)

1/2 teaspoon habañero pepper sauce
  (Caribbean-style hot sauce), or
  Louisiana hot sauce
Salt

In a small saucepan, heat the butter and sauté the green onions and garlic. Add the wine and boil briskly to reduce the liquids almost completely. Add the heavy cream and simmer until somewhat thickened. Whisk in the Creole mustard and hot sauce, and season to taste with salt. Serve warm.

Notes: Another grainy mustard can be used instead of Creole mustard.

Try blackfin tuna, blue marlin, greater amberjack, shortfin mako shark, and spotted eagle ray with this recipe. For the spotted eagle ray, use 6 6- to 8-ounce skinned wing fillets.

Other Delicious Recipes for Atlantic Sailfish include:

Atlantic Sailfish Croquettes Meunière (see skipjack tuna, page 221)

Atlantic Sailfish Fillets in Saffron-White Wine Sauce (see tarpon, page 338)

Atlantic Sailfish Smothered in Jalapeño-Tequila Sauce (see common jack, page 158)

Blackened Atlantic Sailfish Steaks (see blue marlin, page 235)

Charcoal-Grilled Atlantic Sailfish with Garlic Sauce (see blue marlin, page 236)

Cold Poached Atlantic Sailfish Ravigote with Boiled New Potatoes (see spotted jewfish, page 43)

Étouffée of Atlantic Sailfish (see blackfin tuna, page 218)

Fried Skewered Atlantic Sailfish (see spotted eagle ray, page 276)

Steamed Atlantic Sailfish with Aioli Sauce (see squirrelfish, page 328)

Venetian-Style Broiled Atlantic Sailfish Steaks (see blackfin tuna, page 217)

Wood-Grilled Atlantic Sailfish Steaks with Achiote-Garlic Paste (see black grouper, page 49)

Wood-Grilled Atlantic Sailfish Steaks with Sweet Herbs (see king mackerel, page 197)

Blue Marlin

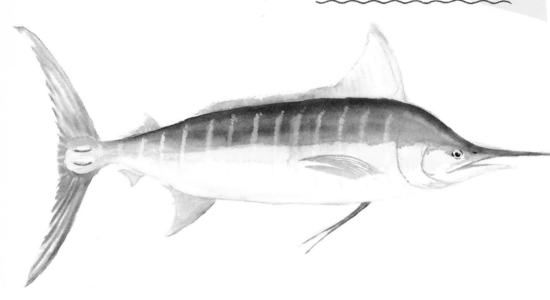

Group: Marlin

Other common name(s):	Maximum weight:	Preferred cooking methods:
Blue	300 pounds	bake
Marlin	*Cuts:*	broil
Latin name:	steak	fry
Makaira nigricans	fillet	grill
Family Istiophoridae	*Meat characteristics:*	poach
Maximum length:	firm, dark, rich	
10 feet	high oil content	

Blackened Blue Marlin Steaks

1 medium onion, minced
2 cloves garlic, minced
1 teaspoon dried thyme
1 teaspoon Hungarian paprika
1 teaspoon freshly ground black pepper

1 teaspoon cayenne pepper
1 tablespoon salt
1/4 cup peanut oil
6 8-ounce blue marlin steaks
2 sticks salted butter

Serves 6

This recipe can be difficult to do at home, as the skillet needs to be on a very hot fire to work perfectly. But don't fear; this dish is excellent cooked on any fire, even if you don't get the full "blackened" effect. There will be a lot of smoke, so be sure that your oven exhaust fan is turned on.

Combine the onion, garlic, thyme, paprika, pepper, cayenne, salt, and oil, and blend into a paste consistency. Rub the blue marlin steaks with the paste. Heat a wide, heavy skillet until it is smoking hot. Lay some of the steaks into the skillet and cook for about 5 minutes on each side, or until the fish is cooked through and "blackened."

Hold the cooked fish on a warm plate in a warm oven until you have cooked all the steaks. Put the butter into the same skillet and melt. You want the blackened herbs in the skillet in the butter, so scrape them up with a wooden spoon.

To serve, put the blue marlin steaks on warm plates and spoon the melted butter over the top.

Note: Atlantic sailfish, blacktip shark, skipjack tuna, and swordfish also work wonderfully with this recipe.

Charcoal-Grilled Blue Marlin with Garlic Sauce

3/4 cup salted butter
3/4 cup peanut oil
18 large cloves garlic, peeled and thinly
    sliced

6 8-ounce blue marlin steaks
Salt and freshly ground black pepper
Vegetable oil for grilling

Serves 6

Light the charcoal 1 hour before cooking. In a wide sauté pan, heat the butter and oil until medium-hot, then add the garlic. Cook at a medium heat, stirring regularly, until the garlic turns golden, but not brown, about 3 minutes. Pour the mixture through a strainer in a pan to stop the garlic from cooking. Reserve the garlic. Keep the butter-oil mixture hot.

When the charcoal is ready, oil the grill rack. Season the fish lightly with salt and pepper, paint it with the strained butter-oil, and place it on the grill rack. Cover the grill and cook for approximately 5 minutes. Remove the grill cover, turn the fish over, baste with the butter-oil mixture, and re-cover the grill. Cook for 5 minutes more, or until the fish is white and flaky all the way through when broken with the tines of a fork.

Transfer to warm serving plates. Add the cooked garlic back to the remaining hot butter-oil and spoon over the fish.

Note: Atlantic sailfish, blacktip shark, largetooth sawfish, and ling cobia also work well prepared this way.

236

Other Delicious Recipes for Blue Marlin include:

Blue Marlin Boudin (see Atlantic moonfish, page 152)

Blue Marlin with Oyster and Crabmeat Sauce Gratiné (see pinfish, page 256)

Blue Marlin Poached in Orange-Curry Marinade (see shortfin mako shark, page 291)

Blue Marlin with Potatoes, Bacon, and Garlic (see scalloped hammerhead shark, page 286)

Blue Marlin and Tomato Bisque (see yellowfin tuna, page 226)

Broiled Blue Marlin Steaks with Creole Mustard and Chive Cream Sauce (see Atlantic sailfish, page 232)

Caribbean Blue Marlin with Rice (see American eel, page 128)

Creole Bisque of Blue Marlin (see tilefish, page 348)

Fried Skewered Blue Marlin (see spotted eagle ray, page 276)

Grilled Blue Marlin with Tomato-Red Wine Sauce (see Atlantic spadefish, page 325)

Poached Blue Marlin Fillets with Drawn Butter (see king mackerel, page 199)

Wood-Grilled Blue Marlin Steaks with Mexican Seasonings (see bluefish, page 66)

Striped Mullet

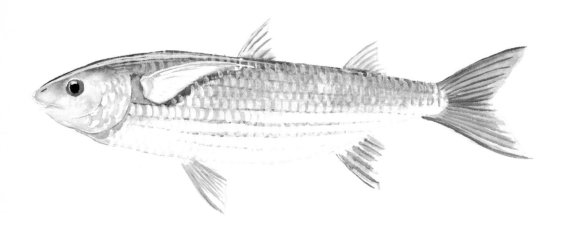

Group: Mullet

Other common name(s):
Mullet

Latin name:
Mugil cephalus
Family Mugilidae

Maximum length:
1 foot 6 inches

Maximum weight:
3 pounds

Cuts:
whole
fillet

Meat characteristics:
firm, white, flaky
medium-to-high oil
content

Preferred cooking methods:
broil
fry
grill
poach
sauté

Fried Cornmeal-Battered Striped Mullet Fillets

1 cup milk

1 egg

1 1/2 cups finely ground yellow cornmeal

2 teaspoons salt

1 teaspoon freshly ground black pepper

1/2 teaspoon cayenne pepper

Peanut oil for frying

2 1/4 pounds 1/2-inch-thick striped
    mullet fillets, skinned

Tartar Sauce (page 375) and Cocktail
    Sauce (page 375)

3 lemons, halved

Serves 6

Blend the milk and egg in one mixing bowl and the cornmeal, salt, black pepper, and cayenne in another. In a wide, heavy frying pan, heat 1/2 inch oil to 350° to 375°. Dip the striped mullet fillets in the milk and egg wash and then dredge them in the seasoned cornmeal. Fry on both sides, without crowding the fish in the pan, until they are golden, about 2 1/2 minutes per side. Drain the fish on absorbent paper.

Serve with lemon halves, and pass the Tartar Sauce and Cocktail Sauce.

Note: Other fish to try with this recipe are gaff-topsail catfish, gulf kingfish, permit, pinfish, scamp, spot drum, spotfin flounder, and spotted sea trout. For the pinfish, use 3 pounds whole fish, scaled and drawn; fry about 5 minutes a side, or until golden.

Variations: The cornmeal-battered fillets are also excellent served with Moulin Rouge Sauce (page 56), Spicy Creole Mayonnaise (page 310), Sweet Mustard-Egg Sauce (page 254), or Two Sisters Sauce (page 184).

Salsa Roja (recipe follows)
6 3/4- to 1-pound whole striped mullet,
   scaled and drawn

Salt and freshly ground black pepper
1/2 cup peanut oil
6 large French bread croutons (page 370)

Serves 6

Prepare the Salsa Roja, and hold aside warm. Rub the striped mullets with salt and pepper. Heat the oil until hot in a heavy skillet and fry fish about 4 minutes on each side, until lightly browned. Drain the fish on absorbent paper.

Serve the fish on the croutons with the warm Salsa Roja spooned over the top.

Salsa Roja

4 large Anaheim chilies (see Note), seeded
3 cloves garlic, mashed
2 large roasted tomatoes (page 370),
   seeded

Salt and freshly ground black pepper

Cut the chilies into flat pieces and roast with the garlic in a dry heated skillet for about 30 seconds on each side.

In a blender, process the tomatoes, chilis, and garlic into a smooth puree. Add a little water if necessary to process the ingredients. Transfer the mixture to a saucepan, season with salt and pepper, and heat. Serve warm.

Note: If Anaheim chilies are not available, you can use serannos or anchos. Or for a mild sauce, use red bell peppers.

Atlantic croaker, Atlantic threadfin, pinfish, sand perch, and white grunt are also excellent fried this way.

Other Delicious Recipes for Striped Mullet include:

Broiled Striped Mullet with Poulette Sauce (see red porgy, page 260)

Corn-Flour-Fried Striped Mullet Fillets (see dog snapper, page 300)

Fried Battered Striped Mullet with Two Sisters Sauce (see permit, page 184)

Fried Striped Mullet Fillets with Bourguignonne Sauce (see hogfish, page 366)

Fried Striped Mullet Fillets with Moulin Rouge Sauce (see scamp, page 56)

Fried Whole Striped Mullet with Creole Mustard Sauce (see creolefish, page 29)

Fried Whole Striped Mullet with Sweet Mustard and Egg Sauce (see pinfish, page 254)

Sautéed Striped Mullet with Citrus-Garlic Sauce (see Atlantic threadfin, page 341)

Striped Mullet Beignets with Rémoulade Sauce (see gray triggerfish, page 353)

Whole Cornmeal-Fried Striped Mullet with Mosca Sauce (see Atlantic croaker, page 93)

Whole Panfried Striped Mullet with Espagnole Sauce (see tripletail, page 361)

Whole Panfried Striped Mullet with Onion, Garlic, and Red Wine Sauce (see pilot fish, page 190)

White Mullet

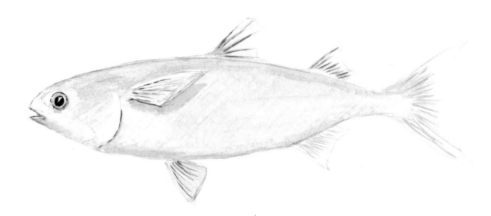

Group: Mullet

Other common name(s):
  Mullet
  Channel Mullet
Latin name:
  Mugil curema
  Family Mugilidae
Maximum length:
  1 foot 2 inches

Maximum weight:
  2 1/2 pounds
Cuts:
  whole
  fillet
Meat characteristics:
  medium-white, flaky
  medium-high oil
  content

Preferred cooking
methods:
  bake
  fry
  grill
  poach
  sauté

Seafood-White Wine Sauce (recipe
  follows)
1/2 cup dry white wine
1 onion, sliced
2 teaspoons salt
5 whole black peppercorns
2 bay leaves
Juice of 1 lemon

2 quarts water
6 1-pound whole white mullets, pan-
  dressed
3 tablespoons grated Swiss cheese
3 tablespoons grated Romano cheese
3 tablespoons grated mozzarella
1/4 cup bread crumbs

Serves 6

This is a classic of old Haute Creole cookery. A bone plate should be supplied to each diner.

Prepare the Seafood-White Wine Sauce, and hold aside warm.

Make a poaching liquor in a wide, heavy skillet: Combine the wine, onion, salt, peppercorns, bay leaves, lemon juice, and water, bring to a boil, and cook for about 3 minutes to allow the seasoning ingredients to flavor the water. Lower the heat to a simmer. Carefully slip the fish into the poaching liquor and bring back to a simmer. Poach about 10 minutes, or until the fish are completely opaque.

Drain the fish and place them in individual oven-proof baking dishes. Spoon the sauce over the poached mullet. Mix the grated cheeses together with the bread crumbs and sprinkle over the fish. Place the dishes under a broiler flame for about 2 minutes, just long enough to melt the cheeses and brown the tops.

Serve immediately.

Seafood-White Wine Sauce

1 cup shucked oysters in their water
1/2 cup chopped green onions
2 tablespoons salted butter
3/4 cup small raw shrimp, peeled and
  deveined

1 cup dry white wine
1 1/2 cups Fish Velouté Sauce (page 373)
Salt and cayenne pepper

Poach the oysters in their water about 2 minutes, just until their edges begin to curl. Strain, reserving the liquid, and set aside.

In a large, heavy saucepan, sauté the green onions in butter until they become limp. Add the shrimp and 1 cup of the white wine, and bring to a boil. Blend in the Fish Velouté and the strained oyster water, and season to taste with salt and cayenne pepper. Serve warm.

Note: Florida pompano, red grouper, red snapper, spotted sea trout, and weakfish are also excellent in this recipe.

Brown Shrimp Sauce (recipe follows)
1 large egg
1 cup milk
1 1/2 cups corn flour (see Note)
1 tablespoon salt

1/2 teaspoon freshly ground black pepper
1/2 teaspoon cayenne pepper
Peanut or vegetable oil for frying
6 8-ounce white mullet fillets, skinned

Serves 6

Prepare the Brown Shrimp Sauce, and hold aside warm. In a bowl, beat the egg together with the milk to make an egg wash. In a flat baking pan, combine the corn flour with the salt, black pepper, and cayenne.

Heat 1/2 inch oil in a wide, heavy skillet to 350°. Dredge the white mullet fillets in the seasoned corn flour, dip in the egg wash, and dredge again in the flour. Shake any excess flour from the fillets and fry for 4 minutes on each side, or until the coating is crisp and golden, and the flesh of the fish is flaky all the way through when broken with a fork. Drain on absorbent paper.

Serve immediately with the warm Brown Shrimp Sauce spooned over the top.

Brown Shrimp Sauce

4 tablespoons salted butter
4 tablespoons all-purpose flour
6 green onions, minced
4 cloves garlic, minced
1/2 cup diced green bell pepper
1/2 cup diced red bell pepper
1 pint fresh mushrooms, sliced
1 1/2 cups beef stock, or beef bouillon

1/4 cup brandy
1/2 cup whipping cream
Salt, freshly ground black pepper, and
    cayenne pepper
1/2 pound raw shrimp, peeled and
    deveined
1 tablespoon chopped fresh parsley

In a saucepan, make a roux: Melt the butter, whisk in the flour, and cook, while whisking, until mixture gives off a bready aroma and acquires a chestnut-brown color. Add the green onions, garlic, green and red bell peppers, and mushrooms, and cook for 5 minutes. Whisk in the beef stock and brandy, and bring to a boil. Add the whipping cream, season to taste with salt, black pepper, cayenne, and simmer gently for 20 minutes. Add the shrimp, and simmer for 5 minutes more. Add the chopped parsley. Serve warm.

Notes: Corn flour is often used in the frying of seafood rather than white flour. It can be bought as plain corn flour in specialty stores or as corn masa or "masa harina" in stores that sell Mexican or Central and South American food products. It is the flour that corn tortillas are made from. It can also be gotten in the form of "fish-fry," which is corn flour that is already seasoned with salt and pepper.

Atlantic croaker, Atlantic threadfin, gray triggerfish, gulf kingfish, mutton snapper, pinfish, sand perch, sheepshead, and squirrelfish may also be used with this recipe.

Other Delicious Recipes for White Mullet include:

Baked Canapé of White Mullet (see Atlantic spadefish, page 323)
Beer-Battered Fried White Mullet (see speckled hind, page 39)
Charcoal-Grilled White Mullet with Tomatillo-Habañero Salsa (see gray triggerfish, page 351)
Fried Whole White Mullet with Sweet Mustard and Egg Sauce (see pinfish, page 254)
Grilled White Mullet Andalouse (see white grunt, page 149)

Panfried White Mullet Fillets with Shrimp Creole Sauce (see Atlantic threadfin, page 342)

Panfried White Mullet with Lobster Cream Sauce (see permit, page 186)

Poached White Mullet with Horseradish and Sour Cream Sauce (see Atlantic croaker, page 95)

White Mullet Smothered in Jalapeño-Tequila Sauce (see common jack, page 158)

Whole Panfried White Mullet with Aurora Sauce (see spot drum, page 114)

Jolthead Porgy

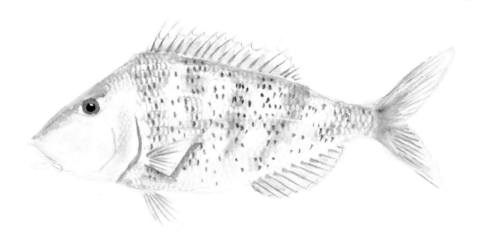

Group: Porgy

Other common name(s):
  Porgy
Latin name:
  Calamus bajonado
  Family Sparidae
Maximum length:
  2 feet 3 inches

Maximum weight:
  9 pounds
Cuts:
  whole
  steak
  fillet
Meat characteristics:
  firm, white
  medium oil content

*Preferred cooking
methods:*
  bake
  fry
  grill
  poach
  sauté

New Orleans-Style Deep-Fried Jolthead Porgy Fillets Meunière

1 1/2 cups half-and-half
3 whole eggs, beaten
1 teaspoon salt
1/2 teaspoon freshly ground white pepper
6 6- to 8-ounce jolthead porgy fillets, skinned
1 1/2 cups all-purpose flour

Peanut oil for frying
1/4 cup hot melted salted butter
3/4 cup freshly squeezed lemon juice
3 tablespoons chopped fresh parsley

Serves 6

Make a batter by whisking the half-and-half together in a wide bowl with the eggs, salt, and white pepper. Dredge the jolthead porgy fillets in the flour, shaking off any excess, immerse them in the batter, then dredge them in flour again. Heat 1/2 inch of oil in a wide, heavy skillet to 375° and fry the fillets, without crowding the pan, for about 7 minutes. When done they will color a golden brown. Drain the cooked fish on absorbent paper. Transfer the fried fillets to warm dinner plates and hold in a hot oven.

Heat the butter in a small saucepan until it begins to brown. Add the lemon juice and pour the mixture over the fish. Garnish the fried jolthead porgy fillets with the chopped parsley and serve immediately.

Note: Also excellent in this recipe are Atlantic moonfish, Florida pompano, gulf flounder, permit, and weakfish.

1 5-pound whole jolthead porgy, scaled
    and drawn
2 tablespoons salted butter, softened
Salt, freshly ground black pepper, and
    cayenne pepper

Spinach Stuffing:
2 tablespoons butter, or olive oil
6 green onions, chopped
2 cloves garlic, minced
2 bunches or bags fresh spinach,
    washed, stemmed, and chopped
2 cups bread crumbs
Juice of 1 lime
1/4 cup water, or more if necessary

Salt, freshly ground black pepper, and
    cayenne pepper
2 eggs, lightly beaten

Cotton string or toothpicks
1 1/2 cups fish stock (page 371), or
    water
2 green onions, minced
1 clove garlic, minced
Juice of 1 lime
1/4 teaspoon mace
1/4 teaspoon dried marjoram
1 to 2 teaspoons arrowroot, or cornstarch
1 tablespoon water
Salt and freshly ground black pepper

Serves 6

Preheat the oven to 375°. Wash and dry the jolthead porgy and rub it inside and out with the softened butter, salt, black pepper, and cayenne. Place the fish in a baking pan. (If you prefer, use a pan that can be brought to the table so you can avoid the problem later of moving the fragile cooked fish to a platter.)

In a saucepan, make the stuffing. Melt the butter or olive oil and sauté the chopped green onions and minced garlic until they become limp. Add the chopped spinach, cover, and simmer for 3 minutes. Fold in the bread crumbs, lime juice, and enough water that the stuffing forms a solid mass. Season with salt, black pepper, and cayenne. Work in the eggs.

Fill the cavity of the jolthead porgy with the spinach stuffing and secure the fish closed with cotton string or toothpicks.

Make a basting liquid for the fish by combining the fish stock, green onions, garlic, and lime juice. Pour it over the fish in the baking pan. Bake the fish for 1 hour, or until the flesh is white and flaky all the way through and the stuffing has set. Baste several times during the baking.

When the fish is done, transfer it to a warm serving platter. Pour the liquids from the baking pan into a small saucepan. Mix 1 or 2 teaspoons arrowroot with the 1 tablespoon water and stir it into the cooking liquids. Bring to a simmer to thicken the sauce, and season with salt and pepper.

Cut the jolthead porgy straight through into six portions, and serve with the sauce spooned over.

Note: Mutton snapper, red drum, red snapper, sheepshead, spotted jewfish, striped bass, tilefish, and weakfish can also be used with this recipe.

Variations
(follow recipe exactly except for the following substitutions and additions):

with Collard Green Stuffing
Substitute 1 bunch collard greens, washed, stemmed, and chopped, for the spinach. Add the collard greens to the sautéed green onions and garlic, cover, and simmer for 10 minutes or until tender.

with Mustard Green Stuffing
Replace the spinach with 1 bunch mustard greens, washed, stemmed, and chopped. Add the mustard greens to the sautéed green onions and garlic, cover, and simmer for 10 minutes or until tender.

with Turnip Green Stuffing
Use 1 bunch washed, stemmed, and chopped turnip greens in place of the spinach. Add the turnip greens to the sautéed green onions and garlic, cover, and simmer for 10 minutes or until tender.

with Watercress Stuffing

Instead of the spinach, use 4 bunches fresh watercress, washed, stemmed, and chopped.

Other Delicious Recipes for Jolthead Porgy include:

Baked Jolthead Porgy with Apples and Onions (see hogfish, page 368)

Baked Shrimp-Stuffed Jolthead Porgy (see black drum, page 98)

Cold Poached Jolthead Porgy Fillets with Green Onion Mayonnaise (see black sea bass, page 23)

Fried Jolthead Porgy Fillets with Moulin Rouge Sauce (see scamp, page 56)

Grilled Jolthead Porgy with Béarnaise Sauce (see queen triggerfish, page 358)

Grilled Jolthead Porgy with Tomato Sauce (see lookdown, page 179)

Hot Jolthead Porgy and Mushroom Salad with Dijon Mustard Dressing (see snook, page 320)

Jolthead Porgy with Pecans (see lookdown, page 181)

Panfried Jolthead Porgy with Lobster Cream Sauce (see permit, page 186)

Poached Jolthead Porgy with Parsley-Lemon Butter (see sheepshead, page 267)

Steamed Whole Jolthead Porgy with Chivry Butter (see bonefish, page 72)

Pinfish

Group: Porgy

Other name(s):
Pinfish

Latin name:
Lagodon rhomboides
Family Sparidae

Maximum length:
16 inches

Maximum weight:
4 pounds

Cuts:
whole
fillet

Meat characteristics:
medium-white, flaky
medium oil content

Preferred cooking methods:
bake
broil
fry
poach
stew

Fried Whole Pinfish with Sweet Mustard and Egg Sauce

Sweet Mustard and Egg Sauce (recipe
  follows)
1 cup milk
1 egg
1 1/2 cups finely ground yellow cornmeal
2 teaspoons salt

1 teaspoon freshly ground black pepper
1/2 teaspoon cayenne pepper
Peanut oil for frying
5 pounds small whole pinfish, scaled and
  drawn
3 lemons, quartered

Serves 6

Prepare the Sweet Mustard and Egg Sauce, and hold aside warm.

Blend the milk and egg in one mixing bowl and the cornmeal, salt, black pepper, and cayenne in another. Pour 1/2 inch of oil into a wide, heavy frying pan and heat the oil to 350° to 375°.

Dip the pinfish in the milk and egg wash and then dredge them in the seasoned cornmeal. Fry on both sides, without crowding the fish in the pan, until they are golden, about 5 minutes per side. Drain the cooked pinfish on absorbent paper.

Serve several fish per person, with Sweet Mustard and Egg Sauce on the side and lemon quarters for squeezing.

Sweet Mustard and Egg Sauce

2 ounces dry mustard
1/2 cup tarragon vinegar

2 medium whole eggs, beaten
1/4 cup sugar

In a bowl, combine the dry mustard with the tarragon vinegar, cover, and let stand for 1 hour.

In a saucepan, combine the beaten eggs with the mustard-vinegar mixture. Add the sugar. Very gently heat the mixture, stirring constantly, until it thickens enough to coat the spoon or whisk. Do not overheat, or allow to come to a boil—it will separate. If the sauce does begin to separate, remove from the heat and whisk in a tablespoon of cold water or milk. Serve warm.

Note: This recipe is also excellent prepared with scamp, speckled hind, striped mullet, or white mullet. Use 2 1/4 pounds 1/2-inch-thick skinned fillets and fry about 2 1/2 minutes per side.

Variations: Fried Whole Pinfish are also excellent served with Moulin Rouge Sauce (page 56), Spicy Creole Mayonnaise (page 310), Tartar Sauce (page 375), or Two Sisters Sauce (page 184).

Oyster and Crabmeat Sauce (recipe
  follows)
2 quarts water, or enough to cover
1 lemon, thinly sliced
1 medium onion, thinly sliced
2 sprigs fresh parsley
2 bay leaves
1 clove garlic, mashed

6 whole black peppercorns
2 tablespoons salt
1/4 teaspoon cayenne pepper
6 6-ounce pinfish fillets
1/4 cup grated Swiss cheese
1/4 cup grated Parmesan cheese
1/2 cup fine bread crumbs

Serves 6

Preheat the oven to 400°. Prepare the Oyster and Crabmeat Sauce, and hold aside warm.

In a wide, heavy skillet, bring the water to a boil with the lemon, onion, parsley, bay leaves, garlic, peppercorns, salt, and cayenne. Let boil for 3 minutes to allow the water to draw the flavor from the seasoning ingredients. Lower the heat to a simmer and lay in the pinfish fillets. Bring back to a simmer and poach for 8 minutes, or until the fish is flaky when broken with a fork.

With a long, wide spatula, carefully remove the poached fillets, drain, and place in individual oven-proof baking dishes. In a small bowl, combine the grated cheeses with the bread crumbs. Spoon the oyster sauce over the pinfish fillets and sprinkle the top with the cheese and bread crumb mixture. Bake for 10 minutes, or until the top is browned and the sauce is bubbly. Serve immediately.

Oyster and Crabmeat Sauce

3 dozen shucked oysters, in their liquor
3 tablespoons salted butter
3 tablespoons all-purpose flour
8 green onions, chopped
1 tablespoon minced fresh parsley

1/2 cup white wine, not too dry
1 pound crabmeat
Salt and freshly ground black pepper to
taste

In a small saucepan, poach the oysters in their own liquor for 2 minutes, just long enough for their edges to begin to curl. Remove the pan from the heat and set aside.

In a large, heavy saucepan, melt the butter and stir in the flour. Cook together for 2 minutes and add the green onions, parsley, and white wine. Add the cooking liquor from the oysters and blend all together. When the mixture is hot, add the crabmeat and oysters and season with salt and pepper. Serve warm.

Note: Try this recipe with blue marlin, mutton snapper, pigfish, queen triggerfish, red snapper, sand perch, sheepshead, squirrelfish, and tripletail.

Other Delicious Recipes for Pinfish include:

Beer-Battered Fried Pinfish (see speckled hind, page 39)
Creole Seafood Gumbo with Pinfish (see sailor's-choice, page 144)
Fried Pinfish with Brown Shrimp Sauce (see white mullet, page 245)
Fried Pinfish Fillets with Bourguignonne Sauce (see hogfish, page 366)
Fried Pinfish Fillets with Moulin Rouge Sauce (see scamp, page 56)
Fried Whole Cornmeal-Battered Pinfish (see striped mullet, page 239)
Fried Whole Pinfish with Creole Mustard Sauce (see creolefish, page 29)

257

Panfried Pinfish Fillets with Shrimp Creole Sauce (see Atlantic threadfin, page 342)

Pinfish Fillets with Lobster-Browned Butter Sauce (see gulf flounder, page 132)

Whole Cracker-Crumb-Coated Panfried Pinfish with Key Lime Sauce (see white grunt, page 147)

Whole Panfried Pinfish with Aurora Sauce (see spot drum, page 114)

Whole Panfried Pinfish with Salsa Roja (see stripped mullet, page 240)

Red Porgy

Group: Porgy

Other common name(s):
  Porgy
  "Snapper" (sic)
  "White Snapper" (sic)
Latin name:
  Pagrus pagrus
  Family Sparidae
Maximum length:
  1 foot 6 inches

Maximum weight:
  3 pounds
Cuts:
  whole
  fillet
Meat characteristics:
  firm, white
  low-to-medium oil
  content

Preferred cooking methods:
  bake
  broil
  fry
  grill
  sauté

Poulette Sauce (recipe follows)
1/4 cup melted salted butter
Juice of 1 lemon

6 6- to 8-ounce red porgy fillets
Salt and freshly ground white pepper
2 teaspoons chopped fresh parsley

Serves 6

Make the Poulette Sauce before broiling the red porgy fillets, and hold aside warm.

Preheat the broiler. Combine the melted butter with the lemon juice and brush a large baking pan with the mixture. Arrange the red porgy fillets in the baking pan. Brush the fish with the butter-lemon mixture and season very lightly with salt and white pepper.

Place the red porgy about 3 inches from the broiler and cook 7 minutes. Baste the fillets several times during the broiling with the pan drippings and butter-lemon mixture.

Carefully transfer the broiled red porgy fillets to warm plates. Combine any remaining pan drippings with the remaining butter-lemon mixture and the Poulette Sauce. Spoon the sauce over the fillets and garnish with chopped parsley.

Poulette Sauce

1 tablespoon salted butter
1/2 cup minced fresh mushrooms
1 tablespoon minced onion
1 1/2 cups Fish Velouté Sauce (page 373)

1/3 cup heavy cream
2 egg yolks
1 tablespoon freshly squeezed lemon juice
1 tablespoon minced fresh parsley

Heat the butter in a saucepan and sauté the minced mushrooms and onion until all the liquid has completely reduced. Add the Fish Velouté and heavy cream and whisk in the egg yolks. Bring to a simmer while whisking, and remove from the heat. Do not boil. Add the lemon juice and minced parsley. Serve warm.

Note: This recipe is also excellent prepared with black drum, black grouper, black sea bass, queen triggerfish, sailor's-choice, sheepshead, southern stingray, or striped mullet. For the southern stingray, use skinned wing fillets.

Colbert Sauce (recipe follows)

6 3/4- to 1-pound red porgies, scaled and drawn

Salt and freshly ground black pepper

1/2 cup peanut oil

6 large French bread croutons (page 370)

Serves 6

Prepare the Colbert Sauce, and hold aside warm.

Dry the red porgies and rub with salt and pepper. Heat the oil until hot in a wide, heavy skillet and fry fish on both sides until lightly browned. Remove the fish from the oil and drain on absorbent paper.

Serve the fish on the croutons with the sauce spooned over.

Colbert Sauce

1/2 cup Tomato Sauce (page 179), or plain (unseasoned) canned tomato sauce

2 tablespoons dry sherry

1 1/2 cups warm Hollandaise Sauce (page 63)

In a saucepan, combine the tomato sauce with the sherry and cook briskly to reduce slightly. Let cool slightly, then blend in the warm Hollandaise. Keep warm until ready to use, without allowing the sauce to simmer, or it will separate.

Other Delicious Recipes for Red Porgy include:

Beer-Battered Fried Red Porgy (see speckled hind, page 39)

Broiled Red Porgy with Balsamic Vinegar (see Atlantic moonfish, page 153)

Broiled Red Porgy Fillets with Cilantro Butter (see weakfish, page 123)

Curried Fillets of Red Porgy (see sailor's-choice, page 143)

Fried Whole Red Porgy with Creole Mustard Sauce (see creolefish, page 29)

Grilled Red Porgy Andalouse (see white grunt, page 149)

Grilled Red Porgy Fillets in Sesame-Brandy Marinade (see scamp, page 58)

Red Porgy Boudin (see Atlantic moonfish, page 152)

Whole Cornmeal-Fried Red Porgy with Mosca Sauce (see Atlantic croaker, page 93)

Whole Panfried Red Porgy with Espagnole Sauce (see tripletail, page 361)

Whole Panfried Red Porgy with Onion, Garlic, and Red Wine Sauce (see pilot fish, page 190)

Sheepshead

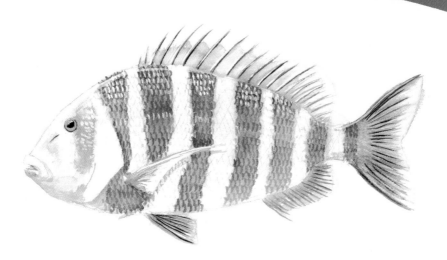

Group: Porgy

Other common name(s):
Sheepshead
Latin name:
Archosargus probato-
cephalus
Family Sparidae
Maximum length:
3 feet

Maximum weight:
20 pounds
Cuts:
whole (small)
steak
fillet
Meat characteristics:
tender, white, flaky
medium oil content

*Preferred cooking
methods:*
bake
fry
poach
steam
stew

2 quarts water, or enough to cover fish (about 2 inches deep in pan)

1 large onion, sliced

1 lemon, sliced

12 whole peppercorns

1 tablespoon salt

2 bay leaves

1/2 teaspoon dried thyme

6 6-ounce sheepshead fillets, skinned

Marguery:

1 stick salted butter

4 tablespoons all-purpose flour

4 green onions, chopped

1/2 cup dry white wine

2 cups reserved poaching liquor

1 pint raw fresh mushrooms, sliced

1 teaspoon salt

1/2 teaspoon freshly ground white pepper

1/4 teaspoon cayenne pepper

1 pound small raw shrimp, peeled and deveined

Serves 6

Pour the water into a wide, shallow saucepan. Add the onion, lemon, peppercorns, salt, bay leaves, and thyme. Bring to a boil and reduce to a simmer. Lay in the sheepshead fillets and poach at a low simmer for 6 to 8 minutes, or until they are opaque all the way through. Carefully remove the fillets and place them on a warm platter with a little of the poaching liquor. Cover and keep warm. Strain the remaining poaching liquor, and reserve 2 cups.

Melt the butter in a saucepan, add the flour, and cook together for 2 minutes to make a roux, allowing the mixture to foam up and cook out the raw flour aroma. Add the green onions, white wine, and reserved poaching liquor. Bring to a boil and add all remaining ingredients, except the shrimp and the poached sheepshead fillets. Reduce the heat and simmer for 10 minutes. Fold the shrimp into the sauce, bring back to a simmer, and remove from the heat. The shrimp will cook and pinken in only moments. Adjust the seasonings if desired.

Transfer the sheepshead fillets to warm dinner plates and spoon the Marguery over them.

Note: Black drum, Florida pompano, spotted sea trout, weakfish, and yellow-tail snapper are also excellent prepared this way.

Parsley-Lemon Butter (recipe follows)

1 5-pound whole sheepshead, scaled and
   drawn

1/2 lemon

2 quarts water, or enough to cover fish
   (about 2 inches deep in the skillet)

1 lemon, thinly sliced

1 medium onion, thinly sliced

2 sprigs fresh parsley

2 bay leaves

1 clove garlic, mashed

6 whole black peppercorns

1 tablespoon salt

1/4 teaspoon cayenne pepper

Serves 6

Prepare the Parsley-Lemon Butter, and hold aside warm. Wash and dry the sheepshead, rub inside and out with the lemon half, and hold aside.

In a wide, heavy skillet, bring the water to a boil with the lemon, onion, parsley, bay leaves, garlic, peppercorns, salt, and cayenne. Let boil for 3 minutes to allow the water to draw the flavor from the seasoning ingredients. Lower the heat to a simmer and lay in the sheepshead. Bring back to a simmer and poach for 30 minutes, or until the sheepshead is flaky when broken with a fork.

With two large spatulas, carefully remove the poached sheepshead, drain, and transfer to a warm platter. Bring the whole fish to the table to serve. Divide the top fillet into three portions, then remove the bones and serve up the bottom fillet in three portions. Spoon Parsley-Lemon Butter over each serving.

Parsley-Lemon Butter

1 1/2 sticks salted butter

Juice of 2 lemons

2 tablespoons chopped fresh parsley

In a small saucepan, melt the butter and stir in the lemon juice and chopped parsley. Serve warm.

267

Note: American eel, jolthead porgy, lookdown, red drum, spotfin flounder, and spotted eagle ray also work well with this recipe. Use 6 8-ounce pieces skinned and drawn American eel; 6 8-ounce skinned spotted eagle ray wing fillets; or 6 1-pound scaled and drawn whole lookdowns and spotfin flounders. The American eel and spotfin flounder require a 10 minute poaching time; the lookdown will take approximately 15 minutes. The fish should be completely cooked and flaky when broken with a fork.

Other Delicious Recipes for Sheepshead include:

Baked Sheepshead in Creole Court-Bouillon (see red drum, page 110)

Braised Sheepshead Burgundy-Style (see spotted sea trout, page 117)

Broiled Sheepshead with Poulette Sauce (see red porgy, page 260)

Ceviche of Sheepshead (see creolefish, page 28)

Cold Poached Sheepshead Fillets with Spicy Creole Mayonnaise (see red snapper, page 309)

Fried Sheepshead with Brown Shrimp Sauce (see white mullet, page 245)

Fried Sheepshead Fillets with Moulin Rouge Sauce (see scamp, page 56)

Sheepshead Garlic Soup (see skipjack tuna, page 223)

Sheepshead with Oyster and Crabmeat Sauce Gratiné (see pinfish, page 256)

Whole Baked Sheepshead with Chanterelles (see spotfin flounder, page 136)

Whole Baked Sheepshead with Spinach Stuffing (see jolthead porgy, page 250)

Whole Panfried Sheepshead with Peanut Sauce (see gaff-topsail catfish, page 78)

Southern Stingray

Group: Ray

Other common name(s):
Stingray
Stingaree

Latin name:
Dasyatis americana
Family Dasyatidae

Maximum length:
6 feet across (wing tip
to wing tip)

Maximum weight:
150 pounds

Cuts:
wing fillet

Meat characteristics:
white, delicate
low oil content

*Preferred cooking
methods:*
bake
poach
sauté
stew

Charcoal-Grilled Southern Stingray with Plantation Groundnut Sauce

Plantation Groundnut Sauce (recipe follows)
6 6- to 8-ounce pieces southern stingray wing fillet, skin on

Peanut oil for grilling
3 lemons, halved

Serves 6

Plantation Groundnut Sauce is an old Southern recipe. The groundnuts—so called because the nuts grow underground—are peanuts. The recipe was named before the term *peanut* was commonly adopted by Americans to refer to this popular nut.

Light the charcoal 1 hour before cooking. Make the Plantation Groundnut Sauce, and hold aside warm.

Using a chef's knife, scrape the stingray fillet pieces of any slick coating that may remain on the skin. Set aside.

When the coals are ready, brush the grill rack and the stingray fillets with peanut oil and grill the fillets for 8 minutes, turning once midway during the cooking.

Transfer the stingray fillets to a warm platter. Each diner can perform the remaining operation, or you can do it for everyone. Carefully lift away and discard the skin from the fillets and place each serving on a warm plate. Spoon Plantation Groundnut Sauce beside each fillet and serve, with lemon halves as garnish.

Plantation Groundnut Sauce

2 tablespoons peanut oil
1 large onion, chopped
3 medium tomatoes, diced
1 small eggplant, skinned and diced
2 large cloves garlic, minced

1 cup roasted shelled peanuts
1/4 cup water
2 teaspoons sugar
2 teaspoon cider vinegar
Salt and cayenne pepper

Heat the peanut oil in a skillet and sauté the onion until transparent. Add the tomatoes, eggplant, and garlic, cover, and simmer for about 20 minutes, or until the eggplant is completely cooked and beginning to break down into a mash.

Process the peanuts into a paste with the water and sugar in a blender or food processor. Add the peanut paste and the cider vinegar to the sauce and season to taste with salt and cayenne pepper. Cover and simmer very gently for another 10 minutes. Serve warm.

Note: Atlantic moonfish, gulf flounder, and yellowfin tuna are also excellent grilled this way. Use 6 6- to 8-ounce pieces fillet.

2 tablespoons olive oil

1 pound southern stingray wing fillet, skinned and diced

1 medium carrot, julienned

1 small green bell pepper, seeded and julienned

2 green onions, julienned

1 medium white onion, julienned

1 stalk celery, julienned

3 medium tomatoes, julienned

2 tablespoons all-purpose flour

1 tablespoon minced fresh parsley

1/2 teaspoon dried thyme

1 large bay leaf

2 garlic cloves, minced

2 tablespoons tomato paste

1/2 cup dry white wine

1 1/2 quarts fish stock (page 371)

Salt, freshly ground black pepper, and cayenne pepper

Serves 6

In a large saucepan or soup pot, heat the olive oil and sauté the diced southern stingray fillet with the carrot, green bell pepper, green onion, white onion, celery, and tomatoes for 2 minutes. Stir in the flour and cook together for 2 to 3 minutes. Stir in the parsley, thyme, bay leaf, garlic, tomato paste, white wine, and fish stock, and season with salt, freshly ground black pepper, and cayenne to taste. Bring the chowder to a boil, turn down the heat, and simmer for 7 minutes.

Serve immediately.

Note: Try this recipe with common jack, king mackerel, largetooth sawfish, pilot fish, rainbow runner, scalloped hammerhead shark, snook, swordfish, and tarpon. Use 1 pound skinned fillets, diced.

Other Delicious Recipes for Southern Stingray include:

Baked Canapé of Southern Stingray (see Atlantic spadefish, page 323)

Broiled Southern Stingray with Cilantro Butter (see weakfish, page 123)

Broiled Southern Stingray with Poulette Sauce (see red porgy, page 260)

Caribbean Southern Stingray Salad (see mutton snapper, page 305)

Creole Seafood Gumbo with Southern Stingray (see sailor's-choice, page 144)

Curried Fillets of Southern Stingray (see sailor's-choice, page 143)

Fillet of Southern Stingray with Browned Butter, Lemon Juice, and Caper Sauce (see blacktip shark, page 296)

Hot Southern Stingray and Artichoke Salad and Russian Dressing with Caviar (see largetooth sawfish, page 279)

Marinated Southern Stingray Salad with Giardeniera (see squirrelfish, page 329)

Sautéed Battered Southern Stingray Fillets with Lemon-Butter Sauce (see red snapper, page 311)

Steamed Southern Stingray with Cypriote Sauce (see scalloped hammerhead shark, page 284)

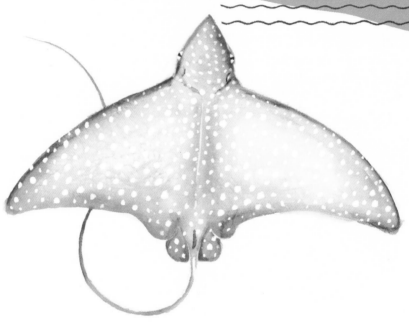

Spotted Eagle Ray

Group: Ray

Other common name(s):
  Stingray
  Eagle Ray
Latin name:
  Aetobatus narinari
  Family Myliobatidae
Maximum length:
  9 feet across (wing tip
  to wing tip)

Maximum weight:
  500 pounds
Cuts:
  wing fillet
Meat characteristics:
  white, delicate
  low oil content

Preferred cooking methods:
  fry
  poach
  steam
  stew

2 cups dry white wine

1 quart fish stock (page 371)

2 pounds spotted eagle ray wings, skinned and cut into 2-inch lengths

4 whole allspice

3 bay leaves

1/2 teaspoon dried thyme

1/4 teaspoon dried oregano

1 stick salted butter

3 onions, chopped

4 cloves garlic, minced

4 tablespoons all-purpose flour

Salt, freshly ground black pepper, and cayenne pepper

1 tablespoon minced fresh parsley

12 French bread croutons (page 370)

Serves 6

Pour the white wine and fish stock into a skillet and bring to a boil. Boil for 5 minutes, turn down to a simmer, and poach the eagle ray in the simmering liquid for 8 minutes. Remove the poached ray with a slotted spoon and hold aside warm, first trimming off and discarding any trailing pieces. Add the allspice, bay leaves, thyme, and oregano to the cooking liquid, bring to a boil, and reduce by half.

In another saucepan, melt the butter and sauté the onions and garlic until they begin to color. Whisk in the flour and continue cooking until lightly browned. Whisk 1 cup of the reduced white wine and fish stock into the roux mixture, then add the remaining liquid. Bring to a boil and let thicken. Season to taste with salt, black pepper, and cayenne and add the minced parsley.

Divide the croutons among six warm soup bowls, top with the hot spotted eagle ray, and ladle the sauce over all.

Note: This stew is also excellent with American eel, king mackerel, shortfin mako shark, and snook. Use 2 pounds skinned fillet cut into 1 x 2-inch strips.

2 1/4 pounds spotted eagle ray wing fillet,
    skinned
Juice of 1 lemon
12 strips bacon
6 metal skewers

2 teaspoons salt
1 teaspoon freshly ground white pepper
1 cup hot melted salted butter
3 lemons, halved

Serves 6

Cut the spotted eagle ray into thirty-six cubes to be skewered. Sprinkle them with lemon juice. Hold aside.

Cut the strips of bacon crosswise into three pieces each and cook in a wide, heavy skillet for 1 or 2 minutes, so that the bacon is still soft but has released some of its drippings. Remove the bacon to a plate to cool and reserve the pan drippings.

Wrap each spotted eagle ray cube with a piece of bacon and load six cubes onto each skewer. Combine the salt and pepper and sprinkle over all sides of the skewered fish.

Reheat the bacon drippings in the skillet and fry the skewered fish about 5 minutes on each side, or until the spotted eagle ray is lightly browned and the bacon is cooked.

Place onto warm plates, remove the skewers, top with the melted butter, and serve with the lemon wedges.

Note: Also try Atlantic sailfish, blackfin tuna, blue marlin, common jack, tilefish, wahoo, or yellowfin tuna. Use 2 1/4 pounds fillets or steaks.

Variations

(follow recipe exactly except for the following substitutions and additions):

Grilled Skewered Spotted Eagle Ray

Cook over a charcoal grill instead of on the stove. Do not precook the bacon; the drippings will baste the fish.

Other Delicious Recipes for Spotted Eagle Ray include:

Breaded Spotted Eagle Ray with Creole Tomato Sauce (see black grouper, page 47)

Broiled Spotted Eagle Ray with Creole Mustard and Chive Cream Sauce (see Atlantic sailfish, page 232)

Fillet of Spotted Eagle Ray with Browned Butter, Lemon Juice, and Caper Sauce (see blacktip shark, page 296)

Fried Spotted Eagle Ray with Black Anchovy Butter (see Atlantic bonito, page 212)

Matelote of Spotted Eagle Ray (see American eel, page 126)

Panfried Spotted Eagle Ray with Peanut Sauce (see gaff-topsail catfish, page 78)

Poached Spotted Eagle Ray with Parsley-Lemon Butter (see sheepshead, page 267)

Spotted Eagle Ray with Lime and Onion (see sand perch, page 34)

Spotted Eagle Ray Poached in Orange-Curry Marinade (see shortfin mako shark, page 291)

Spotted Eagle Ray Poached in Sherry (see snook, page 319)

White Bisque of Spotted Eagle Ray with Sherry (see largetooth sawfish, page 281)

Largetooth Sawfish

Group: Sawfish

Other common name(s):
  Sawfish
  Louisiana Sawfish
Latin name:
  Pristis perotetti
  Family Pristidae
Maximum length:
  20 feet

Maximum weight:
  800 pounds
Cuts:
  steak
  fillet
Meat characteristics:
  firm, medium-white
  medium oil content

Preferred cooking methods:
  broil
  fry
  grill
  sauté
  stew

Hot Largetooth Sawfish and Artichoke Salad and Russian Dressing with Caviar

1/2 cup pecan pieces
2 1/4 pounds largetooth sawfish fillet, skinned
1 teaspoon salt
1/2 teaspoon freshly ground black pepper
1/4 teaspoon cayenne pepper
2 cloves garlic, pressed

Russian Dressing with Caviar (recipe follows)
2 cups sliced cooked artichoke hearts (see Note)
6 large lettuce leaves
2 cups shredded Romaine or Boston lettuce
3 lemons, halved
2 tablespoons chopped fresh parsley

Serves 6

Preheat the oven to 400°. Spread the pecans on a baking sheet in a single layer and toast in the oven for 5 minutes, or until they begin to darken slightly. Hold aside.

Cut the largetooth sawfish fillet into strips the size of your finger and season them with salt, black pepper, cayenne, and pressed garlic. Hold aside while preparing the Russian Dressing.

In a wide, heavy skillet, combine the largetooth sawfish strips, sliced artichoke hearts, and Russian Dressing. Cook the mixture over medium heat for 4 minutes, or until the fish strips are completely opaque.

Place a lettuce leaf on each of six plates, fill the leaves with shredded lettuce, and spoon the hot largetooth sawfish mixture over the lettuce mounds. Sprinkle with the pecan pieces. Garnish the salads with the half lemons and chopped parsley.

2/3 cup Mayonnaise (see page 374)

1/3 cup fresh Tomato Catsup (page 290),
    or bottled catsup

2 tablespoons minced celery

2 tablespoons minced green onions

1 tablespoon minced fresh parsley

1/4 cup red or black lumpfish, or whitefish
    roe, or caviar

1/4 teaspoon freshly ground white pepper

In a small bowl, blend the mayonnaise together with the catsup. Add the celery, green onions, and parsley and blend all well together. Fold in the roe or caviar and continue to fold—carefully so as not to crush the fish eggs—until well mixed together. Season with white pepper to taste.

Notes: You can use artichoke hearts from a jar.

Bluefish, mutton snapper, snook, southern stingray, spotted jewfish, and yellowfin tuna are also excellent prepared this way. For the southern stingray, use skinned wing fillet.

1 stick salted butter
1/2 cup all-purpose flour
6 green onions, chopped
1 rib celery, minced
1 1/2 quarts hot fish stock (page 371), or
    shellfish stock (page 372)
1 pound largetooth sawfish fillet, skinned
    and chopped

1 cup whipping cream
1/2 cup dry sherry
1 bay leaf
1/4 teaspoon dried marjoram
Salt, freshly ground white pepper, and
    cayenne pepper
1 tablespoon minced fresh parsley

Serves 6

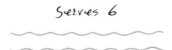

In a large saucepan, melt the butter and blend in the flour. Cook together for 2 minutes without coloring. Add the chopped green onions and celery and cook together for 2 minutes more. Whisk in the hot stock and simmer for 5 minutes. Add the chopped largetooth sawfish fillet, cream, sherry, bay leaf, and marjoram, and season to taste with salt, white pepper, and cayenne. Bring the bisque to a simmer and cook for 20 minutes. Adjust the seasoning if necessary.

Serve the bisque with a sprinkling of minced parsley on top.

Note: Atlantic bonito, blackfin tuna, blacktip shark, common jack, gray triggerfish, greater amberjack, scalloped hammerhead shark, skipjack tuna, and spotted eagle ray can also be used with this recipe.

Other Delicious Recipes for Largetooth Sawfish include:

Bahamian Largetooth Sawfish Chowder (see southern stingray, page 372)

Baked Crabmeat-Stuffed Largetooth Sawfish Fillet (greater amberjack, page 168)

Baked Largetooth Sawfish with Bacon and Onion (see red grouper, page 52)

Charcoal-Grilled Largetooth Sawfish with Garlic Sauce (see blue marlin, page 236)

Grilled Largetooth Sawfish with Criolla Sauce (see black sea bass, page 25)

Hot Largetooth Sawfish and Mushroom Salad with Dijon Mustard Dressing (see snook, page 320)

Largetooth Sawfish and Potato Salad with Chive Vinaigrette (see yellowfin tuna, page 227)

Largetooth Sawfish with Puerto Rican Sauce (see swordfish, page 333)

Panfried Largetooth Sawfish with Antiboise Sauce (see blacktip shark, page 294)

Sautéed Steak of Largetooth Sawfish with Crabmeat and Butter (see common dolphin, page 90)

Sautéed Largetooth Sawfish Steaks Marseilles-Style (see rainbow runner, page 194)

Tamales with Largetooth Sawfish and Roasted Tomato and Chili Sauce (see common jack, page 156)

Scalloped Hammerhead Shark

Group: Hammerhead Shark

Other common name(s):
Hammerhead

Latin name:
Sphyrna lewini
Family Sphyrnidae

Maximum length:
13 feet 9 inches

Maximum weight:
225 pounds

Cuts:
steak
fillet

Meat characteristics:
firm, white
medium oil content

Preferred cooking methods:
broil
fry
grill
steam

Cypriote Sauce (recipe follows)
Water
6 1-inch-thick 6- to 8-ounce pieces
scalloped hammerhead shark fillet

Salt and freshly ground white pepper
Juice of 1 lemon
2 tablespoons chopped fresh parsley

Serves 6

Prepare the Cypriote Sauce and refrigerate for at least 1 hour.

Pour water to about a 1-inch depth in a saucepan large enough to hold your shark fillet pieces in a steamer basket or colander. Try out the basket or colander in the pan to be sure that the water does not come into it from the bottom. Cover the pan and bring the water to a boil.

Rub the shark fillet pieces with salt, white pepper, and lemon juice. Lay them in the colander or steamer basket and place it into the boiling water. Cover and steam for 10 minutes.

Remove the colander from the pot and transfer the fish to warm plates. Garnish with the chopped parsley and serve the Cypriote Sauce on the side.

Cypriote Sauce

1/2 cup Tomato Sauce (page 179)
2 large hard-boiled eggs, shelled
2 anchovy fillets

1 cup Mayonnaise (page 374)
1/4 teaspoon ground fennel seed
Salt (optional)

In a small saucepan, simmer the Tomato Sauce until it is reduced by half. Remove from the heat to cool.

Sieve the hard-boiled eggs, or mince them very finely. Mash the anchovies or finely mince them.

In a small bowl, blend the mayonnaise together with the cooled reduced Tomato Sauce. Add the eggs, anchovies, and ground fennel seed. Season with additional salt, if desired.

Cover tightly and store in the refrigerator for at least an hour, or overnight if possible, to allow the flavors to meld.

Note: Snook, southern stingray, and striped bass also work well in this recipe. For the southern stingray, use skinned wing fillet.

2 pounds scalloped hammerhead shark fillet or steak, skinned and cut into 3/4-inch cubes

2 teaspoons salt

1 teaspoon freshly ground black pepper

1/2 teaspoon cayenne pepper

1 cup all-purpose flour

1/2 pound bacon, cut crosswise into 1/2-inch pieces

1/2 cup peanut oil

2 medium onions, chopped

1 entire head garlic, peeled and chopped

2 pounds unpeeled potatoes, scrubbed and sliced into 1/4-inch-thick rounds

Salt and freshly ground black pepper to taste

2 tablespoons chopped fresh parsley

Serves 6

Rub the scalloped hammerhead shark cubes with the salt, pepper, and cayenne and dredge in the flour. Hold aside.

Heat the bacon in a wide, heavy skillet with the peanut oil to render the fat. When it is cooked but not yet crisp, remove it to a side dish with a slotted spoon. Add the scalloped hammerhead pieces to the fat and fry about 8 minutes, until golden and completely cooked. Remove the fish, drain on absorbent paper, and hold aside.

Add the onions, garlic, and potatoes to the hot fat and cook them together until the potatoes are cooked through, but not mushy. Don't break up the potato slices when cooking. When the potatoes are almost done, spoon off the excess fat and season with salt and pepper.

Return the bacon and the scalloped hammerhead shark to the skillet. Cover and simmer together on low heat for about 5 minutes more. Check the seasonings.

Serve sprinkled with the chopped parsley.

Note: Also try blackfin tuna, blue marlin, hard-tail jack, king mackerel, snook, tarpon, or wahoo with this recipe.

Variations
(follow recipe exactly except for the following substitutions and additions):

with Chayote, Bacon, and Garlic
In place of the potatoes, use 4 chayote (also called mirlitons) skinned, seeded, and diced. (If chayote is unavailable, you can use yellow squash.)

with Pumpkin, Bacon, and Garlic
Replace the potatoes with 2 pounds pumpkin meat sliced into 1 x 1 x 1/4-inch-thick squares.

with White Beans, Bacon, and Garlic
Replace the potatoes with 4 cups cooked white beans (great northerns).

with Zucchini, Bacon, and Garlic
Substitute 2 pounds of zucchini, sliced into 1/4-inch-thick rounds, for the potatoes.

Other Delicious Recipes for Scalloped Hammerhead Shark include:

Bahamian Scalloped Hammerhead Shark Chowder (see southern stingray, page 272)
Caribbean Scalloped Hammerhead Shark Salad (see mutton snapper, page 305)
Étouffée of Scalloped Hammerhead Shark (see blackfin tuna, page 218)
Hot Scalloped Hammerhead Shark and Mushroom Salad with Dijon Mustard Dressing (see snook, page 320)
Scalloped Hammerhead Shark Smothered in Jalapeño-Tequila Sauce (see common jack, page 158)
Scalloped Hammerhead Shark-Stuffed Hand Tortillas (see bluefish, page 68)
Steamed Scalloped Hammerhead Shark with Chivry Butter (see bonefish, page 72)
White Bisque of Scalloped Hammerhead Shark with Sherry (see largetooth sawfish, page 281)
Wood-Grilled Scalloped Hammerhead Shark Steaks with Sweet Herbs (see king mackerel, page 197)

Shortfin Mako Shark

Group: Mackerel Shark

Other common name(s):	Maximum weight:	Preferred cooking
Mako	1,000 pounds	methods:
Latin name:	*Cuts:*	broil
Isurus oxyrinchus	steak	fry
Family Lamnidae	fillet	poach
Maximum length:	*Meat characteristics:*	sauté
12 feet	firm, medium-white	stew
	low oil content	

Soda-Fried Shortfin Mako Shark "Chips" with Fresh Tomato Catsup

1 1/2 cups all-purpose flour, sifted
1 1/2 teaspoons baking soda
1 1/2 teaspoons salt
1 teaspoon sugar
1/2 teaspoon cayenne pepper
1 egg white, well beaten

1 1/2 cups cold water
Fresh Tomato Catsup (recipe follows)
1 1/2 pounds shortfin mako shark fillet
Peanut oil for frying
3 lemons, quartered

Serves 6

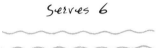

Combine the flour with the baking soda, salt, sugar, and cayenne. In a separate bowl, whisk the well-beaten egg white together with the cold water. Whisk in the flour mixture. Cover the bowl and refrigerate for 15 minutes to set the batter.

Prepare the Fresh Tomato Catsup and hold aside. Pat the fish fillets dry and slice them diagonally into 1/2-inch-thick "chips."

When you are ready to cook the fish chips, heat 3/4 inch of oil (enough to submerge the "chips") in a wide, heavy skillet to 375°. Whisk the chilled batter together briefly. Dip the fish chips in the batter and carefully immerse them in the heated oil. Do not crowd the pan. Fry only about 2 minutes, or until the chips are golden brown and completely opaque. Use a slotted spoon to transfer the chips to drain on absorbent paper.

Serve on warm dinner plates with Fresh Tomato Catsup and lemon quarters.

Fresh Tomato Catsup

6 large very ripe tomatoes
1 rib celery, stringed and chopped
1/2 small red bell pepper, seeded and
    chopped
1 medium onion, chopped
1 hot pepper (cayenne, tabasco, or other),
    seeded and minced
2 bay leaves
8 whole black peppercorns

6 whole allspice
6 whole coriander
1 teaspoon mustard seeds
1 teaspoon minced fresh ginger
1/8 teaspoon ground mace
1/8 teaspoon ground cardamom
1/4 cup cider vinegar
1 1/2 tablespoons brown sugar
1 1/2 teaspoons salt

Chop the tomatoes finely, or puree them in a food mill, reserving all juices and jelly released during the process. Transfer the raw tomato puree to a saucepan and bring to a gentle simmer. Cook for 5 minutes and remove from the heat to cool. Strain the cooled puree through cheesecloth or a fine sieve. You should end up with 3 cups puree.

Combine the tomato puree and all the remaining ingredients in a heavy saucepan. Bring to a boil, turn down to a simmer, and cook, covered, for about 30 minutes. Uncover the pan and continue simmering until the catsup is reduced to half. Strain the sauce, adjust the seasonings if desired, and transfer to a covered container or bottle until ready for use.

The fresh catsup can be served hot, room temperature, or cold, but must be stored in the refrigerator, where it will keep for several weeks in a tightly capped jar.

Note: This soda-fry recipe is also excellent with common dolphin, Spanish mackerel, and spotted jewfish.

Orange-Curry Marinade (recipe follows)

6 8-ounce pieces shortfin mako shark fillet

Hot sauce, preferably Caribbean-style
habañero pepper sauce

Serves 6

Prepare the Orange-Curry Marinade in a skillet or poaching pan wide enough to hold the fish. Add the fish and poach at a simmer for 10 minutes, or until the fish is cooked completely through.

Transfer the poached fish to wide soup bowls, cutting it in half crosswise if necessary for the fit, and pour the cooking marinade over it. Serve, passing the hot sauce as condiment.

Orange-Curry Marinade

1 1/2 cup quarts fish stock (page 371), or
water

2 cups freshly squeezed orange juice

1/4 cup freshly squeezed lime juice

1 small hot pepper, minced

2 large cloves garlic, minced

1 large onion, chopped

6 green onions, chopped

4 whole cloves

4 whole allspice

4 bay leaves

1 tablespoon salt

2 teaspoons curry powder

Combine all the marinade ingredients in a pan and simmer for 10 minutes. Adjust the seasonings.

Note: This recipe is also excellent with blue marlin, king mackerel, speckled hind, spotted eagle ray, and wahoo. For the king mackerel, you may use either fillet or steak. For the sand perch, use 6 1-pound scaled and drawn whole fish and increase the poaching time to 20 minutes. For the spotted eagle ray, use 6 8-ounce pieces skinned wing fillet.

Variations: Shortfin mako shark is also excellent poached in Lime and Onion Marinade (page 34), Red Wine Marinade (page 35), Sherry Marinade (page 319), or White Wine Marinade (page 35).

Other Delicious Recipes for Shortfin Mako Shark include:

Broiled Shortfin Mako Shark Steaks with Creole Mustard and Chive Cream Sauce (see Atlantic sailfish, page 232)

Ceviche of Shortfin Mako Shark (see creolefish, page 28)

Cold Poached Shortfin Mako Shark Ravigote with Boiled New Potatoes (see spotted jewfish, page 43)

Creole Étouffée of Shortfin Mako Shark (see Atlantic sailfish, page 230)

Matelote of Shortfin Mako Shark (see American eel, page 126)

Shortfin Mako Shark Garlic Soup (see skipjack tuna, page 223)

Shortfin Mako Shark Poached in Sherry (see snook, page 319)

Shortfin Mako Shark with Puerto Rican Sauce (see swordfish, page 333)

Shortfin Mako Shark Smothered in Jalapeño-Tequila Sauce (see common jack, page 158)

Shortfin Mako Shark Stew with White Wine (see spotted eagle ray, page 275)

Steamed Shortfin Mako Shark with Aioli Sauce (see squirrelfish, page 328)

Steamed Shortfin Mako Shark Fillets with Espagnole Mayonnaise (see mutton snapper, page 303)

Blacktip Shark

Group: Requiem Shark

Other common name(s):
  Shark
  Blacktip
Latin name:
  Carcharhinus limbatus
  Family
  Carcharhinidae
Maximum length:
  8 feet 3 inches

Maximum weight:
  190 pounds
Cuts:
  steak
  fillet
Meat characteristics:
  firm, white
  medium-to-high oil
  content

Preferred cooking methods:
  broil
  fry
  grill
  poach
  sauté

Antiboise Sauce (recipe follows)
2 tablespoons light-flavored olive oil
2 tablespoons salted butter
Salt

6 6- to 8-ounce pieces blacktip shark fillet
3/4 cup all-purpose flour
Juice of 2 lemons

Serves 6

Prepare the Antiboise Sauce, and refrigerate for at least 1 hour. Heat a large skillet or sauté pan and add the olive oil and butter. Lightly salt the shark fillet pieces and dredge them in flour, shaking away any excess.

When the oil and butter are hot, lay the prepared fish pieces in the pan and cook for about 5 minutes. Carefully turn the fish pieces over, cover the pan, and continue cooking for another 3 minutes or so.

Transfer the shark to warm plates. Stir the lemon juice into the Antiboise Sauce and serve on the side.

Antiboise Sauce

1 cup Mayonnaise (page 374)
2 tablespoons tomato paste
2 teaspoons anchovy paste, or finely
  minced anchovy

1/2 teaspoon dried tarragon, or 1 1/2
  teaspoons chopped fresh or vinegar-
  packed tarragon leaves

In a small bowl, combine the mayonnaise thoroughly with the tomato paste, anchovy paste, and tarragon. Cover tightly or transfer to a jar and refrigerate for an hour or so before using to allow the flavors to meld together. (If you are using dried tarragon, it would be best to allow the sauce to chill overnight to give the flavor of the herb more time to expand.)

Note: Greater amberjack, largetooth sawfish, swordfish, and yellowfin tuna are also excellent sautéed this way.

Fillet of Blacktip Shark with Browned Butter, Lemon Juice, and Caper Sauce

6 6- to 8-ounce pieces blacktip shark fillet
Salt and freshly ground black pepper
1 stick salted butter
2 tablespoons freshly squeezed lemon juice
   (see Note)

1/4 cup capers
2 tablespoons chopped fresh parsley

Serves 6

Sprinkle the blacktip shark fillet pieces liberally with salt and freshly ground black pepper. In a wide, heavy skillet, melt the butter and heat until it begins to color. Cook the fish fillets for 15 minutes, turning once, until opaque all the way through. Transfer the fillets to warm plates and hold them in a warm oven.

To the remaining butter in the skillet, add the lemon juice and capers. Heat together for a minute.

To serve, spoon the sauce over the blacktip shark fillets and garnish with the chopped parsley.

Notes: The lemon juice can be replaced with a vinegar of your choice or with lime juice.

Hard-tail jack, rainbow runner, spotted eagle ray, spotted jewfish, southern stingray, swordfish, and yellowfin tuna also work wonderfully with this recipe. For the spotted eagle ray and southern stingray, use 6 6- to 8-ounce pieces skinned wing fillet.

Other Delicious Recipes for Blacktip Shark include:

Blackened Blacktip Shark Steaks (see blue marlin, page 235)

Blacktip Shark Chowder with Potatoes and Tomatoes (see greater amberjack, page 170)

Blacktip Shark Garlic Soup (see skipjack tuna, page 223)

Blacktip Shark Poached in Sherry (see snook, page 319)

Blacktip Shark and Tomato Bisque (see yellowfin tuna, page 226)

Charcoal-Grilled Blacktip Shark with Garlic Sauce (see blue marlin, page 236)

Creole Bisque of Blacktip Shark (see tilefish, page 348)

Poached Blacktip Shark Fillets with Drawn Butter (see king mackerel, page 199)

Ragout of Blacktip Shark au Gratin (see swordfish, page 332)

Tamales with Blacktip Shark and Roasted Tomato and Chili Sauce (see common jack, page 156)

White Bisque of Blacktip Shark with Sherry (see largetooth sawfish, page 281)

Wood-Grilled Blacktip Shark Steaks with Achiote-Garlic Paste (see black grouper, page 49)

Dog Snapper

Group: Snapper

Other common name(s):
Snapper

Latin name:
Lutjanus jocu
Family Lutjanidae

Maximum length:
2 feet 5 inches

Maximum weight:
30 pounds

Cuts:
whole (small)
steak
fillet

Meat characteristics:
tender, white, flaky
low oil content

Preferred cooking methods:
bake
fry
poach
steam

1/2 cup peanut oil
2 teaspoons salt
1 teaspoon freshly ground white pepper
6 small soft-shell crabs, dressed
6 6- to 8-ounce dog snapper fillets

1 cup Drawn Butter (page 199; see Note)
2 tablespoons chopped fresh parsley
3 lemons, halved

Serves 6

Blend the oil with the salt and pepper and rub it onto the crabs and dog snapper fillets.

Heat a large, heavy skillet to very hot and cook the crabs and dog snapper fillets in the dry skillet for about 3 minutes on each side.

Place the cooked snapper fillets on warm plates, top each with a crab, and spoon on the drawn butter. Sprinkle with the chopped parsley and garnish with lemon halves.

Notes: For 1 cup Drawn Butter, you will need to start out with 2 1/2 sticks salted butter.

This recipe is also excellent with Florida pompano, red drum, red snapper, and spotted sea trout.

Peanut oil for frying
1 large egg
1 cup milk
1/2 cup corn flour (see Note)
1 tablespoon salt

1/2 teaspoon freshly ground black pepper
1/2 teaspoon cayenne pepper
6 6- to 8-ounce pieces dog snapper fillet
3 lemons, halved
1 1/2 cups Tartar Sauce (page 375)

Serves 6

Heat 1/2 inch oil in a wide, heavy skillet to 350°. In a bowl, beat the egg together with the milk to make an egg wash. In another bowl or dish, combine the cornmeal with the salt, black pepper, and cayenne.

Dredge the dog snapper fillets in the seasoned corn flour, dip in the egg wash, and dredge again in the corn flour. Shake any excess flour from the fish and fry, without crowding the pan, for 4 minutes on each side, or until the coating is crisp and golden, and the flesh of the fish is flaky all the way through when broken with a fork. Drain on absorbent paper.

Serve on warm plates with lemon halves and Tartar Sauce.

Notes: Corn flour is often used in the frying of seafood rather than white flour. It can be bought as plain corn flour in specialty stores or as corn masa or "masa harina" in stores that sell Mexican or Central and South American food products. It is the flour that corn tortillas are made from. It can also be gotten in the form of "fish-fry," which is corn flour that is already seasoned with salt and pepper.

Try this recipe with great barracuda, permit, striped mullet, tilefish, and white grunt.

Variations: In place of corn flour, use one of the following: 1 cup cornstarch, 1 1/2 cups French bread crumbs, 1 1/2 cups seasoned Italian bread crumbs, or 1 1/2 cups rolled cracker crumbs.

Other Delicious Recipes for Dog Snapper include:

Baked Crabmeat-Stuffed Dog Snapper (see gulf kingfish, page 106)

Baked Dog Snapper with Apples and Onions (see hogfish, page 368)

Baked Dog Snapper with Bacon and Onion (see red grouper, page 52)

Breaded Fillets of Dog Snapper with Green Mayonnaise (see red drum, page 109)

Ceviche of Dog Snapper (see creolefish, page 28)

Dog Snapper Fillets with Artichokes and Mushrooms in Brown Lemon-Butter Sauce (see black drum, page 100)

Dog Snapper with Pecans (see lookdown, page 181)

Grilled Dog Snapper with Béarnaise Sauce (see queen triggerfish, page 358)

Poached Dog Snapper Fillets with Creamy Pimiento-Butter Sauce (see ling cobia, page 85)

Ragout of Dog Snapper au Gratin (see swordfish, page 332)

Steamed Dog Snapper with Aioli Sauce (see squirrelfish, page 328)

Mutton Snapper

Group: Snapper

Other common name(s):
Snapper

Latin name:
Lutjanus analis
Family Lutjanidae

Maximum length:
2 feet 6 inches

Maximum weight:
25 pounds

Cuts:
whole (small)
steak
fillet

Meat characteristics:
tender, white, flaky
low oil content

Preferred cooking methods:
bake
fry
sauté
steam

Steamed Mutton Snapper Fillets with Espagnole Mayonnaise

Espagnole Mayonnaise (recipe follows)
1/4 cup chopped Spanish olives
1 tablespoon balsamic vinegar
6 6- to 8-ounce mutton snapper fillets

Salt and freshly ground white pepper
Juice of 1 lemon
18 whole Spanish olives
6 sprigs fresh parsley

Serves 6

Prepare the Espagnole Mayonnaise and combine with the chopped Spanish olives and the balsamic vinegar. Transfer to a covered container and refrigerate until ready for use.

Rub the mutton snapper fillets lightly with salt, white pepper, and lemon juice. Arrange the fillets in a steamer basket or colander, and place in a saucepan. Add enough water to come to the bottom of the colander, yet not touch the fish. Remove the basket of fish and bring the water to a boil. Return the basket of fish to the pot of steaming water, cover (with foil if there is no top to fit), and steam the fish for 8 minutes.

Carefully transfer the steamed snapper fillets to warm dinner plates and garnish with the whole Spanish olives and the parsley sprigs. Serve the Espagnole Mayonnaise on the side.

Espagnole Mayonnaise

1 cup Mayonnaise (page 374), or other
   rich mayonnaise

1 cup cold Espagnole Sauce (page 361)
Salt and freshly ground black pepper

Combine the mayonnaise with the Espagnole Sauce. Season to taste with salt and pepper if desired. Cover tightly and refrigerate until ready for use.

303

Note: Black grouper, sailor's-choice, shortfin mako shark, Spanish mackerel, and swordfish also work well in this recipe.

2 quarts water, or enough to cover fish
   (about 1 inch deep in skillet)
1 lemon, thinly sliced
1 medium onion, thinly sliced
2 sprigs fresh parsley
2 bay leaves
1 clove garlic, mashed
6 whole black peppercorns
2 teaspoons salt
1/4 teaspoon cayenne pepper
6 6-ounce pieces mutton snapper fillet,
   skinned

Dressing:
1 egg
1/2 cup cider vinegar

1 1/2 cups olive oil
1 1/2 teaspoons sugar
1 teaspoon salt
1/2 teaspoon dry mustard
1/4 teaspoon cayenne pepper
1/2 teaspoon freshly ground black pepper

Juice of 1 lemon
1 head romaine lettuce, washed and
   prepped
2 ripe avocados, peeled and sliced
2 grapefruits, peeled and sectioned
Black olives

Serves 6

In a wide skillet, bring the water to a boil with the lemon, onion, parsley, bay leaves, garlic, peppercorns, salt, and cayenne. Let boil for 3 minutes to allow the water to draw the flavor from the seasoning ingredients. Lower the heat to a simmer and lay in the mutton snapper fillets. Poach for 10 minutes, or until the fish is flaky when broken with a fork.

With a long spatula, carefully remove the fillets from the water and drain. Cover and chill.

Process the dressing ingredients in a blender until lightly emulsified. Cover and refrigerate until ready to serve.

In a bowl, break the cold poached mutton snapper apart into bite-sized pieces. Sprinkle with the lemon juice, cover, and hold aside.

Line six plates with the lettuce leaves. Place the avocado slices and grapefruit sections in a star pattern over the lettuce. Spoon the mutton snapper meat into the center and pour the dressing over the salads. Garnish the center with black olives.

Note: Atlantic moonfish, black drum, ling cobia, red grouper, scalloped hammerhead shark, skipjack tuna, southern stingray, and swordfish also work wonderfully with this recipe. For the southern stingray, use skinned wing fillet.

Variations
(follow recipe exactly except for the following substitutions and additions):

Mutton Snapper Salad with Corn and Orange and a Curry Vinaigrette
Omit the sugar from the dressing and replace the cayenne pepper with 1 teaspoon curry powder and the black pepper with 1/2 teaspoon freshly ground white pepper. In place of the avocados and grapefruits, use 3 ears cooked corn (kernels removed from the cob) and 2 large oranges, peeled and sectioned. To assemble the salads, toss the fish pieces, corn, and orange sections with the curry vinaigrette in a bowl before spooning onto the lettuce leaves.

Mutton Snapper Salad with Orange and Cucumber and a Lime Dressing
Use 1/2 cup freshly squeezed lime juice instead of lemon, 1 1/2 cups corn or peanut oil instead of olive oil, 1 head bibb lettuce rather than romaine, with 3 large peeled and sectioned oranges and 2 peeled and sliced cucumbers instead of avocados and grapefruit. Sprinkle 1 tablespoon lime juice on the fish and use the rest in the dressing. To assemble the salads, place the cucumber slices and orange sections in a star pattern over the lettuce, spoon the fish into the center, pour the lime vinaigrette over the salad, and garnish the center with cherry tomatoes.

Mutton Snapper Salad with Tomato
Use 2 tablespoons freshly squeezed lemon juice on the fish. Substitute 1/2 cup red wine vinegar for the cider vinegar in the dressing and omit the sugar. Replace the

avocados and grapefruit with 6 ripe tomatoes, sliced into 4 rounds each. When assembling the salads, arrange the tomato slices in overlapping circles over the lettuce.

Mutton Snapper Salad with Tomato and Red Onion and a Citronette Dressing
Substitute 1 head butternut lettuce for the romaine and 3 ripe tomatoes sliced into 4 rounds each and 3 small red onions, peeled and thinly sliced, for the avocados and grapefruit. Use 1/2 cup freshly squeezed lemon juice. Sprinkle 1 tablespoon lemon juice on the fish and use the rest in the dressing. To assemble the salads, arrange the tomato rounds and red onion slices in an overlapping circular pattern over the lettuce and spoon the fish into the center. Pour the Citronette Dressing over the salads and garnish with green olives.

Other Delicious Recipes for Mutton Snapper include:

Breaded Mutton Snapper with Creole Tomato Sauce (see black grouper, page 47)
Fried Mutton Snapper with Brown Shrimp Sauce (see white mullet, page 245)
Hot Mutton Snapper and Artichoke Salad and Russian Dressing with Caviar
    (largetooth sawfish, page 279)
Hot Mutton Snapper and Mushroom Salad with Dijon Mustard Dressing (see
    snook, page 320)
Mutton Snapper with Creole Sauce Piquante (see wahoo, page 209)
Mutton Snapper Fillets in Saffron-White Wine Sauce (see tarpon, page 338)
Mutton Snapper with Oyster and Crabmeat Sauce Gratiné (see pinfish, page 256)
Mutton Snapper and Potato Salad with Chive Vinaigrette (see yellowfin tuna,
    page 227)
Poached Mutton Snapper Fillets with Hollandaise Sauce (see striped bass,
    page 63)
Whole Baked Mutton Snapper with Chanterelles (see spotfin flounder, page 136)
Whole Baked Mutton Snapper with Spinach Stuffing (see jolthead porgy, page 250)
Whole Steamed Mutton Snapper Marinière (see weakfish, page 122)

Red Snapper

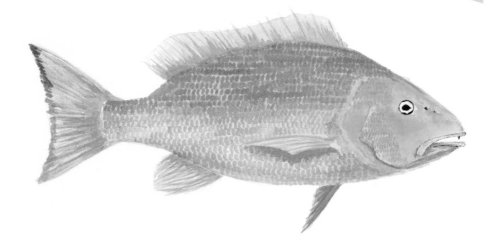

Group: Snapper

Other common name(s):
  Snapper
Latin name:
  Lutjanus campechanus
  Family Lutjanidae
Maximum length:
  2 feet 6 inches

Maximum weight:
  25 pounds
Cuts:
  whole (small)
  steak
  fillet
Meat characteristics:
  tender, white, flaky
  low oil content

Preferred cooking methods:
  bake
  poach
  sauté
  stew

1 1/2 quarts water, or enough to cover fish (about 1 inch deep in pan)
1 cup dry white wine
1 small onion, thinly sliced
1 small green bell pepper, seeded and thinly sliced
4 sprigs fresh parsley
1 tablespoon salt

1/2 teaspoon cayenne pepper
6 whole allspice
4 bay leaves
6 6- to 8-ounce red snapper fillets, skinned
Spicy Creole Mayonnaise (recipe follows)
3 lemons, halved

Serves 6

Pour the water into a large, wide saucepan and add the wine, onion, bell pepper, and parsley sprigs. Season with the salt and cayenne and add the allspice and bay leaves. Bring the liquid to a boil, cover, and boil for about 5 minutes to allow the ingredients to release their flavor into the liquid.

Remove the cover and bring down to a simmer. Lay the red snapper fillets into the liquid, bring back to a gentle simmer, and cook for about 8 minutes, or until the flesh of a fillet flakes apart when pierced with the tines of a fork. Carefully lift the fillets onto a platter. Allow the fillets and the poaching liquor to come to room temperature.

When the poaching liquor and the fillets are cool, transfer the fillets to a pan in which they will fit without crowding. Add enough poaching liquor to cover. Cover the pan with a lid or foil and refrigerate for 6 hours or overnight. Prepare the Spicy Creole Mayonnaise and refrigerate.

To serve, remove the cold fillets from the now-thickened liquid and place them on individual plates. Nap with the Spicy Creole Mayonnaise, garnish with lemon halves, and serve.

Spicy Creole Mayonnaise

2 whole large egg yolks
1/2 teaspoon salt
1/4 teaspoon freshly ground white pepper
1/2 teaspoon cayenne pepper

2 tablespoons tarragon vinegar
1 cup light-flavored olive oil
1/4 cup Creole mustard

In a bowl, beat the egg yolks, salt, white pepper, and cayenne together with 1 tablespoon of the tarragon vinegar. Briskly beat in the olive oil, 1 teaspoon at a time, until you have added 1/4 cup and the mixture is beginning to emulsify. Continue beating in the oil 1 tablespoon at a time until you have added 1/2 cup.

Now add the remaining tablespoon tarragon vinegar and beat in the rest of the oil 1 tablespoon at a time. Fold in the Creole mustard.

Cover tightly and refrigerate until ready to use.

Note: Black drum, red grouper, sheepshead, spotted sea trout, and striped bass are also excellent prepared this way.

Variations: Cold Poached Red Snapper Fillets are also delicious napped with Cocktail Sauce (page 375), Moulin Rouge Sauce (page 56), Sweet Mustard and Egg Sauce (page 254), Tartar Sauce (page 375), or Two Sisters Sauce (page 184).

Sautéed Battered Red Snapper Fillets with Lemon-Butter Sauce

Batter:
1 cup milk
2 whole eggs
1 teaspoon salt
1/2 teaspoon freshly ground white pepper

3 sticks salted butter
6 6-ounce red snapper fillets, skinned
3/4 cup all-purpose flour
1/2 cup freshly squeezed lemon juice
2 tablespoons minced fresh parsley

Serves 6

In a mixing bowl, make the batter by combining the milk, eggs, salt, and pepper.

Melt the butter in a wide, heavy skillet. Dredge the red snapper fillets in the flour, dip in the batter, and dredge in the flour again. Sauté in the hot butter until golden brown on each side, about 6 minutes altogether.

Place the cooked red snapper fillets on warm dinner plates. Pour the lemon juice into the pan with the liquids and heat for a moment. Spoon the sauce over the red snapper fillets and serve, garnished with minced parsley.

Note: Try this recipe with Atlantic threadfin, greater amberjack, ling cobia, queen triggerfish, southern stingray, and spotted sea trout. For the southern stingray, use skinned wing fillets.

311

Other Delicious Recipes for Red Snapper include:

Baked Crabmeat-Stuffed Red Snapper (see gulf kingfish, page 106)

Baked Red Snapper in Creole Court-Bouillon (see red drum, page 110)

Braised Red Snapper Burgundy-Style (see spotted sea trout, page 117)

Grilled Red Snapper Andalouse (see white grunt, page 149)

Red Snapper Chowder with Potatoes and Tomatoes (see greater amberjack, page 170)

Red Snapper Fillets Florentine (see tilefish, page 346)

Red Snapper Fillets with Lobster-Browned Butter Sauce (see gulf flounder, page 132)

Red Snapper Fillets Stuffed with Shrimp Soufflé (see spotfin flounder, page 135)

Red Snapper with Oyster and Crabmeat Sauce Gratiné (see pinfish, page 256)

Red Snapper and Potato Salad with Chive Vinaigrette (see yellowfin tuna, page 227)

Red Snapper with Seafood-White Wine Sauce Gratiné (see white mullet, page 243)

Skillet-Grilled Red Snapper Fillets Pontchartrain (see dog snapper, page 299)

Whole Baked Red Snapper with Spinach Stuffing (see jolthead porgy, page 250)

Yellowtail Snapper

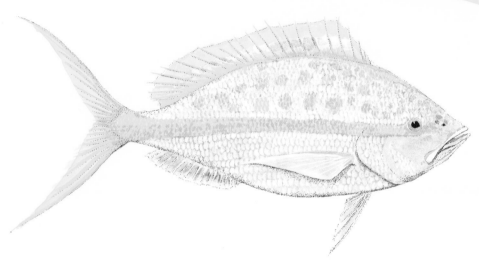

Group: Snapper

Other common name(s):
  Yellowtail
  Snapper

Latin name:
  Ocyurus chrysurus
  Family Lutjanidae

Maximum length:
  2 feet 6 inches

Maximum weight:
  7 pounds

Cuts:
  whole
  steak
  fillet

Meat characteristics:
  tender, white, flaky
  low oil content

Preferred cooking methods:
  bake
  fry
  sauté

3 cups Mornay Sauce (recipe follows)
6 6-ounce yellowtail snapper fillets
Salt and freshly ground white pepper
1/2 cup dry white wine
2 bay leaves

4 French shallots, minced
Parchment or aluminum foil
2 tablespoons softened salted butter
3/4 cup grated Gruyère cheese

Serves 6

Season the yellowtail snapper fillets with salt and white pepper.

Heat the wine in a heavy, wide skillet with the bay leaves and shallots. When it boils, add the snapper, cover the fish with a piece of parchment or foil, and then cover the pan. Simmer for about 5 minutes.

Butter six warm ovenproof plates. Carefully drain the cooked fillets, reserving the liquid, and transfer to the plates.

Reduce the remaining liquids by half. Prepare the Mornay Sauce, whisk the reduced liquids into it, and nap the fillets. Sprinkle with the Gruyère cheese and place the dishes under a broiler to melt the cheese and lightly brown the sauce.

Serve immediately.

Mornay Sauce

1 cup reduced fish stock (page 372)
2 cups Béchamel Sauce (page 374)
2 egg yolks
1/4 cup heavy cream

1/2 cup grated Parmesan cheese
1/2 cup grated Gruyère cheese
2 tablespoons salted butter

Combine the fish stock with the Béchamel Sauce and simmer for about 10 minutes. Remove from heat and let cool slightly.

In a bowl, beat the egg yolks together with the heavy cream. Whisk some of the warm sauce into the egg yolk-cream mixture, then whisk the mixture back into the saucepan with the remaining sauce. Fold in the cheeses and finish with the butter. Allow the cheeses to melt, but do not allow the sauce to come to a simmer or it will separate. *Use immediately.*

Note: Black sea bass, red grouper, and spotted jewfish are also excellent prepared this way.

Herbed Garlic Yellowtail Snapper

6 6- to 8-ounce pieces yellowtail snapper
    fillet
1 lemon
1/2 cup all-purpose flour
3/4 cup light-flavored olive oil
2 teaspoons freshly ground black pepper
1 teaspoon salt

1 teaspoon dried oregano
1 teaspoon dried rosemary
1 teaspoon dried thyme
4 bay leaves
12 cloves garlic, mashed
1 cup dry white wine
French bread

Serves 6

Rub the yellowtail snapper fillets with lemon and dust them lightly with flour.

In a wide, heavy skillet, heat the olive oil together with the black pepper, salt, oregano, rosemary, thyme, bay leaves, and garlic cloves. When hot, add the fish and cook for 4 minutes on each side. Transfer the fillets to warm serving plates and hold in a warm oven.

Add the white wine to the skillet, bring to a boil, and reduce for 3 minutes.

Spoon the pan sauce over the fish and serve with plenty of French bread to mop up the sauce.

Note: Atlantic bonito, Atlantic croaker, common jack, hogfish, rainbow runner, speckled hind, and swordfish may also be used with this recipe.

Variations

(follow recipe exactly except for the following substitutions and additions):

with Basil-Garlic Sauce

Replace the oregano, rosemary, and thyme with 1/4 cup chopped fresh basil leaves.

with Dill-Garlic Sauce

Instead of the oregano, rosemary, and thyme use 1/2 cup chopped fresh dill.

with Lemon Chive, and Garlic Sauce

In place of the oregano, rosemary, and thyme use 1/2 cup chopped fresh lemon chives.

with Bell Pepper and Garlic Sauce

For the oregano, rosemary, and thyme leaves substitute 1 cup chopped bell peppers.

Other Delicious Recipes for Yellowtail Snapper include:

Baked Canapé of Yellowtail Snapper (see Atlantic spadefish, page 323)

Beer-Battered Fried Yellowtail Snapper (see speckled hind, page 39)

Fillet of Yellowtail Snapper Baked en Papillote with a Shrimp, Crabmeat, and White Wine Sauce (see Florida pompano, page 161)

Gulf Coast Bouillabaisse with Yellowtail Snapper (see pigfish, page 140)

Sautéed Yellowtail Snapper Fillets with Artichokes and Mushrooms in Brown Lemon-Butter Sauce (see black drum, page 100)

Whole Panfried Yellowtail Snapper with Colbert Sauce (see red porgy, page 262)

Yellowtail Snapper Fillet Marguery (see sheepshead, page 265)

Yellowtail Snapper Fillets with Cucumbers and Spinach (see gulf kingfish, page 104)

Yellowtail Snapper en Papillote with Black Olives (see striped bass, page 61)

Yellowtail Snapper en Papillote with Fennel (see pigfish, page 139)

Snook

Group: Snook

Other common name(s):
none

Latin name:
Centropomus
undecimalis
Family
Centropomidae

Maximum length:
4 feet

Maximum weight:
50 pounds

Cuts:
whole (small)
steak
fillet

Meat characteristics:
firm, white
medium oil content

Preferred cooking methods:
braise
grill
poach
sauté
stew

Snook Poached in Sherry

Sherry Marinade (recipe follows)   6 8-ounce pieces snook fillet, skinned

Serves 6

In a wide, heavy skillet or poaching pan large enough to hold all the fish, prepare the Sherry Marinade. Add the fish and poach at a simmer for 10 minutes.

Transfer the fish to wide soup bowls, cutting them in half crosswise if necessary for the fit, pour the cooking marinade over them, and serve.

Sherry Marinade

1 1/2 quarts fish stock (page 371), or
   shellfish stock (page 372)
2 cups dry sherry
1/4 cup freshly squeezed lemon juice
4 large cloves garlic, crushed

1 large onion, sliced
4 green onions, chopped
4 whole allspice
2 bay leaves
1 tablespoon salt

Combine all the ingredients, and simmer for 10 minutes. Adjust seasonings.

Note: Blacktip shark, king mackerel, shortfin mako shark, spotted eagle ray, striped bass, and swordfish are also excellent in this recipe. For the king mackerel, you may use either fillet or steak. For the spotted eagle ray, use 6 8-ounce pieces skinned wing fillets.

Variations: Snook is also excellent poached in Lime and Onion Marinade (page 34), Orange-Curry Marinade (page 291), Red Wine Marinade (page 35), or White Wine Marinade (page 35).

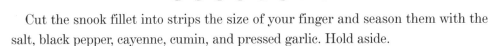

Hot Snook and Mushroom Salad with Dijon Mustard Dressing

2 1/2 pounds snook fillet, skinned
1 tablespoon salt
1 teaspoon freshly ground black pepper
1 teaspoon cayenne pepper
1 teaspoon cumin powder
2 cloves garlic, pressed
Dijon Mustard Dressing (recipe follows)

1/2 cup pecan pieces
2 cups sliced fresh mushrooms
6 large lettuce leaves
2 cups shredded Romaine or Boston
  lettuce
3 lemons, halved
2 tablespoons chopped fresh parsley

Serves 6

Cut the snook fillet into strips the size of your finger and season them with the salt, black pepper, cayenne, cumin, and pressed garlic. Hold aside.

Preheat the oven to 400°. Prepare the Dijon Mustard Dressing and hold aside. Spread the pecans in a single layer on a baking sheet and toast for 5 minutes, or until the nuts darken just slightly.

In a wide, heavy skillet, combine the snook strips, sliced mushrooms, and Dijon dressing. Cook the mixture over medium heat for 4 minutes, or until the fish strips are completely opaque.

Place a lettuce leaf on each of six plates, fill the leaves with shredded lettuce, and spoon the hot snook mixture over the lettuce mounds. Sprinkle with the toasted pecan pieces. Garnish the salads with the half lemons and chopped parsley.

Dijon Mustard Dressing

1 tablespoon Dijon mustard
1 tablespoon red wine vinegar
2/3 cup light-flavored olive oil
1 clove garlic, minced

1 egg yolk
1 teaspoon salt
1/4 teaspoon freshly ground white pepper

Whisk all the ingredients together in a small bowl.

Variations
(follow recipe exactly except for the following substitutions and additions):

Hot Snook Salad with Toasted Pecans and Creole Mustard Dressing
Use 2 tablespoons Creole mustard in place of the Dijon and increase the amount of pecans to 1 1/2 cups. Omit the mushrooms from the recipe.

Other Delicious Recipes for Snook include:

Bahamian Snook Chowder (see southern stingray, page 272)

Baked Canapé of Snook (see Atlantic spadefish, page 323)

Baked Shrimp-Stuffed Snook (see black drum, page 98)

Hot Snook and Artichoke Salad and Russian Dressing with Caviar (see largetooth sawfish, page 279)

Panfried Snook with Bienville Sauce (see wahoo, page 207)

Snook Poached with Lime and Onion (see sand perch, page 34)

Snook and Potato Salad with Chive Vinaigrette (see yellowfin tuna, page 227)

Snook with Potatoes, Bacon, and Garlic (see scalloped hammerhead shark, page 286)

Snook with Puerto Rican Sauce (see swordfish, page 333)

Snook Stew with White Wine (see spotted eagle ray, page 275)

Steamed Snook with Cypriote Sauce (see scalloped hammerhead shark, page 284)

Whole Steamed Snook Marinière (see weakfish, page 122)

Atlantic Spadefish

Group: Spadefish

Other common name(s):	Maximum weight:	Preferred cooking
Spadefish	10 pounds	methods:
Spades	Cuts:	bake
Latin name:	whole	broil
Chaetodopterus faber	steak	fry
Family Ephippidae	fillet	grill
Maximum length:	Meat characteristics:	sauté
2 feet	tender, white	
	medium oil content	

1 cup milk

2 tablespoons salted butter

2 tablespoons all-purpose flour

8 green onions, chopped

1/2 cup dry white wine

1/8 teaspoon ground nutmeg

Salt and freshly ground white pepper to
    taste

2 tablespoons grated Swiss cheese

2 tablespoons grated Romano cheese

2 tablespoons grated mozzarella cheese

1 1/2 pounds spadefish fillets, skinned and
    chopped (see Notes)

2 cups bread crumbs

6 slices toasted bread, trimmed of crusts

12 anchovy fillets

3 lemons, quartered

6 sprigs fresh parsley

Serves 6

Preheat the oven to 375°. In a small saucepan, scald the milk. Bring it just to the very point of simmering, then turn off the heat. Do not allow to boil. Remove and discard the skin that will form on the surface of the milk. Hold aside.

In a large, heavy saucepan, melt the butter and stir in the flour. Stir and cook without coloring until the mixture becomes foamy, about 2 minutes. Add the green onions and whisk in the white wine. Bring to a boil. Whisk in the hot scalded milk and bring to a boil again, then turn down to a simmer. Add the nutmeg and season with salt and white pepper to taste. Simmer for 12 minutes or so.

Add the grated cheeses and simmer together, stirring until all the cheese is melted; then add the chopped Atlantic spadefish. Simmer for 6 minutes and remove from the heat. Add 1 cup of the bread crumbs, and check the seasoning. Let cool enough to handle and shape.

Divide the mixture into six equal parts and shape into balls. Roll the balls in the remaining bread crumbs and place them on the toasts. Cross two anchovy fillets over the top of each and bake for 15 minutes.

Serve the baked spadefish canapés garnished with lemon quarters and a sprig of parsley.

Notes: Precooked or leftover cooked fish can be used instead of raw fish.

Atlantic moonfish, Atlantic bonito, queen triggerfish, snook, southern stingray, white mullet, and yellowtail snapper also work wonderfully with this recipe. For the southern stingray, use skinned wing fillets.

Tomato-Red Wine Sauce (recipe follows)
Vegetable oil for grilling

6 1-pound whole Atlantic spadefish; scaled and drawn

Serves 6

Light the grill or charcoal 1 hour before cooking. Prepare the Tomato-Red Wine Sauce, and hold aside warm.

When the grill is ready, brush the rack with vegetable oil. Wash and dry the Atlantic spadefish, brush on both sides with vegetable oil, and grill for about 7 minutes, or until they are turning white even on the top side. Brush the top of the fish with oil and carefully turn them over. Cook for another 7 minutes or so, until they are opaque all the way through.

Transfer the grilled Atlantic spadefish to warm plates and serve with the warm Tomato-Red Wine Sauce spooned over.

Tomato-Red Wine Sauce

4 large very ripe tomatoes
3 tablespoons salted butter
3 tablespoons all-purpose flour
1 onion, minced
1/2 cup minced fresh mushrooms
1 medium carrot, minced
1 medium stalk celery, minced
1 whole head garlic, peeled and minced

2 tablespoons minced fresh parsley
2 bay leaves
1/2 teaspoon dried thyme
1 cup dry red wine
1 cup reduced fish stock (page 372), or
  shellfish stock (page 372)
1 teaspoon salt
1/2 teaspoon freshly ground black pepper

Chop the tomatoes finely, or puree them in a food mill, reserving all juices and jelly released during the process. Transfer the raw tomato puree to a saucepan and bring to a gentle simmer. Cook for 5 minutes and remove from the heat to cool.

325

Strain the cooled puree through cheesecloth or a fine sieve. You should end up with 2 cups puree.

In a saucepan, melt the butter and blend in the flour. Cook together until it begins to brown, then add the minced onion, mushrooms, carrot, celery, and garlic. Cook together until browned, then add all the remaining sauce ingredients. Simmer gently for 45 minutes. Serve warm.

Note: Atlantic moonfish, blue marlin, bluefish, speckled hind, and tilefish are also excellent prepared this way.

Other Delicious Recipes for Atlantic Spadefish include:

Atlantic Spadefish Beignets with Rémoulade Sauce (see gray triggerfish, page 353)

Atlantic Spadefish Garlic Soup (see skipjack tuna, page 223)

Atlantic Spadefish with Pecans (see lookdown, page 181)

Beer-Battered Fried Atlantic Spadefish (see speckled hind, page 39)

Broiled Atlantic Spadefish with Balsamic Vinegar (see Atlantic moonfish, page 153)

Cold Poached Atlantic Spadefish Fillets with Green Basil Mayonnaise (see queen triggerfish, page 356)

Creole Seafood Gumbo with Atlantic Spadefish (see sailor's-choice, page 144)

Grilled Atlantic Spadefish with Criolla Sauce (see black sea bass, page 25)

Grilled Atlantic Spadefish with Tomato Butter (see sand perch, page 32)

Grilled Atlantic Spadefish with Tomato-Oyster Sauce (see Florida pompano, page 164)

Grilled Atlantic Spadefish with Tomato Sauce (see lookdown, page 179)

Squirrelfish

Group: Squirrelfish

Other common name(s):
 "Red Snapper" (sic)
 "Snapper" (sic)

Latin name:
 Holocentrus ascensionis
 Family Holocentridae

Maximum length:
 2 feet

Maximum weight:
 4 pounds

Cuts:
 whole
 fillet

Meat characteristics:
 white, flaky
 low oil content

Preferred cooking methods:
 fry
 poach
 steam
 stew

Aioli Sauce (recipe follows)
6 6- to 8-ounce squirrelfish fillets
Salt and freshly ground white pepper

Juice of 1 lemon
6 sprigs fresh parsley
3 lemons, halved

Serves 6

Prepare the Aioli Sauce, and refrigerate until ready to serve.

Rub the squirrelfish fillets lightly with salt, white pepper, and lemon juice. Arrange the fillets in a steamer basket or colander, and place in a saucepan. Add enough water to come to the bottom of the colander, yet not touch the fish. Remove the basket of fish and bring the water to a boil. Return the basket of fish to the pot of steaming water, cover (use foil if there is no top to fit), and steam the fish for about 8 minutes.

Carefully transfer the steamed squirrelfish fillets to warm dinner plates, garnish with parsley sprigs and lemon halves, and serve, with the Aioli Sauce on the side.

Aioli Sauce

4 cloves garlic, pressed or finely minced
1 1/4 cups Mayonnaise (page 374)

Blend the pressed garlic into the mayonnaise. Cover tightly and refrigerate for at least an hour before using to allow the flavors to meld.

Note: American eel, Atlantic sailfish, dog snapper, shortfin mako shark, and skipjack tuna are also excellent prepared this way. For the American eel, use skinned fillet.

3 quarts water, or enough to cover the fish

1 medium onion, sliced

6 bay leaves

6 whole allspice

3 tablespoons salt

2 teaspoons cayenne pepper

6 pounds scaled and drawn whole squirrelfish, one or several

2 cups light-flavored olive oil

1 1/2 cups white vinegar

16 cloves garlic, peeled and crushed

2 cups chopped onions

1 teaspoon salt

1/2 teaspoon freshly ground black pepper

3 cups chilled giardeniera (see Note)

6 large outer lettuce leaves

Serves 6

This recipe is prepared the day before so that it can marinate overnight.

In a large pot, bring the water to a boil with the onion, bay leaves, allspice, salt, and cayenne. Let boil for 5 minutes to allow the flavors to be dispersed in the water. Lay in the squirrelfish, bring back to a simmer, and poach for 20 minutes. Carefully remove the fish from the poaching liquid, drain, and set aside to cool. When cool enough to handle, remove all meat from the fish and break it into bite-sized pieces.

In a large bowl, mix the olive oil and vinegar together and add the garlic, onions, salt, and pepper. Fold in the fish pieces, cover, and marinate in the refrigerator overnight.

To assemble the salad, fold the giardeniera into the marinated squirrelfish and spoon out onto lettuce-leaf-lined plates.

Notes: The giardeniera, which is an Italian pickled vegetable salad, can be found in the pickled section of large grocery stores, or sometimes fresh in a good Italian market.

Try this recipe with Atlantic threadfin, blackfin tuna, bonefish, spot drum, southern stingray, or yellowfin tuna. Use 2 1/4 pounds blackfin or yellowfin tuna and 4 1/2 pounds skinned southern stingray wings. Cooking times are the same except for the Atlantic threadfin which should be poached approximately 10 minutes or until completely cooked.

Variations
(follow recipe exactly except for the following substitutions and additions):

with Olives
Use 3 cups chilled olive salad, fresh or from a jar, instead of giardeniera.

Other Delicious Recipes for Squirrelfish include:

"Chops" of Squirrelfish (see spotted sea trout, page 118)
Cold Poached Squirrelfish Fillets with Green Basil Mayonnaise (see queen triggerfish, page 356)
Fried Squirrelfish with Brown Shrimp Sauce (see white mullet, page 245)
Fried Squirrelfish Fillets with Bourguignonne Sauce (see hogfish, page 366)
Grilled Squirrelfish Andalouse (see white grunt, page 149)
Grilled Squirrelfish with Béarnaise Sauce (see queen triggerfish, page 358)
Grilled Squirrelfish with Tomato Butter (see sand perch, page 32)
Squirrelfish Croquettes Meunière (see skipjack tuna, page 221)
Squirrelfish Fillets Simmered in Leek and Tomato Sauce (see hard-tail jack, page 174)
Squirrelfish Garlic Soup (see skipjack tuna, page 223)
Squirrelfish wtih Oyster and Crabmeat Sauce Gratiné (see pinfish, page 256)
Squirrelfish, Tomato, and Pepper Soup (see red grouper, page 53)

Swordfish

Group: Swordfish

Other common name(s):
none

Latin name:
Xiphias gladius
Family Xiphiidae

Maximum length:
15 feet

Maximum weight:
1,200 pounds

Cuts:
steak
fillet

Meat characteristics:
firm, dark, rich
high oil content

Preferred cooking methods:
bake
broil
fry
grill
sauté

2 pounds swordfish fillet or steak, skinned
   and cut into 3/4-inch cubes
Salt and freshly ground white pepper
Juice of 1 lemon
1 cup milk
1 cup heavy cream
4 tablespoons salted butter
4 tablespoons all-purpose flour

1/8 teaspoon freshly grated nutmeg
1 teaspoon salt
1/4 teaspoon freshly ground white pepper
1/16 teaspoon cayenne pepper
1/3 cup grated Swiss cheese
1/3 cup grated white American cheese
1/3 cup French bread crumbs

Serves 6

Preheat the oven to 400°. Season the swordfish cubes lightly with salt and white pepper and sprinkle with lemon juice. Hold aside. Bring the milk and heavy cream to a simmer in a small saucepan, and hold aside warm.

In another saucepan, melt the butter, blend in the flour, and stir and cook for 1 minute, letting the flour bubble up. Carefully whisk in the warm milk and cream mixture and blend well. Add the nutmeg, salt, white pepper, and cayenne, and simmer for just a few minutes, until you have a sauce with a relatively thick consistency. Fold in the fish and bring back to a simmer. Check the seasoning and remove from the heat. Spoon the mixture into six individual ovenproof dishes.

In a separate bowl, combine the grated Swiss and American cheeses with the French bread crumbs. Sprinkle this evenly over the top of the ragout. Bake for 12 minutes, or until the cheese mixture is nicely browned and the sauce is bubbly.

Serve immediately.

Note: Try this recipe with black grouper, blacktip shark, common dolphin, dog snapper, greater amberjack, ling cobia, spotted jewfish, or tilefish.

Puerto Rican Sauce (recipe follows)
6 6-to-8-ounce pieces swordfish fillet
1/2 cup olive oil

Salt and cayenne pepper
2 cloves garlic, minced

Serves 6

Prepare the Puerto Rican Sauce, and hold aside warm.

In a wide, heavy skillet, heat the olive oil. Season the swordfish with salt and cayenne and quickly sauté them for 4 minutes. Turn the fillets, add the garlic, and sauté 4 minute more, or until nicely browned.

Serve the swordfish with the Puerto Rican Sauce spooned over.

Puerto Rican Sauce

1/4 cup olive oil
1 large onion, chopped
3 large fresh tomatoes, skinned (see Note), seeded, and chopped
1/2 cup pimiento-stuffed green olives, minced

2 tablespoons capers, minced
1 1/2 cups fish stock (page 371), or water
1 tablespoon red wine vinegar
2 bay leaves
1 teaspoon salt, or to taste
1/4 teaspoon cayenne pepper, or to taste

In a heavy saucepan, heat the olive oil and sauté the chopped onion until it begins to color. Add the remaining ingredients, cover, and simmer gently for 30 minutes, adding additional water if the sauce becomes too dry. Serve warm.

Notes: To skin the tomatoes, immerse them in boiling water for 1 to 2 minutes, then plunge them into cold water.

Blackfin tuna, gulf kingfish, largetooth sawfish, red grouper, snook, and Spanish mackerel also work wonderfully with this recipe.

Variations
(follow recipe exactly except for the following substitutions and additions):

Swordfish with Stewed Chayote
Replace the tomatoes and olives with 4 large chayote (a.k.a. mirliton) skinned, seeded, and diced.

Other Delicious Recipes for Swordfish include:
Bahamian Swordfish Chowder (see southern stingray, page 272)
Blackened Swordfish Steaks (see blue marlin, page 235)
Caribbean-Style Swordfish Stew (see pilot fish, page 189)
Caribbean Swordfish Salad (see mutton snapper, page 305)
Fillet of Swordfish with Browned Butter, Lemon Juice, and Caper Sauce (see blacktip shark, page 296)
Marinated Escabèche of Swordfish (see hard-tail jack, page 176)
Panfried Swordfish with Antiboise Sauce (see blacktip shark, page 294)
Steamed Swordfish Fillets with Espagnole Mayonnaise (see mutton snapper, page 303)
Swordfish Beignets with Rémoulade Sauce (see gray triggerfish, page 353)
Swordfish Poached in Sherry (see snook, page 319)
Venetian-Style Broiled Swordfish Steaks (see blackfin tuna, page 217)
Wood-Grilled Swordfish Steaks with Achiote-Garlic Paste (see black grouper, page 49)

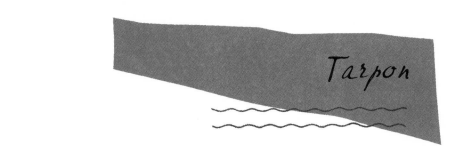

Tarpon

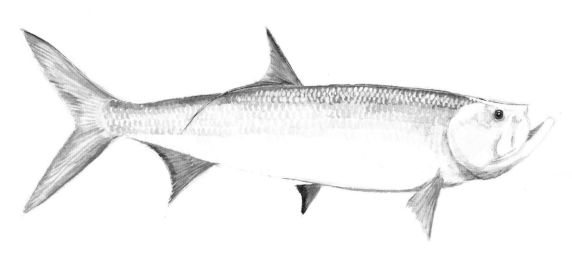

Group: *Tarpon*

Other common name(s):	*Maximum weight:*	*Preferred cooking*
none	300 pounds	*methods:*
Latin name:	*Cuts:*	bake
Megalops atlanticus	fillet	braise
Family Elopidae	*Meat characteristics:*	sauté
Maximum length:	dense, firm	steam
8 feet	high oil content	stew

Broth:

2 tablespoons olive oil

1 large onion, roughly chopped

2 medium carrots, roughly chopped

2 sticks celery, roughly chopped

1 small green bell pepper, seeded and
    chopped

1 small red bell pepper, seeded and
    chopped

2 leeks (white part only), thinly sliced

1 dozen fresh okra pods, sliced

2 tablespoons tomato paste

2 medium tomatoes, skinned (see Note),
    seeded, and diced

1 cup brandy

1/2 cup dry white wine

1/2 cup Herbsaint, or Pernod

2 tablespoons filé powder (see Note), or
    to taste

2 quarts fish stock (page 371)

Salt and freshly ground black pepper

1/2 cup dry white wine

1 tablespoon chopped French shallots

1 tablespoon chopped garlic

2 tablespoons chopped fresh parsley

2 pounds tarpon fillet, skinned, boned,
    and cut into 3/4-inch cubes

Serves 6

Begin the pot au feu by making the broth. Heat the olive oil in a large saucepan or soup pot. Sauté the onion, carrots, celery, green and red bell peppers, and leeks for 5 minutes. Add the okra pods and continue to sauté. When the vegetables are nearly transparent, stir in the tomato paste and tomatoes, and cook briefly.

Being very careful, add the brandy and ignite it to burn out the alcohol and flavor the cooking vegetables. Add the white wine and Herbsaint. Season with filé powder to taste. Then add the fish stock and simmer until vegetables are cooked. Season with salt and pepper.

In a separate soup pot, combine the white wine with the shallots, garlic, and parsley. Add the cubed tarpon and simmer, stirring several times, for only about 2 minutes. Then add the contents of this pot to the pot au feu broth and simmer until the tarpon is tender, approximately 15 minutes.

To serve, ladle the soup, with the vegetables and tarpon, into large, warm soup bowls.

Notes: To skin the tomatoes, immerse them in boiling water for 1 to 2 minutes, then plunge them into cold water.

Filé powder is powdered sassafras leaves, used as a thickening, coloring, and flavoring agent. It comes to New Orleans Creole cuisine from the Louisiana Indians.

American eel, Atlantic bonito, greater amberjack, hard-tail jack, and wahoo all work wonderfully in this recipe.

Tarpon Fillets in Saffron-White Wine Sauce

6 8-ounce pieces tarpon fillet
1 teaspoon salt
1/2 teaspoon ground white pepper
1/4 teaspoon cayenne pepper

1/2 teaspoon ground thyme
1/2 teaspoon ground marjoram
Saffron-White Wine Sauce (recipe follows)

Serves 6

Rub the tarpon fillets with the salt, pepper, cayenne, thyme, and marjoram. Hold aside.

Prepare the Saffron-White Wine Sauce in a heavy skillet large enough to hold the fish. Lay the tarpon fillets into the pan with the sauce and simmer for 20 minutes, or until the fish is tender and completely opaque.

Serve in shallow bowls with the sauce from the pan spooned over.

Saffron-White Wine Sauce

1/2 cup olive oil
2 medium onions, chopped
6 green onions, chopped
1 small bell pepper, seeded and chopped
2 ribs celery, minced
4 cloves garlic, minced
1 tablespoon minced fresh parsley
1/4 cup all-purpose flour

2 cups fish stock (page 371)
2 cups dry white wine
1/2 teaspoon dried thyme
2 bay leaves
1/4 teaspoon crumbled Spanish saffron
Salt, freshly ground white pepper, and
cayenne pepper

In a skillet, heat the oil and sauté the chopped onions, green onions, bell pepper, celery, garlic, and parsley just until they become limp. Whisk in the flour and cook together for 4 minutes, then whisk in the fish stock and white wine. Add the thyme, bay leaves, and saffron, and season to taste with salt, pepper, and cayenne. Simmer for 20 minutes.

338

Note: Atlantic sailfish, king mackerel, mutton snapper, permit, skipjack tuna, tilefish, and yellowfin tuna should also be tried with this recipe. For the permit, use 6 6-ounce fillets. Simmer the Atlantic sailfish, king mackerel, and skipjack tuna with the sauce for 12 minutes or until cooked, and the permit for 10 minutes.

Other Delicious Recipes for Tarpon include:

Bahamian Tarpon Chowder (see southern stingray, page 272)

Caribbean-Style Tarpon Stew (see pilot fish, page 189)

"Chops" of Tarpon (see spotted sea trout, page 118)

Cold Poached Tarpon Ravigote with Boiled New Potatoes (see spotted jewfish, page 43)

Creole Bisque of Tarpon (see tilefish, page 348)

Tarpon Beignets with Rémoulade Sauce (see gray triggerfish, page 353)

Tarpon Garlic Soup (see skipjack tuna, page 223)

Tarpon with Potatoes, Bacon, and Garlic (see scalloped hammerhead shark, page 286)

Tarpon-Stuffed Hand Tortillas (see bluefish, page 68)

Tarpon Tamales with Piquant Green Sauce (see Spanish mackerel, page 203)

Tarpon, Tomato, and Pepper Soup (see red grouper, page 53)

Atlantic Threadfin

Group: Threadfin

Other common name(s):
Threadfin

Latin name:
Polydactylus
octonemus
Family Polynemidae

Maximum length:
6 inches

Maximum weight:
1/2 pound

Cuts:
whole
fillet

Meat characteristics:
tender, white, flaky
low-to-medium oil
content

**Preferred cooking
methods:**
bake
fry
sauté

6 8-ounce Atlantic threadfins, or more if
   they are small, scaled and drawn
2 teaspoons salt
1 teaspoon freshly ground black pepper

1 teaspoon ground cumin
4 tablespoons light-flavored olive oil
Citrus-Garlic Sauce (recipe follows)

Serves 6

Wash and dry the Atlantic threadfins.

Combine the salt, pepper, and cumin and rub it onto the threadfins. Heat the olive oil in a wide sauté pan or skillet. Sauté the fish for about 8 minutes, turning once halfway through the cooking. Transfer the fish to a warm platter and hold in a warm oven.

Serve the Atlantic threadfin on warm dinner plates with the warm Citrus-Garlic Sauce spooned over.

Citrus-Garlic Sauce

4 tablespoons salted butter
1 tablespoon minced garlic
1/2 cup freshly squeezed orange juice
2 tablespoons freshly squeezed lime juice

2 tablespoons freshly squeezed lemon juice
Salt and freshly ground black pepper
   (optional)

Add the butter to the pan. When it is melted and hot, add the garlic and sauté for 1/2 minute. Stir in the orange, lime, and lemon juices, bring to a boil, and turn down to a simmer. If desired, season to taste with salt and pepper.

Note: Atlantic moonfish, pigfish, sailor's-choice, sand perch, and striped mullet also work well in this recipe.

Panfried Atlantic Threadfin Fillets with Shrimp Creole Sauce

Shrimp Creole Sauce (recipe follows)
2 eggs
1/2 cup water
6 6-ounce Atlantic threadfin fillets
Salt and freshly ground black pepper

1 1/2 cups French bread crumbs
4 tablespoons salted butter
1/4 cup peanut oil
2 tablespoons minced fresh parsley

Serves 6

Prepare the Shrimp Creole Sauce, and hold aside warm.

Beat the eggs together with the water to make an egg wash. Lightly season the Atlantic threadfin fillets with salt and black pepper, dip them in the egg wash, and dredge in the bread crumbs. Melt the butter in the peanut oil in a wide, heavy skillet and fry the fillets 4 minutes on each side, or until they are golden brown.

Transfer the cooked Atlantic threadfin fillets to warm dinner plates, spoon the Shrimp Creole Sauce over the top, and sprinkle with the chopped parsley.

Shrimp Creole Sauce

1 stick salted butter
1 large green bell pepper, seeded and
    chopped
2 large onions, chopped
2 ribs celery, finely chopped
4 large tomatoes, chopped
1/2 cup dry white wine

3 bay leaves
1/2 teaspoon dried thyme
1 pound medium-to-small raw shrimp,
    peeled and deveined
Salt, freshly ground black pepper, and
    cayenne pepper

In a sauté pan, melt the butter and sauté the green peppers, onions, and celery for 3 minutes. Add the tomatoes, wine, bay leaves, and thyme, and simmer for 15 minutes. Add the shrimp, and simmer for 5 minutes more. Season to taste with salt, black pepper, and cayenne. Serve warm.

Note: Hogfish, pinfish, queen triggerfish, red drum, spotfin flounder, and white mullet also work well with this recipe.

Variations
(follow recipe exactly except for the following substitutions and additions):

with Crawfish Creole Sauce
Replace the shrimp with 1 pound crawfish tail meat.

with Oyster Creole Sauce
Use 3 dozen shelled raw oysters in place of the shrimp. After adding the oysters to the sauté mixture, simmer for 2 minutes or just until the edges of the oysters begin to curl.

with Scallop Creole Sauce
Substitute for the shrimp 1 pound small bay scallops.

Other Delicious Recipes for Atlantic Threadfin include:
Atlantic Threadfin Poached with Lime and Onion (see sand perch, page 34)
Breaded Atlantic Threadfin with Creole Tomato Sauce (see black grouper, page 47)
Breaded Fillet of Atlantic Threadfin with Green Mayonnaise (see red drum, page 109)
Fried Atlantic Threadfin with Brown Shrimp Sauce (see white mullet, page 245)
Fried Battered Atlantic Threadfin with Two Sisters Sauce (see permit, page 184)
Grilled Atlantic Threadfin Fillets in Sesame-Brandy Marinade (see scamp, page 58)
Marinated Atlantic Threadfin Salad with Giardeniera (see squirrelfish, page 329)
Sautéed Battered Atlantic Threadfin Fillets with Lemon-Butter Sauce (see red snapper, page 311)

Whole Broiled Atlantic Threadfin with Balsamic Vinegar (see Atlantic moonfish, page 153)

Whole Cornmeal-Fried Atlantic Threadfin with Mosca Sauce (see Atlantic croaker, page 93)

Whole Panfried Atlantic Threadfin with Espagnole Sauce (see tripletail, page 361)

Whole Panfried Atlantic Threadfin with Salsa Roja (see striped mullet, page 240)

Tilefish

Group: Tilefish

Other common name(s):
none

Latin name:
Lopholatilus chamaeleonticeps
Family Malacanthidae

Maximum length:
3 feet

Maximum weight:
50 pounds

Cuts:
whole (small)
steak
fillet

Meat characteristics:
firm, white
low oil content

Preferred cooking methods:
bake
fry
poach
stew

Creamed Spinach:
2 tablespoons salted butter
2 10-ounce bags fresh spinach, washed,
   trimmed, and chopped
3 tablespoons salted butter
3 tablespoons all-purpose flour
1 cup hot milk
1 teaspoon salt
1/2 teaspoon freshly ground white pepper

1 medium onion, sliced
1/2 cup dry white wine
2 cloves garlic, mashed
2 bay leaves
1 tablespoon salt
6 6-ounce pieces tilefish fillet, skinned
1/2 cup bread crumbs
1/4 cup grated Swiss cheese
1/4 cup grated Parmesan cheese

Hollandaise Sauce (page 63)
2 quarts water, or enough to cover fish
   (about 2 inches deep in pan)

Serves 6

Preheat the oven to 400°. Melt the 2 tablespoons butter in a large saucepan and add the spinach. Cover the pot and simmer for 10 minutes, or until the spinach completely collapses. Hold aside.

In another saucepan, melt the 3 tablespoons butter and blend in the flour. Stir and cook for 2 minutes without coloring the flour. Carefully whisk in the hot milk and simmer for 7 minutes, or until the sauce is thickened. Add this sauce to the cooked spinach and season with the salt and white pepper. Cover and simmer for 10 minutes. Set aside and keep warm.

Prepare the Hollandaise, and hold aside warm.

To poach the tilefish, place the water, onion, white wine, garlic, bay leaves, and salt in a wide saucepan, and bring to a boil. Reduce to a simmer, lay the tilefish fillets into the simmering liquid, and poach for 8 minutes. Carefully remove the fillets with a slotted spoon or spatula to a warm plate. Cover with a warm damp towel and keep warm.

To assemble the dish, spoon the creamed spinach into six individual oven-proof ramekins or soufflé dishes, top with a tilefish fillet, and spoon on the Hollandaise. Blend the bread crumbs and cheeses and sprinkle over the Hollandaise. Place in the oven for 7 minutes, or until the cheese is melted and the tops begin to brown.

Serve immediately.

Note: Florida pompano, gulf flounder, red snapper, and spotted sea trout are also excellent prepared this way.

1 pound tilefish fillet, skinned and diced
1/2 cup peanut oil
1/2 cup salted butter
1/2 cup flour
2 large yellow onions, finely chopped
8 green onions, finely chopped
2 medium carrots, finely chopped
2 quarts fish stock (page 371), or water
2 large tomatoes, finely chopped

2 tablespoons chopped fresh parsley
4 cloves garlic, minced
1/4 teaspoon dried thyme
2 bay leaves
Salt
1 teaspoon freshly ground black pepper
1/2 teaspoon cayenne pepper
1 tablespoon chopped fresh parsley

Serves 6 to 8

Heat the butter and peanut oil together in a large, heavy saucepan and stir in the flour. Cook together, stirring constantly, over moderate heat for approximately 15 minutes, or until a dark red-brown or mahogany color has been acquired. This is a brown roux.

Add the yellow onions, green onions, and carrots and cook together until nicely browned. Whisk in the fish stock, or water. Add the tomatoes, parsley, garlic, thyme, and bay leaves and season with the salt, black pepper, and cayenne. Cover and simmer for 45 minutes. Add the diced tilefish, cover, and simmer for 10 minutes, or until the fish pieces are tender.

Stir in the chopped parsley, and serve.

Note: Atlantic bonito, black drum, blacktip shark, bluefish, blue marlin, lookdown, pilot fish, and tarpon also work well in this recipe.

Other Delicious Recipes for Tilefish include:

Cold Poached Tilefish Fillets with Green Basil Mayonnaise (see queen triggerfish, page 356)

Corn-Flour-Fried Tilefish Fillets (see dog snapper, page 300)

Fried Skewered Tilefish (see spotted eagle ray, page 276)

Grilled Tilefish Fillets in Sesame-Brandy Marinade (see scamp, page 58)

Grilled Tilefish with Tomato-Red Wine Sauce (see Atlantic spadefish, page 325)

Poached Tilefish with Marquis Sauce (see speckled hind, page 37)

Ragout of Tilefish au Gratin (see swordfish, page 332)

Tilefish Fillets with Cucumber and Spinach (see gulf kingfish, page 104)

Tilefish Fillets in Saffron-White Wine Sauce (see tarpon, page 338)

Whole Baked Tilefish with Spinach Stuffing (see jolthead porgy, page 250)

Whole Steamed Tilefish Marinière (see weakfish, page 122)

Gray Triggerfish

Group: Triggerfish (Leatherjackets)

Other common name(s):
Triggerfish

Latin name:
Balistes capriscus
Family Balistidae

Maximum length:
1 foot

Maximum weight:
2 pounds

Cuts:
whole
fillet

Meat characteristics:
tender, white, flaky
low-to-medium oil
content

*Preferred cooking
methods:*
fry
sauté
steam

Charcoal-Grilled Gray Triggerfish with Tomatillo-Habañero Salsa

Tomatillo-Habañero Salsa (recipe follows)

6 1-pound gray triggerfish, scaled and drawn

1/4 cup light-flavored olive oil

Serves 6

Light the charcoal 1 hour before cooking. Prepare the Tomatillo-Habañero Salsa at the same time so the flavors have time to meld.

When the coals are ready, brush the gray triggerfish with a little olive oil, and the grill rack as well to prevent the fish from sticking. Grill the gray triggerfish for about 7 minutes on one side. Carefully turn the fish over and cook for another 5 minutes.

Transfer the fish to warm dinner plates and serve with the room-temperature Tomatillo-Habañero Salsa on the side. The skin of the fish should be removed by each diner. Bone plates would facilitate the enjoyment of this dish.

Tomatillo-Habañero Salsa

8 large tomatillos, husked and finely chopped

1 medium yellow onion, finely chopped

Juice of 3 limes

2 cloves garlic, pressed

1 fresh habanero (Scotch bonnet) pepper, seeded and minced, or more, according to your taste

1 tablespoon minced fresh cilantro

Salt

Combine the tomatillos and onion with the lime juice, garlic, habañero pepper, and cilantro. Season to taste with salt. Transfer the salsa to a covered container and hold at room temperature for at least an hour before using.

Note: Atlantic moonfish, lookdown, skipjack tuna, and white mullet are also excellent grilled this way.

Gray Triggerfish Beignets with Rémoulade Sauce

2 cups all-purpose flour
1 tablespoon baking powder
4 green onions (both white part and
    green), minced
4 tablespoons minced pimiento
2 cloves garlic, minced
1 1/2 cups water

1 tablespoon olive oil
1 1/2 pounds gray triggerfish fillet,
    skinned and chopped
1 teaspoon salt
1/2 teaspoon Louisiana hot sauce
Rémoulade Sauce (recipe follows)
Peanut oil for frying

Serves 6

In a large bowl, make the batter. Combine the flour, baking powder, green onions, pimiento, garlic, water, olive oil, gray triggerfish, salt, and hot sauce. Cover the bowl with a damp towel, and set aside for 30 minutes.

Prepare the Rémoulade Sauce, cover with plastic wrap, and hold aside at room temperature.

Heat 1 inch of oil in a wide, heavy skillet to 375°. Mix the beignet batter again slightly and drop tablespoonfuls of the mixture into the 375° oil. Do not crowd the skillet. Fry until the beignets are lightly browned on both sides. Drain on absorbent paper and serve with the Rémoulade Sauce.

Rémoulade Sauce

1 cup light-flavored olive oil, or peanut oil
1/3 cup vinegar
1 teaspoon salt
1/2 teaspoon cayenne pepper
1 tablespoon Hungarian paprika

3/4 cup Creole mustard
6 green onions (both white part and
    green), minced
2 tablespoons minced fresh parsley
1 rib celery, minced

In a bowl, whisk together the olive oil, vinegar, salt, cayenne, and paprika. Blend in the Creole mustard, green onions, parsley, and celery. Cover with plastic wrap until ready to use.

Notes: Any unused Rémoulade Sauce can be stored in a tightly capped jar in the refrigerator for up to a week. The flavor actually improves in a day or two.

Also try this recipe with Atlantic croaker, Atlantic spadefish, gaff-topsail catfish, lookdown, striped mullet, swordfish, and tarpon.

Variations: Gray triggerfish beignets are also excellent served with Aioli Sauce (page 328), Cocktail Sauce (page 375), or Tartar Sauce (page 375).

Other Delicious Recipes for Gray Triggerfish include:

Broiled Gray Triggerfish (see gulf flounder, page 131)
"Chops" of Gray Triggerfish (see spotted sea trout, page 118)
Fried Gray Triggerfish with Brown Shrimp Sauce (see white mullet, page 245)
Gray Triggerfish Croquettes Meunière (see skipjack tuna, page 221)
Gray Triggerfish with Lobster Cream Sauce (see permit, page 186)
Grilled Gray Triggerfish with Tomato Butter (see sand perch, page 32)
White Bisque of Gray Triggerfish with Sherry (see largetooth sawfish, page 281)

Queen Triggerfish

Group: Triggerfish

Other common name(s):
Triggerfish

Latin name:
Balistes vetula
Family Balistidae

Maximum length:
1 foot 8 inches

Maximum weight:
4 pounds

Cuts:
whole
fillet

Meat characteristics:
tender, white
low-to-medium oil
content

Preferred cooking methods:
fry
poach
sauté

Cold Poached Queen Triggerfish Fillets with Green Basil Mayonnaise

1 1/2 quarts water, or enough to cover fish (about 1 inch deep in skillet)
1 lemon, thinly sliced
1 medium onion, thinly sliced
2 sprigs fresh parsley
2 bay leaves
1 clove garlic, mashed
6 whole black peppercorns

2 teaspoons salt
1/4 teaspoon cayenne pepper
6 6-ounce pieces queen triggerfish fillets, skinned
Green Basil Mayonnaise (recipe follows)

3 lemons, quartered

Serves 6

In a wide skillet, bring the water to a boil with the lemon, onion, parsley, bay leaves, garlic, peppercorns, salt, and cayenne. Let boil for 3 minutes to allow the water to draw the flavors from the seasoning ingredients. Lower the heat to a simmer and lay in the fillets. Poach for 10 minutes, or until the fish is flaky when broken with a fork. With a long spatula, carefully remove the fillets from the water, drain, cover, and refrigerate for several hours, or until chilled.

Prepare the Green Basil Mayonnaise, and refrigerate until ready to serve.

To serve, nap the queen triggerfish fillets with the Green Basil Mayonnaise and garnish with the lemon quarters.

Green Basil Mayonnaise

1 egg
1 tablespoon Dijon mustard
3 tablespoons tarragon vinegar
3 tablespoons minced fresh parsley
1 green onion, minced
1 teaspoon salt

1 teaspoon ground white pepper
1 tablespoon minced fresh tarragon, or 1 teaspoon dried tarragon
1/4 cup minced fresh basil, or 1 1/4 tablespoons dried basil
1 cup peanut or corn oil

In a blender, combine all the sauce ingredients except the oil, and blend on a low speed. Turn up the speed to high and pour in the oil in a thin stream, until it is all added and the sauce is emulsified. Refrigerate until ready to use.

Note: Atlantic spadefish, Florida pompano, rainbow runner, sailor's-choice, squirrelfish, tilefish, and weakfish also work well with this recipe.

Variations: Cold Poached Queen Triggerfish Fillets are also delicious served with Aioli Sauce (page 328), Espagnole Mayonnaise (page 303), or Spicy Creole Mayonnaise (page 310).

Béarnaise Sauce (recipe follows)

6 1-pound whole queen triggerfish, scaled and drawn

Vegetable oil for grilling

Salt and freshly ground white pepper

Serves 6

Light the grill or charcoal 1 hour before cooking. Prepare the Béarnaise Sauce, and hold aside warm.

When the grill is ready, brush the rack with vegetable oil. Brush the queen triggerfish on both sides with oil and season lightly with salt and white pepper. Grill for about 6 minutes on each side.

Remove the grilled queen triggerfish to warm plates and serve with the Béarnaise Sauce on the side.

Béarnaise Sauce

1/4 cup minced white onion

2 tablespoons minced fresh tarragon leaves

2 tablespoons minced fresh parsley

1/4 cup tarragon vinegar

6 large egg yolks, lightly beaten

3 tablespoons freshly squeezed lemon juice

1 teaspoon salt

1/2 teaspoon cayenne pepper

3 sticks salted butter

Put the minced onion, tarragon, parsley, and tarragon vinegar in a saucepan and reduce the liquid completely. Let cool and remove to a double boiler. Add the egg yolks, lemon juice, salt, and cayenne. Cut the butter sticks in half and add one of the six pieces to the egg yolk mixture. Heat the water in the bottom of the double boiler without ever letting it come to a boil. Whisk the mixture until the first piece of butter is completely melted; then add the next piece. Continue this process until you have used all the butter pieces. Keep whisking over the heat until the sauce has thickened. Remove from heat and continue whisking until the sauce has cooled slightly.

Note: Black drum, dog snapper, jolthead porgy, squirrelfish, and tripletail are also excellent grilled this way.

Other Delicious Recipes for Queen Triggerfish include:

Baked Canapé of Queen Triggerfish (see Atlantic spadefish, page 323)

Broiled Queen Triggerfish with Balsamic Vinegar (see Atlantic moonfish, page 153)

Broiled Queen Triggerfish with Poulette Sauce (see red porgy, page 260)

Grilled Queen Triggerfish Andalouse (see white grunt, page 149)

Grilled Queen Triggerfish with Criolla Sauce (see black sea bass, page 25)

Grilled Queen Triggerfish with Tomato Butter (see sand perch, page 32)

Grilled Queen Triggerfish with Tomato-Oyster Sauce (see Florida pompano, page 164)

Grilled Queen Triggerfish with Tomato Sauce (see lookdown, page 179)

Gulf Coast Bouillabaisse with Queen Triggerfish (see pigfish, page 140)

Panfried Queen Triggerfish Fillets with Shrimp Creole Sauce (see Atlantic threadfin, page 342)

Queen Triggerfish with Oyster and Crabmeat Sauce Gratiné (see pinfish, page 256)

Sautéed Battered Queen Triggerfish Fillets with Lemon-Butter Sauce (see red snapper, page 311)

Tripletail

Group: Tripletail

Other common name(s):
"Blackfish" (sic)

Latin name:
Lobotes surinamensis
Family Lobotidae

Maximum length:
3 feet 6 inches

Maximum weight:
28 pounds

Cuts:
whole (small)
fillet
steak

Meat characteristics:
firm, white, flaky
medium oil content

Preferred cooking methods:
bake
broil
fry
grill
poach

Espagnole Sauce (recipe follows)
6 3/4- to 1-pound whole tripletails, scaled
  and drawn

Salt and freshly ground black pepper
3/4 cup peanut oil
6 large French bread croutons (page 370)

Serves 6

Prepare the Espagnole Sauce, and hold aside warm.

Wash and dry the tripletails and rub with salt and pepper. Heat the oil until hot in a heavy skillet and fry the fish about 4 minutes on a side, until lightly browned. Drain on absorbent paper.

Serve the fish on the croutons with the Espagnole Sauce spooned over.

Espagnole Sauce

3 tablespoons salted butter
1/2 cup finely chopped onion
1/2 cup finely chopped carrot
3 tablespoons all-purpose flour
3 cups beef or chicken stock, or bouillon
1 cup Tomato Sauce (page 179), or plain
  (unseasoned) canned tomato sauce
2 cloves garlic, minced
1/2 teaspoon dried thyme

1 small stalk celery
2 bay leaves
3 sprigs parsley
1 teaspoon sugar
1 teaspoon water
3 tablespoons red wine vinegar
1/4 teaspoon anchovy paste
Salt and freshly ground black pepper

In a saucepan, melt the butter and sauté the onion and carrot until they begin to color. Add the flour and cook until brown. Add the stock, tomato sauce, garlic, thyme, celery, bay leaves, and parsley.

In another small saucepan, cook the sugar with the water, stirring constantly, until it caramelizes (colors light brown). Remove from the heat and immediately add the vinegar. Mix in the anchovy paste, add this mixture to the ingredients of the other saucepan, and bring to a simmer. Season to taste with salt and pepper, cover, and simmer for 30 minutes. Pass the sauce through a strainer. Serve warm.

Note: Atlantic threadfin, pinfish, striped mullet, and white grunt are also excellent prepared this way.

Poached Tripletail Fillets with Rockefeller Sauce

Rockefeller Sauce (recipe follows)
2 quarts water, or enough to cover fish
   (about 2 inches deep in pan)
1 large onion, sliced
1 lemon, sliced
12 black peppercorns

1 tablespoon salt
2 bay leaves
1/2 teaspoon dried thyme
6 6- to 8-ounce skinned tripletail fillets, or
   a single large skinned fillet cut into 6
   portions

Serves 6

Rockefeller Sauce was created by my great-grandfather, Jules Alciatore, in 1899 when he was proprietor of the family's restaurant, Antoine's, in New Orleans. Make the Rockefeller Sauce before poaching the fish, and hold aside warm.

Preheat the oven to 400°. In a wide shallow saucepan, bring the water, onion, lemon, peppercorns, salt, bay leaves, and thyme to a boil, and reduce to a simmer. Poach the tripletail fillets at a low simmer for about 8 minutes, or until they are opaque all the way through.

Carefully remove the fillets from the poaching liquor and place them on oven-proof plates. Spoon the Rockefeller Sauce over the fish, completely covering their top sides. You can add a more decorative look by piping the sauce through a fluted pastry bag. Bake for about 7 minutes, or until the sauce is bubbly and browned lightly on the top.

Serve immediately.

Rockefeller Sauce

1/2 stick salted butter
4 tablespoons all-purpose flour
1 cup bottled clam juice
2 cups finely minced stemmed fresh
   parsley
16 green onions, finely minced
8 ribs celery, stringed and finely minced

4 tablespoons tomato paste
1 tablespoon sugar
1 tablespoon red wine vinegar
1/2 teaspoon cayenne pepper
Salt and freshly ground white pepper
1/2 cup bread crumbs

Melt the butter in a heavy saucepan. Add the flour and cook for 2 minutes, allowing the mixture to foam up and cook out the raw flour smell. Whisk in the clam juice, then fold in the parsley, green onions, and celery. Add the tomato paste, sugar, vinegar, and cayenne and a dash of salt and white pepper. Simmer very, very slowly for 1 hour and 15 minutes. Add the bread crumbs, and adjust the seasonings if necessary. Serve warm.

Note: Black sea bass, hogfish, and red drum also work well in this recipe.

Other Delicious Recipes for Tripletail include:

Baked Tripletail with Bacon and Onion (see red grouper, page 52)

Beer-Battered Fried Tripletail (see speckled hind, page 39)

Caribbean Tripletail with Rice (see American eel, page 128)

Cold Poached Tripletail Fillets with Green Onion Mayonnaise (see black sea bass, page 23)

Fried Tripletail Fingers with Pink Horseradish Mayonnaise (see gaff-topsail catfish, page 80)

Grilled Tripletail with Béarnaise Sauce (see queen triggerfish, page 358)

Gulf Coast Bouillabaisse with Tripletail (see pigfish, page 140)

Poached Tripletail Fillets with Maltaise Sauce (see common dolphin, page 88)

Tripletail with Oyster and Crabmeat Sauce Gratiné (see pinfish, page 256)

Whole Panfried Tripletail with Onion, Garlic, and Red Wine Sauce (see pilot fish, page 190)

Hogfish (male)

Group: Wrasse

Other common name(s):
    none
Latin name:
    Lachnolaimus
    maximus
    Family Labridae
Maximum length:
    3 feet

Maximum weight:
    36 pounds
Cuts:
    whole (small)
    steak
    fillet
Meat characteristics:
    firm, white, flaky
    low-to-medium oil
    content

*Preferred cooking
methods:*
    bake
    braise
    fry
    stew

Fried Hogfish Fillets with Bourguignonne Sauce

Bourguignonne Sauce (recipe follows)
1 egg
1 1/2 cups milk
2 cups corn flour (see Note)
2 teaspoons salt

1 teaspoon freshly ground white pepper
1/2 teaspoon cayenne pepper
Peanut oil for frying
6 6-to-8-ounce hogfish fillets

Serves 6

Prepare the Bourguignonne Sauce, and hold aside warm.

In a bowl, beat the egg and milk together to make an egg wash. In a separate bowl, combine the corn flour with the salt, white pepper, and cayenne. Heat 1/2 inch oil in a heavy, wide skillet to 350°. Dip the hogfish fillets into the egg wash, coating completely, then dredge in the seasoned corn flour. Fry, without crowding the skillet, for approximately 6 minutes, or until golden brown on all sides. Drain on absorbent paper.

Transfer the hogfish fillets to warm plates, spoon Bourguignonne Sauce over each, and serve.

Bourguignonne Sauce

1 cup finely minced fresh parsley
1 cup finely minced green onions
1/2 cup finely minced garlic

1 cup Drawn Butter (page 199; see Note)
Salt to taste

In a small saucepan, combine the parsley, green onions, garlic, and Drawn Butter. Bring to a boil, season with salt, and hold aside warm until ready to use.

Notes: Corn flour is often used in the frying of seafood rather than white flour. It can be bought as plain corn flour in specialty stores or as corn masa flour or "masa harina" in stores that sell Mexican or Central and South American food products. It is the flour that corn tortillas are made from. It can also be gotten in the form of "fish-fry," which is corn flour that is already seasoned with salt and pepper.

For 1 cup Drawn Butter, you will need to start with 2 1/2 sticks salted butter.

Atlantic bonito, gaff-topsail catfish, pinfish, spot drum, squirrelfish, and striped mullet are also delicious in this recipe.

Variations: Fried hogfish fillets are also good served with Béarnaise Sauce (page 358), Black Anchovy Butter (page 212), Beurre Noir Sauce (page 213), Pink Horseradish Mayonnaise (page 80), Ravigote Mayonnaise (page 44), Rémoulade Sauce (page 353), or Tartar Sauce (page 375).

1 6- to 7-pound whole hogfish, scaled and
   drawn
1 tablespoon salt
1 teaspoon freshly ground black pepper
1/2 teaspoon dried thyme
4 apples, cored and quartered

4 onions, quartered
2 ribs celery, chopped
8 cloves garlic, chopped
Salt and freshly ground black pepper
8 strips bacon
1 cup fish stock (page 371), or water

Serves 6

Preheat the oven to 350°. Wash and dry the hogfish and rub it inside and out with the salt, pepper, and thyme. Lay it into a baking pan.

Combine the apples, onions, celery, and garlic in a bowl and sprinkle with salt and pepper. Stuff the hogfish with the mixture and spread what remains in the roasting pan surrounding the fish. Lay the bacon strips across the top of the hogfish. Bake for 50 minutes, or until nicely browned. Baste the fish with pan drippings during cooking to keep it moist.

With a long, wide spatula, remove the fish and pan vegetables to a warm serving platter. Deglaze the pan with fish stock or water, and season to taste with salt and pepper.

Divide the hogfish into serving portions at the table. Cut off the top fillet, divide it into three servings, remove the bones, and cut the bottom fillet into three portions. Divide the apples and onions among the plates as a vegetable, and spoon the pan juices over all.

Note: Bluefish, dog snapper, jolthead porgy, pilot fish, scamp, and spotted jewfish also work well with this recipe.

Other Delicious Recipes for Hogfish include:

Baked Shrimp-Stuffed Hogfish (see black drum, page 98)

Breaded Fillets of Hogfish with Green Mayonnaise (see red drum, page 109)

Breaded Hogfish with Creole Tomato Sauce (see black grouper, page 47)

Fried Hogfish with Black Anchovy Butter (see Atlantic bonito, page 212)

Fried Hogfish Fingers with Pink Horseradish Mayonnaise (see gaff-topsail catfish, page 80)

Herbed Garlic Hogfish (see yellowtail snapper, page 316)

Hogfish Fillets wtih Artichokes and Mushrooms in Brown Lemon-Butter Sauce (see black drum, page 100)

Hogfish Fillets Simmered in Leek and Tomato Sauce (hard-tail jack, page 174)

Hogfish Garlic Soup (see skipjack tuna, page 223)

Panfried Hogfish Fillets with Shrimp Creole Sauce (see Atlantic threadfin, page 342)

Poached Hogfish Fillets with Rockefeller Sauce (see tripletail, page 363)

A FEW ESSENTIALS

This chapter contains a few basic preparations you will need for the fish recipes in this book.

French Bread Croutons

Butter 1/2-inch-thick rounds of French bread and toast them on a baking sheet in a preheated 400° oven for 3 or 4 minutes, or until crisp and just beginning to color.

Roasted Tomatoes

Roast firm, whole tomatoes on a fork over an open flame on the stovetop or on a grill or in the broiler until the skin chars and splits. Turn as they blacken so they will char evenly. Peel off the skin under running tapwater.

Fish Stocks

Fish stock—called *fumet de poisson* in Haute Creole and French cuisine—is a seasoned broth in which fish or fish bones have been cooked. Stocks have been called the foundation of fish cookery; they are used as the basis of sauces and soups and for poaching. Any liquid in which fish has been cooked is technically a stock; however, stock is usually prepared specially by cooking fish bones. You can collect bones for the stock in a plastic bag in the freezer, adding to the bag until you have enough.

Since stocks are fairly time-consuming to prepare, they are often made in advance (whenever you have a nice collection of bones) and frozen in usable quantities.

There is no one way to make fish stock, and no set list of ingredients. Presented here is one basic simple fish stock, and a number of classic variations on it. When fish or shellfish stock are called for in a recipe in this book, you can use simple, enhanced, white wine, red wine, or reduced stock—whichever most appeals to you, or you have time to prepare. Remember, though, that the richer the stock, the fuller the flavor of the finished sauce or recipe.

Salt and Pepper: A Note
I do not add salt or pepper to a stock because I prefer not to have to worry about balancing out their intensity in whatever preparation I am adding the stock to. If you prefer to salt and pepper your stock, go right ahead and do it.

Simple Fish Stock

2 1/2 quarts water
6 pounds fish heads (degilled), tails, fins, and bones, raw
1 large onion, sliced

1/2 cup chopped parsley, leaves and stems
2 bay leaves
1 teaspoon dried thyme

Place all the ingredients in a large soup pot or stock pot. Bring slowly to a gentle simmer and cook uncovered for 30 minutes. Skim off and discard any foam that may form on the top of the stock.

Strain the stock and use immediately, refrigerate if to be used within a day or two, or freeze.

Enhanced Fish Stock

If you want a richer stock, you can add to the simple stock all or some of the following:

2 sliced carrots
2 sliced celery ribs
1 cup fresh mushroom stems and pieces

1 cup green onion tops
2 cloves garlic, crushed
Juice of 1 lemon

371

White or Red Wine Fish Stock

To the enhanced stock, add:

2 cups dry white or red wine

Note: If you use a red wine stock, it will tint the exterior of the fish flesh.

Reduced or Rich Fish Stock

To make a richer, more intensely flavored stock, reduce any of the stocks above by half by boiling the strained stock briskly. Reduced, or rich, stocks are excellent for poaching fish.

Shrimp Stock

Follow the recipe for any of the fish stocks. Instead of fish parts, use:

Shrimp heads and shells, raw, from 2 or
  more pounds shrimp.

Notes: The more heads and shells, the richer the stock.

Shellfish Stock

Follow the recipe for any of the fish stocks. Instead of fish parts, use:

2 or more pounds shells, raw, from any
  combination of shrimp, crabs, crawfish,
  and Florida lobster

Clam Juice or Fresh Oyster Water

Bottled clam juice or fresh oyster water (available from oyster purveyors) can be used as the stock for seafood sauces when there are no shells or fish parts available to make a fresh stock. Clam juice is fairly salty, so you should taste it before adding any salt to the dish you are preparing.

Chicken Stock

It is not an uncommon practice to use a chicken stock in place of a fish stock in a fish preparation to achieve a more "textured" flavor, or simply when there is no fish or seafood stock available. Follow the recipe for any of the fish stocks. Instead of fish parts, use:

2 to 3 pounds chicken bones, wings, necks,
  and giblets (no livers), raw

You can also use canned chicken broth or chicken bouillon cubes or paste, if you don't mind their saltiness; taste them before salting the dish you are preparing.

Velouté Sauce

There are two basic white sauces for cooking fish in French cuisine, one stock-based and one milk- or cream-based. Fish Velouté is stock-based. It is used by itself and as the base of many sauces used in fish preparations (for example, Seafood-White Wine Sauce, page 244).

4 tablespoons salted butter
4 tablespoons all-purpose flour
2 cups hot fish stock (page 371), shrimp
  stock (page 372), shellfish stock (page
  372), or chicken stock (above)

Salt and freshly ground white pepper

Melt the butter in a saucepan and blend in the flour. Stir and cook for a minute or so, until this "roux" bubbles up and begins to smell bready rather than floury. Whisk in the hot stock. Cook uncovered at a low simmer for about 10 minutes, until the sauce is medium-thick. Season to taste with salt and pepper.

Béchamel Sauce

This the basic milk-based white sauce of Creole and French cuisine. This classic sauce is used by itself or as the basis of many other traditional sauces important to fish cookery (for example, Mornay Sauce, page 314).

2 cups milk or half-and-half	Salt and freshly ground white pepper
4 tablespoons salted butter	Pinch freshly grated nutmeg (optional)
4 tablespoons all-purpose flour	

In a small saucepan, scald the milk or half-and-half. Bring it just to the point of simmering, then turn off the heat. Do not allow to boil. Remove and discard the skin that will form on the surface of the milk. Hold aside.

Melt the butter in a heavy saucepan and stir in the flour. Stir and cook together for a minute or so, or until the mixture bubbles up and takes on a bready rather than a floury aroma. Whisk in the scalded milk or half-and-half and cook at a gentle simmer for 3 minutes, until the sauce achieves a medium-thick consistency. Season to taste with salt and white pepper, and add a pinch of freshly ground nutmeg if desired.

Mayonnaise

This is another basic of fish cookery, upon which a great many other wonderful sauces are based—a number of which are included in this book.

2 large egg yolks, or 1 large whole egg	Salt and freshly ground white pepper
1 cup light olive oil	Dash cayenne (optional)
2 tablespoons lemon juice	

Put the yolks or whole egg in a bowl and beat them well with a whisk. Beat in 1 tablespoon of the oil very well. Continue beating in the next 3 tablespoons of the oil one at a time, allowing the sauce to completely emulsify, or thicken. Continue adding the oil a little at a time, beating constantly, until all the oil is added. Beat in the lemon juice. Season to taste with salt and white pepper, and a dash cayenne if desired. Transfer to a tightly covered container and refrigerate until ready to use.

Note: This mayonnaise can also be made very easily in a blender.

Cocktail Sauce

Serve with raw oysters or boiled or fried seafood.

3/4 cup catsup
1/4 cup prepared horseradish
1/4 cup freshly squeezed lemon juice

2 teaspoons Louisiana hot sauce, or to taste

In a bowl, combine all the ingredients. Transfer to a tightly capped jar and refrigerate.

Tartar Sauce

Tartar Sauce is used with hot and cold seafood, and can be used as a dressing for salads or cold vegetables.

1 egg
1 tablespoon Dijon mustard
1 tablespoon white vinegar
1 cup peanut or corn oil
2 tablespoons freshly squeezed lemon juice
3 tablespoons minced fresh parsley

3 tablespoons chopped sour pickles, or cornichons
2 green onions, minced
2 tablespoons capers, chopped
Salt and freshly ground white pepper

In a mixing bowl or blender container, combine the egg, mustard, and vinegar and whisk or process for a few seconds. Add 1 tablespoon of the oil and process it in. Continue adding the oil a little at a time, whisking or processing continually, until all the oil is used. Fold in the lemon juice, parsley, pickles, green onions, and capers. Season to taste with salt and white pepper. Transfer to a tightly covered container and refrigerate until ready to use.

BEYOND THE RECIPES:
THE BASICS OF COOKING FISH

This chapter presents basic instructions for cooking fish, to help you become further acquainted with Gulf Coast fish and expand your repertoire beyond the recipes in this book.

You can use any of the sauces in the book in conjunction with these basic cooking instructions to create your own delicious Gulf Coast fish recipes. All the separate sauces in the book are listed in categories at the end of the chapter for easy reference.

In deciding how to cook a particular fish, you need to consider its meat type and its size and cut. As I pointed out in the Introduction, oil content and texture can greatly affect the cooking method. The higher the oil content, the drier the cooking method that can be used. Broiling is the driest of cooking methods; grilling is also dry. Conversely, the lower the oil content, the more moisture that needs to be added in cooking. Steaming, poaching, and stewing or cooking in a soup are the moistest methods. If a fish has a firm, dense texture, it will not fall apart when cooked and can be grilled or used in a stew, whereas a flaky fish, which can fall apart when cooked, is best baked or cooked in a broth or sauce. Delicate fish are best cooked quickly, in a manner that does not involve much handling, such as sautéing or pan-frying.

Texture and oil content need to be considered together. For example, a fish with a high oil content and a firm, dense texture, such as swordfish, will work well grilled, but a fish with a high oil content and a flaky texture, such as pinfish, may not.

Following these meat-type guidelines, you should be able to experiment successfully as you familiarize yourself with the Gulf Coast fish. Meat characteristics for each fish are given in the fish chapters, and preferred cooking methods are listed.

377

In addition, for easy reference, the fish in this book are categorized by oil content and texture in a chart in the appendix.

You should realize, however, that although these meat-type guidelines are generally accepted principles of fish cookery, they are not hard-and-fast rules, and can be successfully "violated" depending upon how you handle the fish and the accompanying ingredients you choose. Because I have been cooking these fish all my life, I "break the rules" with great success—as you will find demonstrated in a number of the recipes in this book. Consider the guidelines a learning tool to help you as you get to know the Gulf Coast fish.

Cut and size have a more unforgiving effect on cooking method. Steaks or fillets under 3/4 inch thick could overcook if deep-fried, baked, grilled, or broiled; on the other hand, a thick chunk or a large whole fish could be underdone in the middle and overdone on the outside if grilled.

The following chart suggests cooking methods that work well with standard cuts of fish:

Steaks: no thinner than 1/2 inch, no thicker than 2 inches—grill, barbecue, broil, bake, panfry, sauté, steam

Fillets: thin (up to 3/4 inch)—sauté, panfry, deep-fry, poach, microwave
thick (3/4 inch to 2 inches)—grill, barbecue, broil, bake, sauté, poach, steam, stew, braise, microwave

Large chunks: poach, stew, braise

Whole Fish, with head: small (up to 1 1/2 pounds)—poach, steam
medium (1 1/2 pounds to 2 1/2 pounds)—bake, poach, steam
large (3 pounds to 8 pounds)—bake, poach, steam

Whole Fish, pan-dressed: panfry, deep-fry, bake, poach, steam, barbecue

Cooking Times

Cooking times are similar for all methods of cooking (except microwaving): 8 to 10 minutes per inch thickness of fish, at the thickest part of the fish.

The rule of thumb has traditionally been 10 minutes per inch, but I often prefer to have fish less cooked so that more of the juices and flavor remain. Eight minutes per inch is best for red-fleshed fish, like tuna, which I prefer pink on the inside. A minute or two of additional cooking will bring it to a more done stage if you want. White-fleshed fish, however, need to be cooked the full 10 minutes per inch.

Testing for Doneness

Test for doneness by inserting the tip of a small knife or a metal skewer into the thickest part of the fish. When it is cooked through, the meat will be opaque rather than translucent. White fish will no longer be pinkish; red fish will be gray or white. The fibers of the meat will separate easily when pressed with the tines of a fork. The meat of whole fish will come away from the bone.

If the fish is fairly thick, you can test for doneness by inserting a metal skewer into the center of the thickest part, holding it there a few seconds, and then touching it to the palm of your hand: If it's hot, the fish is done.

Basic Cooking Methods

BAKING:

Any type, size, and cut of fish can be baked. I prefer to use whole, scaled fish. The oven temperature varies from chef to chef, anywhere from 350 to 450 degrees. My preference is the lower end of the heat range: 350–375 degrees. Fish can be baked in either a covered pan or an uncovered pan. If you want a little crispness to the exterior, bake the fish uncovered at 350 degrees; if you want to preserve more of the moisture of the flesh cover the pan and cook at 375 degrees. It's simply a matter of choice.

When baking dark, rich, high-oil-content fish such as mackerel, you may want to bake the fish on a rack in the pan. This way the oils released from the flesh during cooking will not be reabsorbed as they would be if the fish remained on the bottom of the pan. For anyone who prefers their high-oil-content fish with less of the fish oil taste, this method is preferable.

BROILING:

Broiling is the term used for cooking quickly at very high heat under the broiler of your oven. Broiling works best with high-oil-content fish because the high heat (500 degrees or higher) can dry out the flesh. However, broiling also works well with leaner fish as long as you take care to keep them moist during the cooking. Fillets or steaks 3/4 inch to 2 inches thick, or whole fish that weigh up to 1 pound, are preferable—thicker fish may get overdone on the outside before they are done in the middle; thinner pieces may dry out all the way through. Broil higher-oil-content, firm-fleshed fish about 3 inches from the broiler element. Leaner, flakier, more tender fish should be farther from the heat—4 inches from the element is best.

Fillets and steaks under 1 inch thick should not be turned during the broiling. Whole fish or fillets and steaks of 1 inch or more should be turned just once, halfway through the cooking. Be careful not to break the fish in the turning process: Use a large, wide spatula, or two spatulas, so the whole fish is supported. Baste the fish several times during the broiling with oil, butter, or a marinade or stock to keep the flesh moist. Even so, the top of the fish will crisp somewhat. Preheat the broiler, and even the broiling pan or dish, so that full cooking begins immediately.

DEEP-FRYING:

Deep-frying means cooking the fish totally immersed in hot oil. The fish is first coated with a batter to seal in the juices and preserve the moisture of the flesh. Deep-frying works best with small pieces of fish, small whole dressed fish that weigh up to 1 pound, or skinned white-fleshed, low-oil-content fish fillets that weigh up to 8 ounces. The batter will strengthen the fish in the cooking, helping it to remain intact.

Deep-frying can be done in either a heavy skillet or a deep-fryer. I prefer to use peanut oil for deep-frying. The oil should be preheated to at least 375 degrees, and as high as 425 degrees, depending on the size of the fish. Small pieces or small dressed fish should be cooked at the higher temperature, while thicker fillets or whole fish should be cooked at the lower temperature to ensure that they cook thoroughly without the outside becoming overcooked. The temperature is important, so use a thermometer to check it.

When deep-frying, do not allow the fish to press against each other. If you crowd the pan, the temperature of the oil will drop considerably and the batter will not seal immediately, thus absorbing more of the cooking oil than is desirable. If you are deep-frying in batches, check the oil between batches to make sure it is hot enough.

PANFRYING:

Panfrying means cooking the fish over high heat in just enough oil to cover the bottom of the pan. It is a good method for cooking small pan-dressed whole fish, fillets, and steaks. A panfried fish is not coated with a thick batter as for deep-frying, but is seasoned with salt and pepper and, if desired, a light dusting of flour, corn flour, or cornmeal. A light-flavored oil works the best—my preference is peanut oil, although light-flavored olive oil is also nice.

In panfrying the fish are turned over only once, halfway through the cooking.

SAUTÉING:

Sautéing is very much like panfrying except I use butter or a light-flavored olive oil that will become the basis of a sauce for the cooked fish. Fillets or steaks are the preferred cuts. In sautéing, I do not always dust the fish with flour, corn flour, or cornmeal as in panfrying, but simply season it with salt, white pepper, and maybe a little cayenne for flavor. Add a simple squeeze of fresh lemon juice to the pan drippings and you have a most delicious sauce for sautéed fish.

STEAMING:

Steaming is a most healthful way to cook fish—particularly if you are avoiding fats, even healthful fish oils—because the oil is released into the bottom of the pan as the fish cooks, separating it from the flesh. In steaming, a whole, filleted, or steaked fish is cooked on a rack in a long or wide covered pot over boiling water. The rack should be high enough that the water does not touch the fish, even when boiling.

Season the fish if desired, bring the water to a boil, place the fish on the rack in the pot, and cover the pot. Do not turn the fish during cooking. When transferring the cooked fish to serving plates, be careful not to let it break apart—two long spatulas work well for the operation.

Steaming is my preferred method for cooking white-fleshed fish, especially if I want to use a mild sauce, or even a hollandaise, because it preserves the delicate flavor of the fish.

POACHING:

Poaching is another very healthful way to prepare fish if you are avoiding fats, because oil is not needed in the cooking. It works best with whole fish and skinned fillets. The fish is cooked immersed in a simmering liquid in a covered pan. The liquid should not be allowed to boil—the agitation of boiling causes the fish to break apart. The poaching liquid is seasoned to impart additional flavors to the cooked fish. After the fish is cooked it is transferred to a platter or serving plates with two long spatulas, a somewhat delicate procedure as care must be taken that the fish does not break apart. The poaching liquid can then be reduced and used as a base for an accompanying sauce, provided that it was not overly seasoned with salt and pepper.

The simplest poaching liquid is water seasoned with salt, pepper, and herbs. For a richer liquid—called in French cuisine a court-bouillon, or "short boil"—add a combination of other seasonings such as onion and garlic, lemon, wine, mushrooms, carrots, celery, parsley, or even tomatoes and boil 3 minutes or so before adding the fish to draw out the flavors into the liquid. For an even richer poaching liquid, use a fish stock or a sauce.

BRAISING:

Braising is a term used to describe the process of cooking fish in a roaster or Dutch oven on a bed of chopped vegetables such as onions, carrots, and celery. Enough stock or wine is added so that the vegetable bed is covered without the fish itself being immersed. The fish is placed on the vegetables and the pot is covered. When the cooking is done, the remaining liquid can be used alone for a sauce or can be thickened and seasoned. If desired, the pan vegetables can be incorporated into the sauce for a richer flavor.

Large fillets and large chunks are best for braising.

GRILLING:

Grilling can be done several different ways. There is the solid steel grill, the slotted grill, and the wire grill commonly used outdoors. The heat source is either electric, gas, or charcoal. On the solid steel grill, it is best to use fillets or steaks with the skin left on. On the slotted or wire grill, fillets and steaks with the skin on and whole dressed fish are all good choices.

Dark, rich, firm, high-oil-content fish are perfect for grilling. They hold together well, and the highly flavored oils are left behind in the cooking, which gives a lighter taste to the cooked fish. Leaner, less firm fish can also be grilled successfully as long as you handle them carefully and keep them moist. Baste even the high-oil-content fish with a light oil or butter several times during the cooking to keep the exterior from drying out before the fish is cooked through.

You will need to light the grill 1 hour before you plan to cook. The rack must be very clean or the fish will stick to it and collect the ash. When the grill is ready, brush the rack with vegetable oil before you lay on the fish.

BARBECUING:

Barbecuing fish is grilling it over live charcoal. The fish is cooked on a wire rack, and is usually covered during the cooking. The barbecue "pit" is lit an hour before cooking, and the wire rack is brushed with vegetable oil when the coals are ready. A piece of water-soaked sweet wood, such as pecan or hickory, might be added to the coals to give the fish a smoked flavor. The fish should be basted with butter, a light oil, or a sauce during the cooking.

Whole dressed fish, thick fish steaks, or a thick fillet are the best for barbecuing. I often take the whole large fillets from big fish and leave the skin and scales on while cooking. The cut side of the fish is basted and grilled briefly, and then the fillet is turned over so that the remaining cooking is done with the scale/skin side on the rack. You will find that the cooked fish will easily come away from the skin for serving. This method also helps retain more of the flavor and moisture.

MICROWAVING:

Although I have not included any recipes for microwaving in this book, I do occasionally microwave fish. I treat microwaving fish the same way that I treat steaming fish. I prefer to use skinned fillets of tender, white flaky fish with low oil content. I place the fillet in a covered microwaveable dish with a little stock, wine, or even flavored vinegar. This helps give the fillet a chance to cook more evenly while at the same time imparting additional flavors. The dish should be rotated a quarter turn halfway through the cooking.

One 1/2-inch-thick fillet should cook in about 2 to 3 minutes at 100 percent power; an 1-inch fillet will take 3 1/2 to 4 1/2 minutes. Add about 1 1/2 minutes for each additional piece of fish cooked at the same time. Note: Microwave ovens often vary in cooking times; you will have to determine what works best for yours.

SMOKING:

I have not included instructions or recipes for smoking fish because individuals who use the process have their own specialized equipment and recipes.

Using Sauces

A simply cooked fish is delicious; add a good sauce and it becomes divine. Sauces are the painter's palette of fish cookery, allowing scope for creativity and imagination. This book contains sauces aplenty from the American Gulf Coast for you to choose among, from classic Haute Creole to zesty Tex/Mex.

In deciding what sauce to use with a particular fish, it helps to consider the characteristics of the fish meat. Here are some general guidelines:

Low-oil-content, white, delicate (bland) fish need mild sauces that will not overpower their natural flavor (e.g., butter-based, milk- or cream-based, white wine based; broths). Mild herbs, onions, garlic, greens, or mild cheeses make good seasonings.

High-oil-content, dark (richer, stronger tasting) fish can take stronger tasting, more robust sauces or butters (e.g., citrus-, mustard-, red wine-, or tomato-based). Cilantro and other pungent herbs, hot peppers, or horseradish make good seasonings.

Medium-oil-content fish go well with hollandaise- and mayonnaise-based sauces.

Again, as with the advice given about types of fish to use with different cooking methods, these guidelines are merely suggestions to help you as you familiarize yourself with the Gulf Coast fish. Ultimately, the sauces and flavorings used with particular fish are a matter of personal taste. Use these guidelines if you feel you need them; otherwise—experiment!

THE SAUCES IN THIS BOOK:

To make it easier for you to find the Gulf Coast sauces in this book that are separable from the recipes, they are listed below.

Butter-Based Sauces
Black Anchovy Butter (page 212)
Brown Lemon-Butter Sauce (page 100)
Browned Butter, Lemon Juice, and Caper Sauce (page 296)
Beurre Noir Sauce (page 213)
Drawn Butter (page 199)
Parsley-Lemon Butter (page 267)

Cream/Milk-Based Sauces
Béchamel Sauce (page 374)
Creamy Pimiento-Butter Sauce (page 85)
Creole Mustard and Chive Cream Sauce (page 232)
Horseradish and Sour Cream Sauce (page 95)
Mornay Sauce (page 314)
Moulin Rouge Sauce (page 56)
Poulette Sauce (page 260)

Hollandaise-Based Sauces
Hollandaise Sauce (page 63)
Béarnaise Sauce (page 358)

Seasoned Butters
Chivry Butter (page 72)
Cilantro Butter (page 123)
Garlic-Chive Butter (page 124)
Rosemary Butter (page 124)
Tarragon Butter (page 124)
Tomato Butter (page 32)

Pastes—For Grilling or Broiling
Achiote-Garlic Paste (page 49)
Creole Garlic Paste (page 50)
Italian Herb-Garlic Paste (page 50)
Mexican Paste (page 66)
Sweet Herb Paste (page 197)

Dressings and Vinaigrettes—for salads; vinaigrettes can also be used as marinades
  for baking, broiling, or grilling, or as a poaching liquor
Chive Vinaigrette (page 227)
Citronette Dressing (page 307)
Creole Mustard Dressing (page 321)
Curry Vinaigrette (page 306)
Dijon Mustard Dressing (page 320)
Lime Dressing (page 306)
Russian Dressing with Caviar (page 280)

Marinades—use as poaching liquor or for baking, broiling, or grilling
Lime and Onion Marinade (page 34)
Orange-Curry Marinade (page 291)
Red Wine Marinade (page 35)
Sesame-Brandy Marinade (page 58)
Sherry Marinade (page 319)
White Wine Marinade (page 35)

APPENDIX

Gulf Coast Fish Categorized by Meat Type

In the following chart, I have categorized the fish in this book according to the color, texture, and oil content of their meat. Fish with similar meat types can easily be substituted for one another in any recipe. This list can also be a helpful reference when deciding on a particular cooking method or sauce.

White, tender, delicate
Low oil content
    Spotted Eagle Ray
    Southern Stingray

White, tender, delicate
Medium-to-high oil content
    Florida Pompano

White, tender
Low oil content
    Sand Perch

White, tender
Low-to-medium oil content
    Queen Triggerfish

White, tender
Medium oil content
    Sailor's-Choice
    Atlantic Spadefish

White, tender, flaky
Low oil content
    Great Barracuda
    Spotfin Flounder
    Spotted Sea Trout
    Dog Snapper

    Mutton Snapper
    Red Snapper
    Yellowtail Snapper
    Weakfish

White, tender, flaky
Low-to-medium oil content
    Gulf Flounder
    Pigfish
    Atlantic Threadfin
    Gray Triggerfish

White, tender, flaky
Medium oil content
    Gaff-Topsail Catfish
    Permit
    Sheepshead

White, flaky
Low oil content
    Spot Drum
    Gulf Kingfish
    Squirrelfish

White, flaky
Low-to-medium oil content
    Speckled Hind
    Scamp

White, firm, flaky
Low oil content
    White Grunt
    Atlantic Croaker
    Black Grouper

White, firm, flaky
Low-to-medium oil content
    Creolefish
    Red Grouper
    Hogfish
    Red Drum

White, firm, flaky
Medium oil content
    Black Drum
    Tripletail

White, firm, flaky
Medium-to-high oil content
    Striped Mullet

White, firm
Low-to-medium oil content
    Black Sea Bass

White, firm
Low oil content
    Striped Bass
    Tilefish

White, firm
Low-to-medium oil content
    Red Porgy

White, firm
Medium oil content
    Bonefish
    Common Dolphin
    Lookdown
    Pilotfish
    Jolthead Porgy
    Scalloped Hammerhead
    Shark
    Snook

White, firm
Medium-to-high oil content
    Blacktip Shark

White, firm
High oil content
    American Eel

~~~~~~~~~~~~~~~~~~~~

Medium-white, flaky
Medium-to-high oil content
    White Mullet
    Pinfish

~~~~~~~~~~~~~~~~~~~~

Medium-white, firm, flaky
Low-to-medium oil content
    Spotted Jewfish

~~~~~~~~~~~~~~~~~~~~

Medium-white, firm
Low oil content
    Shortfin Mako Shark

Medium-white, firm
Low-to-medium oil content
    Ling Cobia

Medium-white, firm
Medium oil content
    Greater Amberjack
    Atlantic Moonfish
    Largetooth Sawfish
    Wahoo

~~~~~~~~~~~~~~~~~~~~

Medium-white, firm, dense
High oil content
    Tarpon

~~~~~~~~~~~~~~~~~~~~

Dark, rich, tender
High oil content
    Blue

~~~~~~~~~~~~~~~~~~~~

Dark, rich, firm
Medium-to-high oil content
    Common Jack

Dark, rich, firm
High oil content
    Atlantic Bonito
    Hard-Tail Jack
    King Mackerel
    Spanish Mackerel
    Blue Marlin
    Rainbow Runner
    Atlantic Sailfish
    Blackfin Tuna
    Skipjack Tuna
    Yellowfin Tuna
    Swordfish

INDEX

with poulette sauce, broiled, 260-61
steaks Marseilles-style, sautéed, 194-95
steaks with criolla sauce, grilled, 25-26
with tomato butter, grilled, 32-33
blacktip shark:
with antiboise sauce, panfried, 294-95
with browned butter, lemon juice and caper
    sauce, fillet of, 296
chowder with potatoes and tomatoes,
    170-71
Creole bisque of, 348
fillets with drawn butter, poached,
    199-200
with garlic sauce, charcoal-grilled, 236
garlic soup, 223
poached in sherry, 319
ragout of, au gratin, 332
steaks, blackened, 235
steaks with achiote-garlic paste, wood-
    grilled, 49-50
tamales with roasted tomato and chili
    sauce, 156-57
and tomato bisque, 226
white bisque of, with sherry, 281
"blaff," Caribbean, 202
bluefish, 65
with apples and onions, baked, 368-69
and artichoke salad and Russian dressing
    with caviar, hot, 279-80
boudin, 152
Creole bisque of, 348
étouffée of, 218-19
fillets with cilantro butter, broiled, 123-24
marinated escabèche of, 176
matelote of, 126-27
ravigote with boiled new potatoes, cold
    poached, 43-44
steaks with achiote-garlic paste, wood-
    grilled, 49-50
steaks with Mexican seasonings, wood-
    grilled, 66-67
-stuffed bell peppers, 214
-stuffed hand tortillas, 68-69
tamales with piquant green sauce, 203-4
with tomato-red wine sauce, grilled,
    325-26
blue marlin, 234
boudin, 152
Creole bisque of, 348
fillets with drawn butter, poached,
    199-200
fried skewered, 276-77
with garlic sauce, charcoal-grilled, 236

with oyster and crabmeat sauce gratiné,
    256-57
poached in orange-curry marinade, 291-92
with potatoes, bacon and garlic, 286-87
with rice, Caribbean, 128
steaks, blackened, 235
steaks with Creole mustard and chive
    cream sauce, broiled, 232-33
steaks with Mexican seasonings, wood-
    grilled, 66-67
and tomato bisque, 226
with tomato-red wine sauce, grilled,
    325-26
bonefish, 71
beer-battered fried, 39-40
fillets with cucumber and spinach, 104-5
fillets with sorrel, zucchini and
    mushrooms, 74-75
marinated, salad with giardeniera, 329-30
with pecans, 181-82
poached, with horseradish and sour cream
    sauce, 95-96
whole steamed, with chivry butter, 72-73
boudin, 152
bouillabaisse, Gulf Coast, 140-41
bourguignonne sauce, 366-67
braising, 382; see also specific fish
brandy-sesame marinade, 58
broiling, 380; see also specific fish
browned butter, lemon juice and caper
    sauce, 296
brown lemon-butter sauce, 100-101
brown shrimp sauce, 245-46
Burgundy-style braised spotted sea trout,
    117
butter:
black anchovy, 212-13
chivry, 72-73
cilantro, 123-24
drawn, 199-200
garlic-chive, 123-24
parsley-lemon, 267-68
rosemary, 123-24
tarragon, 123-24
tomato, 32-33
brown-lemon sauce, 311, 100,101

canapé of Atlantic spadefish, baked, 323-24
caper, lemon juice and browned butter
    sauce, 296

394

ragout of, au gratin, 332

dolphin, *see* common dolphin

drawn butter, 199-200

"dressed" fish, 13

dressing:
  chive vinaigrette, 227-28
  Dijon mustard, 320-21
  Russian, with caviar, 279-80

eel, *see* American eel

egg and sweet mustard sauce, 254-55

eggplant:
  greater amberjack chowder with tomatoes
    and, 170-71
  grilled ling cobia steaks with onions, green
    bell peppers and, 84

escabèche of hard-tail jack, marinated, 176

espagnole mayonnaise, 303-4

espagnole sauce, 361-62

étouffée:
  of Atlantic sailfish, 218-19
  of Atlantic sailfish, Creole, 230-31
  of blackfin tuna, 218-19
  of blackfin tuna, Creole, 230-31
  of bluefish, 218-19
  of common jack, 218-19
  of gulf kingfish, 218-19
  of gulf kingfish, Creole, 230-31
  of scalloped hammerhead shark, 218-19
  of shortfin mako shark, Creole, 230-31
  of speckled hind, 218-19
  of spotfin flounder, Creole, 230-31
  of wahoo, 218-19
  of wahoo, Creole, 230-31
  of yellowfin tuna, Creole, 230-31

eviscerating of fish, 12

fennel, pigfish en papillote with, 139

filleting of fish:
  flat, 14
  round, 13-14
  skinning fillets, 14

fingers, fried gaff-topsail catfish, with pink
  horseradish mayonnaise, 80-81

fish:
  amount to buy, 6-7
  baking of, 379-80
  barbecuing of, 383
  braising of, 382-83
  broiling of, 380
  buying of, 2-7

chunking of, 15
cleaning of, 10-13
color of, 5
cooking times for, 379
cuts of, 378
deep-frying of, 380-81
defrosting of, 10
degilling of, 13
"dressed," 13
eviscerating (gutting) of, 12
eyes, appearance of, 3
filleting of, 13-14
firmness of, 4
freezing of, at home, 9-10
freshness of, 3-4
frozen, evaluating of, 4-5
gills, appearance of, 3-4
grilling of, 383
handling of, 3, 7
meat types of, 5-6
microwaving of, 384
odor of, 4
oil content of, 5
"pan-dressed," 13
panfrying of, 381
poaching of, 382
sautéing of, 381
scaling of, 11
steaking of, 15
steaming of, 381-82
storing of, 6
storing of frozen, 9-10
substituting types of, 5
texture of, 5, 6

fish markets, evaluating of, 2-3

fish-scalers, 11

fish stock, 370-72
  clam juice or oyster water in place of, 373
  enhanced, 371
  reduced or rich, 372
  shellfish stock, 372
  shrimp stock, 372
  simple, 371
  white or red wine, 372

florentine tilefish fillets, 346-47

Florida pompano, 160
  baked en papillote with a shrimp, crab
    meat and white wine sauce, fillet of,
    161-63
  broiled, 131
  with crabmeat and butter, sautéed fillet of,
    90-91
  fillet Marguery, 265-66

397

with oyster and crabmeat sauce gratiné,
256-57
poached, with parsley-lemon butter,
267-68
whole baked, with chanterelles, 136-37
whole baked, with spinach stuffing, 250-52
whole panfried, with peanut sauce, 78-79
shellfish, stock, 372
sherry:
marinade, 319
white bisque of blackfin tuna with, 281
shortfin mako shark, 288
with aioli sauce, steamed, 328
ceviche of, 28
"chips" with fresh tomato catsup, soda-
fried, 289-90
Creole étouffée of, 230-31
fillets with espagnole mayonnaise,
steamed, 303-4
garlic soup, 223
matelote of, 126-27
poached in orange-curry marinade, 291-92
poached in sherry, 319
with Puerto Rican sauce, 333-34
ravigote with boiled new potatoes, cold
poached, 43-44
smothered in jalapeño-tequila sauce,
158-59
steaks with Creole mustard and chive
cream sauce, broiled, 232-33
stew with white wine, 275
shrimp:
-browned butter sauce, 133
crabmeat and white wine sauce, 161-63
Creole sauce, 342-43
étouffée of blackfin tuna, 218-19
sauce, brown, 245-46
sautéed steak of common dolphin with
butter and, 90-91
spotfin flounder fillets stuffed with, 135
stock, 372
-stuffed baked black drum, 98-99
skipjack tuna, 220
with aioli sauce, steamed, 328
"chops" of, 118-19
croquettes meunière, 221-22
fillets in saffron-white wine sauce, 338-39
garlic soup, 223
Gulf Coast bouillabaise with, 140-41
with rice, Caribbean, 128
salad, Caribbean, 305-6
smothered in jalapeño-tequila sauce,
158-59

steaks, blackened, 235
steaks Marseilles-style, sautéed, 194-95
steaks with onions, green bell peppers and
eggplant, grilled, 84
with tomatillo-habañero salsa, charcoal-
grilled, 351-52
white bisque of, with sherry, 281
snook, 318
and artichoke salad and Russian dressing
with caviar, hot, 279-80
baked canapé of, 323-24
baked shrimp-stuffed, 98-99
with Bienville sauce, panfried, 207-8
chowder, Bahamian, 272
with cypriote sauce, steamed, 284-85
marinière, whole steamed, 122
and mushroom salad with Dijon mustard
dressing, hot, 320-21
poached in sherry, 319
poached with lime and onion, 34-35
with potatoes, bacon and garlic, 286-87
and potato salad with chive vinaigrette,
227-28
with Puerto Rican sauce, 333-34
stew with white wine, 275
sorrel, bonefish fillets with zucchini,
mushrooms and, 74-75
soufflé, shrimp, 135
soup:
Atlantic spadefish garlic, 223
blacktip shark garlic, 223
hogfish garlic, 223
permit, tomato and pepper, 53
pigfish, tomato and pepper, 53
pilot fish and tomato, 193
rainbow runner and tomato, 193
rainbow runner garlic, 223
red grouper, tomato and pepper, 53
sheepshead garlic, 223
shortfin mako shark garlic, 223
skipjack tuna garlic, 223
spotted jewfish garlic, 223
squirrelfish, tomato and pepper, 53
squirrelfish garlic, 223
tarpon, tomato and pepper, 53
tarpon garlic, 223
wahoo garlic, 223
white grunt, tomato and pepper, 53
see also bisque; chowder; stew
sour cream and horseradish sauce, 95-96
southern stingray, 269
and artichoke salad and Russian dressing
with caviar, hot, 279-80

and chili sauce, roasted, 157
and common jack bisque, 226
greater amberjack chowder with eggplant and, 170-71
greater amberjack chowder with potatoes and, 170-71
permit and pepper soup, 53
pigfish and pepper soup, 53
and pilot fish soup, 193
and rainbow runner soup, 193
red grouper and pepper soup, 53
red snapper chowder with potatoes and, 170-71
roasted, 370
squirrelfish and pepper soup, 53
tarpon and pepper soup, 53
and wahoo bisque, 226
wahoo chowder with potatoes and, 170-71
white grunt and pepper soup, 53
and yellowfin tuna bisque, 226
tomato sauce:
Creole, 47-48
grilled lookdown with, 179-80
leek and, 174-75
oyster-, 164-65
red wine-, 325-26
roasted, with chili, 157
tortillas, hand, 68-69
tripletail, 360
with bacon and onion, baked, 52
with béarnaise sauce, grilled, 358-59
beer-battered fried, 39-40
with espagnole sauce, whole panfried, 361-62
fillets with green onion mayonnaise, cold poached, 23-24
fillets with Maltaise sauce, poached, 88-89
fingers with pink horseradish mayonnaise, fried, 80-81
Gulf Coast bouillabaisse with, 140-41
with onion, garlic and red wine sauce, whole panfried, 190-91
with oyster and crabmeat sauce gratiné, 256-57
with rice, Caribbean, 128
with Rockefeller sauce, poached fillets of, 363-64
tuna, see blackfin tuna; skipjack tuna; yellowfin tuna
turnip green stuffing, 251
two sisters sauce, 184-85

velouté sauce, 373-74

Venetian-style broiled blackfin tuna steaks, 217
vinaigrette, chive, 227-28

wahoo, 206
with Bienville sauce, panfried, 207-8
chowder of potatoes and tomatoes, 170-71
with crabmeat and batter, sautéed steak of, 90-91
Creole étouffée of, 230-31
with Creole sauce piquante, 209-10
étouffée of, 218-19
fried skewered, 276-77
garlic soup, 223
poached in orange-curry marinade, 291-92
with potatoes, bacon and garlic, 286-87
pot-au-feu, Creole-style, 336-37
with rice, Caribbean, 128
-stuffed bell peppers, 214
and tomato bisque, 226
watercress stuffing, 251
weakfish, 121
baked shrimp-stuffed, 98-99
fillet marguery, 265-66
fillets meunière, New Orleans-style deep-fried, 249
fillets with artichokes and mushrooms in brown lemon-butter sauce, 100-101
fillets with cilantro butter, broiled, 123
fillets with green basil mayonnaise, cold poached, 356-57
fillets with lobster-browned butter sauce, 132-33
fillets with Moulin Rouge sauce, fried, 56-57
with green mayonnaise, breaded fillets of, 109
marinière, steamed whole, 122
poached with lime and onion, 34-35
with seafood-white wine sauce gratiné, 243-44
with spinach stuffing, whole baked, 250-52
white beans, scalloped hammerhead shark with bacon, garlic and, 286-87
white bisque of largetooth sawfish with sherry, 281
white grunt, 146
cold poached, with green onion mayonnaise, 23-24
corn-flour-fried, fillets, 300-301
with Creole sauce piquante, 209-10
curried fillets of, 143

411

fillets simmered in leek and tomato sauce, 174-75

fillets with lobster-browned butter sauce, 132-33

fingers with pink horseradish mayonnaise, fried, 80-81

grilled, andalouse, 149-50

en papillote with fennel, 139

tomato and pepper soup, 53

whole cracker-crumb-coated panfried, with Key lime sauce, 147-48

whole panfried, with aurora sauce, 114-15

whole panfried, with espagnole sauce, 361-62

whole panfried, with salsa roja, 240-41

white mullet, 242

andalouse, grilled, 149-50

in aurora sauce, whole panfried, 114-15

baked canapé of, 323-24

beer-battered fried, 39-40

with brown shrimp sauce, fried, 245-46

fillets with lobster cream sauce, panfried, 186-87

fillets with shrimp Creole sauce, panfried, 342-43

with horseradish and sour cream sauce, poached, 95-96

with seafood-white wine sauce gratiné, 243-44

smothered in jalapeño-tequila sauce, 158-59

with sweet mustard and egg sauce, fried whole, 254-55

with tomatillo-habañero salsa, charcoal-grilled, 351-52

white wine:

American eel stew with, 275

fish stock, 372

marinade, 35

-saffron sauce, 338-39

-seafood sauce gratiné, 243-44

shortfin mako shark stew with, 275

shrimp and crabmeat sauce, 161-62

snook stew with, 275

spotted eagle ray stew with, 275

wine, *see* red wine; white wine

yellowfin tuna, 225

with antiboise sauce, panfried, 294-95

and artichoke salad and Russian dressing with caviar, hot, 279-80

with browned-butter, lemon juice and caper sauce, fillets of, 296

Creole étouffée of, 230-31

fillets in saffron-white wine sauce, 338-39

fillets with tomato-oyster sauce, grilled, 164-65

fried skewered, 276-77

marinated escabèche of, 176

matelote of, 126-27

and mushroom salad with Dijon mustard dressing, hot, 320-21

with plantation groundnut sauce, charcoal-grilled, 270-71

and potato salad with chive vinaigrette, 227-28

steaks with criolla sauce, grilled, 25-26

and tomato bisque, 226

yellow squash, greater amberjack chowder with yucca and, 170-71

yellowtail snapper, 313

baked canapé of, 323-24

baked en papillote with a shrimp, crabmeat and white wine sauce, fillet of, 161-62

beer-battered fried, 39-40

with Colbert sauce, whole panfried, 262-63

fillet marguery, 265-66

fillets with artichokes and mushrooms in brown lemon-butter sauce, sautéed, 100-101

fillets with cucumbers and spinach, 104-5

fillets with Mornay sauce, 314-15

Gulf Coast bouillabaisse with, 140-41

herbed garlic, 316-17

en papillote with black olives, 61-62

en papillote with fennel, 139

yucca, greater amberjack chowder with yellow squash and, 170-71

zucchini:

bonefish fillets with sorrel, mushrooms and, 74-75

scalloped hammerhead shark with bacon, garlic and, 286-87